Successful Scientific Writing

A Step-by-Step Guide for the Biological an~~d~~

Fourth edition

Thoroughly revised and updated, the new edition of this acclaimed and best-selling guide offers a rich blend of practical advice and real-life examples. The authors draw on 50 years of experience, providing detailed step-by-step guidance designed to help students and researchers write and present scientific manuscripts more successfully through knowledge, practice, and an efficient approach.

Retaining the user-friendly style of the previous editions, this fourth edition has been broadened to include detailed information relevant to today's digital world. It covers all aspects of the writing process, from first drafts, literature retrieval, and authorship to final drafts and electronic publication. A new section provides extensive coverage of ethical issues, from plagiarism and dual publication to honesty in reporting statistics. Both the text and 30 hands-on exercises include abundant examples applicable to a variety of writing contexts, making this a powerful tool for researchers and students across a range of disciplines.

Janice R. Matthews is a writer and educator with a broad background in the biological sciences. Her professional focus is on facilitating clearer communication of scientific material. She has edited books, technical manuals, and hundreds of scientific research papers in the veterinary and biological sciences, both in university settings and for private industry.

Robert W. Matthews is a Josiah Meigs Distinguished Teaching Professor, Emeritus at the University of Georgia, and a member of the UGA Teaching Academy. An insect behavior specialist, his scientific publications number over 175 research articles.

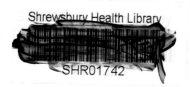

Successful Scientific Writing

A Step-by-Step Guide for the
Biological and Medical Sciences

FOURTH EDITION

Janice R. Matthews
Robert W. Matthews

CAMBRIDGE
UNIVERSITY PRESS

CAMBRIDGE
UNIVERSITY PRESS

University Printing House, Cambridge CB2 8BS, United Kingdom

Cambridge University Press is part of the University of Cambridge.

It furthers the University's mission by disseminating knowledge in the pursuit of education, learning and research at the highest international levels of excellence.

www.cambridge.org
Information on this title: www.cambridge.org/9781107691933

© Cambridge University Press 1996, 2000, 2008, 2014

First published 1996
Second edition 2000
Third edition 2008
Fourth edition 2014
Reprinted 2015

Printed in the United Kingdom by TJ International Ltd, Padstow, Cornwall

A catalog record for this publication is available from the British Library

ISBN 978-1-107-69193-3 Paperback

Contents

Preface to the fourth edition

Why do scientists write? Ask a dozen, and you'll hear a lot of grumpy answers. "Because I have to!" "Haven't you heard about publish or perish?" "If I don't, I'll never get my degree/get promoted/get a grant/reach full professor!" Seldom do you hear, "Because, actually, I sort of enjoy it!" Such an admission seems to run up against a cultural taboo among academics. Researchers accept, even delight in, an associate's exhilaration about his or her discoveries, and pat each other on the back when a paper is accepted for publication or a grant proposal is funded. Seldom do they share similar enthusiasm over the actual writing process that was central to those successes. Yet in their free time, and sensing no contradiction, these same individuals may use similar skills to do crossword or sudoku puzzles for relaxation or use their electronic gadgets to puzzle over word games with friends.

There is joy to be found in any creative act, and generally the more skillful one becomes at it, the greater that joy. Why should scientific writing be any different? Could it be that science's demand that one must write has dampened or killed that joy, in the same way that being forced to do Japanese math puzzles might remove the incentive to do so for pleasure?

Scientific writing makes demands on its practitioner, like any other task done really well. Every facet demands precision and complete accuracy. Rewriting and editing generally require more time than the initial drafting of the content. Yet, does a skilled woodworker complain that sanding takes time? Or a dedicated weaver resent the accuracy required to properly dress a loom?

Scientific writing, too, is a craft, with rules, conventions, and even passing fads. The more completely one understands the basics, the easier mastery becomes. However, this is not enough. We are in a time when the basics of scientific writing and publication are changing extremely quickly, not just in mechanics and rules, but in very outlook. Practices that were once taboo, such as blatant self-promotion and dual publication, have become increasingly acceptable and commonplace. Online journals are springing up like mushrooms, and like fungi, they require careful appraisal to discern the valuable from the potentially toxic. English-language publications are no longer solely paper copy consigned to languish on dusty library shelves, but electronic missives that reach large and diverse audiences around the world.

In response, this fourth edition of *Successful Scientific Writing* has changed more than any of its previous iterations. We've doubled the number of chapters, allowing more explicit advice on ethical issues and on the planning and presentation of research. For relative newcomers to the world of scientific writing, we've added much more guidance on writing and organizing each part of a manuscript's initial draft. Strategies for more effective written and oral presentations have been presented in greater detail. We've collated and expanded the exercises that allow practice in applying concepts to actual examples.

For those who have been writing in the biological and medical fields a bit longer, the new world of electronic publication has received more emphasis in this edition. Other new material ranges from techniques for conducting a more effective and comprehensive literature review to ways to hone and present one's scientific message so that it receives the attention it deserves. We have expanded tips for writers coming from, or addressing their work to, the growing international community of scientists for whom English is an acquired language.

What hasn't changed is our pragmatic, practical outlook that views scientific writing as an interesting craft to be learned. We also remain focused on better ways to work in a systematic and organized fashion. Writing well does take time, but the task doesn't need to be never-ending.

As in earlier editions, we've attempted to approach all these subjects with the light touch and bit of humor (including over two dozen cartoons in this edition) that befit an interesting and potentially pleasurable task. We're aware that to many of you, "enjoyable writing" is an oxymoron. Ours is a minority view, we know, but we'd like to invite you to have an open mind. Perhaps we'll be able to convince you, and perhaps not. Either way, this book will provide the tools, skill set, and insider tips you need to become more skilled in the writing your profession calls upon you to do. If, along with personal success you also come to find some joy and humor in the writing task, we'll feel that we too were successful.

J.R.M.
R.W.M.
January 2014

1   Start with a plan

> Find a subject you care about and which you in your heart feel others should
> care about.
>
> It is this genuine caring, not your games with language, which will be the
> most compelling and seductive element in your style.
>
> KURT VONNEGUT

Most of us were drawn to science because, like Vonnegut, we found a subject
we feel deeply about, not just because we wanted to write about it. However, all
scientists recognize that research must be made known if it is to have lasting
value. This is how science moves forward, with the shared word illuminating
each step of discovery for the sake of others that follow.

"Scientific writing" can be defined narrowly as the reporting of original
research in peer-reviewed journals, or construed more broadly to encompass
other ways that scientists share research information with one another, such as
review articles, abstracts, case study reports, grant proposals and summaries,
posters, and slide-based presentations. (The term "science writing" is often
used for writing about science topics for the general public.) Whatever form it
takes, successful scientific writing must answer basic questions and address
problems raised during the dialogs that identify and define a given subject. It
must be clear, concise, and follow established formats. In many ways, its
language forms a dialect all its own.

What is the most efficient way to write a paper or presentation that
successfully covers all this? This book exists to help you tackle the task, step
by step. In this chapter, we suggest that you back up from actual writing, and
start where your research does – with a question. Learn the most effective ways
of compiling background information. For help defining, organizing, and
planning the content, use techniques borrowed from problem-solving
strategies. Choose a journal so that you have a goal and format. Take charge
of the whole project by using the Process Approach.

Ask fundamental questions first

Although peer-reviewed formal research publication receives major emphasis
in this book, it is only one of many ways scientific data can be shared.
The methods by which scientists transmit their work to one another have

changed and multiplied more in the past three decades than at any time since
the first appearance of scholarly journals back in the late seventeenth century.
Thus, choosing how your study will be disseminated should be your first step
toward presenting it to the world.

Before going any further, a savvy scientific writer asks four questions:

- What message do I want to convey?
- Who will be interested in my message?
- What format is most appropriate for my message?
- Where should this paper be published?

You may be able to answer these questions by yourself, but for an extra margin
of safety, discuss them with a more experienced colleague. All of us can suffer
from the normal human failings of inflating the importance of a message and
overestimating the size and nature of its potential audience.

What message do I want to convey?
By this point, you should be able to answer this question in some detail. What
is my research question, and what is (or probably will be) my answer? This is
not the same as asking the "purpose" of the research. That phrasing can lead to
some tremendously circular and meaningless statements: The purpose of my
research was to obtain data so I could publish them in order to get my degree
so I could do more research and publish some more . . .

Who will be most interested in my message?
Most of us have pretty healthy egos. We think our writing will merit the
attention of far more readers than it will in fact attract. This nearly universal
failing can lead to poor choice of a potential journal, and this poor choice can
lead to delays, requests for major revision, or outright rejection.

Two closely related, bluntly asked questions can help a writer find the most
appropriate audience:

- *So what?* This question could be cast less abruptly in any of several ways.
  What effect will my message have on concepts or practices? Why should
  readers pay attention to it? Will it lead to widespread changes in the way we
  view the world?
- *Who cares?* One could also ask this question more mildly. Who will be the
  most interested in this information? Will it be the specialists in a small field?
  Most practitioners? The scientific world in general?

Be realistic. Don't get caught up in contemplating a vast potential audience that
"needs" to know your information. (In this information-filled world, no one

should be expected to make brain-room for data simply because the facts are currently unknown to him or her.) The more accurately you can answer these questions, the more precise your journal publication options become. And the more precisely you can target a journal, the better the chances for publication.

Where can I most effectively communicate my message?

Most of us are justifiably interested in recognition for our work. The way in which a study is presented and published can determine the nature of that recognition, and in fact whether we receive any recognition at all. This is most clearly demonstrated in the case of the twin concepts of "valid publication" and "priority." For a scientist to receive professional credit for being the first to discover something new, it is not sufficient just to be the first to perceive or detect it – he or she must be the first to publish the information "validly," that is, in a very specific way. This distinction is most important in (but not restricted to) the taxonomic sciences, in which the naming of new organisms hinges on a strict system of priority of valid publication.

Valid scientific publication has several essential components. It is (1) the first publication of research results (2) in a form whereby peers can assess the observations, evaluate the intellectual processes, or repeat the experiment and test its conclusions, (3) appearing in a primary journal or other source document (4) that is readily available within the scientific community. In addition, (5) the scientific paper contains certain specified kinds of information that are (6) organized in a certain stylized manner, i.e., it has a certain format.

What is a "primary journal or other source document that is readily available within the scientific community"? Primary and secondary has nothing to do with quality or importance. Rather, a primary journal is merely one that details first-hand information reported by people directly involved with an action or event. A secondary journal presents information that does not come directly from people involved in the action or event. Rather, a person two or three steps removed from the source reports the information. Some of these secondary publications are significant sources of communication among scientists and the educated public, particularly now that the Internet provides increased accessibility to them.

Communication format: the message determines the medium

In 1964, Marshall McLuhan, a Canadian philosopher of communication theory, coined the phrase "the medium is the message" to help explain the ways people reacted to new media such as television. Our variation on that phrase is to underscore the reality that where scientific material appears is almost as important as what it says. Conversely, where it appears ideally should be determined by what it says.

Research articles and case histories

Though they may be designated by slightly different sets of names, research papers in the biological and medical sciences fall into four general categories – research articles, case histories, reviews, and case-series analyses – and shorter variants with such titles as research notes or brief communications. Each category is most appropriate for different sorts of messages. Because of the very specific nature of requirements for establishing priority of discovery, the first two of these categories form the usual avenue for "valid" publication of original results. This is not to imply that other publication is "invalid" for any other use than this very specialized purpose.

Articles that present original research and case histories are the presentations that usually come to mind when people hear the term "scientific paper." Both types of papers are "primary" because they are based on a scientist's own experiences. A research article generally presents new data obtained through experimentation or observation. A case history usually covers such subjects as a unique or previously unknown syndrome or disease, new information on an illness, an unsuspected causal relationship, or an unexpected outcome such as a possible therapeutic or adverse drug effect. The study may be retrospective (based on analysis of previously accumulated data) or prospective (with a design that pre-dates data collection).

Satisfying a requirement for valid publication, research articles and case histories have a specific set of defining characteristics. Both are structured with distinctive sections that parallel the sequence of a critical argument. They present a question (often formally stated as a hypothesis). They marshal evidence to support various possible answers to the question or tests of the hypothesis. Finally, they attempt to persuade the reader of the truth of a particular choice of answers.

Review articles and case-series analyses

Review articles and case-series analyses, on the other hand, cover principally other scientists' discoveries rather than one's own, so they are "secondary." This is not to downplay their importance, nor to suggest that they are in any way second-rate. Reviews, such as those found in the "*Annual Review of . . .*" series, perform a valuable role by synthesizing the results of a search through literature or other records. Both reviews and case-series analyses may yield new insights, hypotheses, and understanding.

Reviews can be particularly valuable to someone entering a subject for the first time and for communication between scientists. By summarizing and synthesizing existing studies and technologies, they broaden readers' knowledge base. They can also introduce new ways of looking at a topic, and point out flaws or gaps in scientific understanding or in the published literature.

In the past, journals only published reviews that they had invited scientific authorities to write (and some still do). However, many journals now have come to realize that review articles increase the impact factor, visibility, and perceived value of a journal. In response, they have opened the authorship opportunities and broadened the variety of types and lengths of reviews they offer. Online publishing has also loosened previous restraints on the length of published papers, making it both possible and practical to publish longer, more comprehensive reviews when warranted.

Publishing a review article, case-series analysis and other summary research can be valuable to authors as well. Such a publication can benefit a new researcher in establishing credibility in his or her field, and can enable more established scientists to stake a claim in a field tangential to their primary research focus.

The structure and format of reviews and other summary analyses are less standardized than those of a research article. If there is a Methods section, it often states the manner and extent of the search. If a series of cases is being included, it often tells what records were accessed. The organizational sequence of these papers depends on the topic. Commonly, items are covered either in chronological order, from general to particular, or from frequent occurrence to rare. In most cases, the journal will offer quite specific guidance on the form and substance they want to see in a review.

Theses and dissertations

These important documents have a common purpose – serving as a gateway and rite of passage for the highest university degree – but almost no generally accepted rules for their structure or composition. They do, however, generally come in two varieties: compilations and monographs. Monographs are usually the preferred form for humanities, theology, and law. Compilations are increasingly common in medicine, technology, and the natural sciences.

Compilations are collections of research papers on various aspects of the main message of the dissertation. Students and professors alike appreciate this format because it offers a front-loaded solution to a common problem – the daunting post-degree task of repackaging one's lengthy and formal academic dissertation into shorter publishable papers. In the past, as newly minted Ph.D.s left academia and took on new job-related responsibilities, many theses and dissertations simply languished on the shelf and never entered into formal publication channels. Nowadays, about half of the four papers or articles included in a typical biomedical dissertation have already been published, and the other two are either in press, have been submitted, or are manuscripts in final draft form, ready to be submitted (Gustavii, 2008). In addition, compilations mean that some or all of the papers have been subject to peer review and scrutiny beyond that provided by a local departmental committee.

Because much research today results from collaborative work, the compiled articles generally have several authors. The doctoral student is generally listed as first author, but it is important to state which parts of the work were his or her own. (See Chapter 4 for more on authorship.)

Some compilation-based dissertations sandwich the journal articles between introductory and concluding chapters written by the student. Others append reprints of the published articles to a separately written document that provides an overview of the work. However, in either case, the guidelines described in this book generally apply to theses and dissertations.

Grant applications and other proposals

Competing for money is a nearly universal part of an academic research career. To be successful, scientists need money and finding it is generally their own responsibility. Not surprisingly, this can be a major source of stress, but avoiding common mistakes can help tip the balance in one's favor.

The success of grant proposals depends on many factors (Table 1.1). Of these, only a few are really under your direct control: the perceived innovative nature or critical importance of your proposed project, your skill in building a compelling case, and the care with which you write your proposal. The first two of these are up to you and your imagination. Hopefully, the guidelines in this book will help you with the third. For advice on other aspects such as choosing the most appropriate funding source and interacting with potential funders, see sources such as Friedland and Folt (2009), Hofmann (2010), and Schimel (2012). Many online resources are also available that contain profiles, articles, and links related to specific funders.

Writing for a more general audience

Popular books and articles – the name given to secondary accounts designed to entertain as well as to inform – may or may not adhere to the rigorous standards of regular scientific articles. They typically offer only a condensed overview of the methodology used and a summary of the major findings, without presenting actual data. For these reasons, such articles do not

Table 1.1 Some major factors that determine funding success (modified from Hofmann, 2010)

Factor	Ways to influence chances of success
The sponsoring organization	Research the most appropriate potential sponsor; ensure an appropriate match; cultivate relationships; write letter of inquiry and/or pre-proposal.
The innovative nature or critical importance of the proposed project	Be realistic when listing aims, and do not make them too interdependent. Summarize impact as broadly as possible.
The competition level	When possible, research this.
The skills of the grant writer in building a compelling case	Make sure both experts and generalists can clearly follow your well-written text.
The care with which the proposal is developed	Obtain and strictly follow proposal guidelines. Make sure the first page (executive summary or abstract, etc.) is perfect. Provide a feasible experimental plan. Draft a realistic time line. Present a well-reasoned budget.
Good luck	Not too much you can do about this one!
Good timing (in terms of whether the funder and/or society is ready for the idea or approach)	Pay attention to indicators.

generally constitute "valid" publication in the narrow sense of scientific publication. Often, they are called "science" writing, as opposed to "scientific" writing.

Because science writing is intended to be entertaining enough to capture the continued interest of potential readers, its style is much less somber than the usual scientific writing. The use of slang, puns, and other word plays on the English language are accepted and even encouraged. (The book you hold in your hands straddles the divide between science writing and scientific writing. With apologies to those English learners for whom translating humor in another language sometimes may be problematic, we have consciously decided to strive for a light touch on what otherwise could tend to be a very somber subject.)

Distinguishing between science writing and scientific writing is reasonable – they have different purposes and a different audience. However, one would be ill advised to use the term "science writing" or "popular writing" in a disparaging way. Writing (or providing consultation for others who are writing)

popularized accounts based on scientific research should be an important part of every scientist's outreach activities. The wider community is essential to adequate support for scientific endeavors. Scientists and non-scientists alike distrust and fail to appreciate studies that seem esoteric or secretive, but will defend and assist research that they have come to understand and value.

Other publication formats

In recent years, the lag time between acceptance and appearance in primary publication has grown. A gap of 1–3 years now sometimes exists. For work in highly competitive leading edge areas, this is no small consideration. Research notes, short communications, and research briefs have arisen to address the need for quicker, but less comprehensive transmission of results.

Writing variants such as abstracts, transactions, conference proceedings, local bulletins, posters, newsletters, websites, and other such outlets are often viewed as commanding less prestige than classic journal articles. Admittedly, they are not peer-reviewed, and they can be ephemeral in nature. However, they offer much more immediate communication with fellow specialists, and can be particularly valuable in helping one stake an intellectual claim in a rapidly changing field of study.

For practice with message, format, and audience, go to Exercise 1.

So, where *should* this paper be published?

Even after all these considerations have been examined, a lot of choice remains. There are tens of thousands of refereed scientific journals in current publication. Within a single specialized area, they differ in such vital aspects as topic coverage, format, interval and backlog of publication, acceptance rate,

"I'M SORRY BUT THERE ARE NOW 16,000 MEDICAL JOURNALS, AND I NO LONGER HAVE TIME TO SEE ANY PATIENTS."

© ScienceCartoonsPlus.com. Reprinted with permission.

page charges, and presumed prestige. Their readership varies as well. For the greatest efficiency and the best chance of acceptance and prompt publication, search early and well for the best match of topic, journal, and audience you can possibly achieve. Some surveys suggest that 80–90% of papers that are rejected from the author's first journal choice will eventually find a home somewhere if the author perseveres. Nonetheless, one can only imagine how many hours are consumed during this rewriting/re-submission process.

Very often, the most appropriate journal is the one you already most often read, or the one that contains a majority of the references you have identified. Did your literature search indicate that one or more journals were the principal sources of reports related to your research? If so, start there. Refer to those abstracting services or indexes that you used to begin a literature search, and use them to help identify potential avenues for publication.

After you have identified a few promising possibilities, go to the library or Internet and scan some recent issues. Check the table of contents. Look inside the front or back cover of a printed journal, and on the home page or directory of an online one. When you have uncovered some promising possibilities, seek answers to some fundamental questions:

- What type of journal is it?
- What categories of papers appear in the journal?

- Is the general topic of my proposed paper within the journal's scope?
- Is my topic represented in the journal frequently or only rarely?
- What is the journal's acceptance/rejection rate?
- How long does this journal take to publish papers? (How much is editing phase? How much is production phase?)
- What do rankings such as *Journal Citation Reports* indicate about this journal?
- What potential costs or other constraints need to be considered?

Nearly all journals will have two items of special interest – a statement of the journal's scope, and a variably titled set of editorial guidelines we've chosen to call *Instructions to Authors* or *ITAs*. Some printed journals publish these in every issue, others only annually (usually in the first issue of the year). Increasingly, they will appear on the journal's website. Do the scope and guidelines seem appropriate for the topic and type of paper you will be writing? Generally, if a journal is regularly publishing a number of papers on topics similar to yours, you stand a better chance of acceptance than if very few papers related to your topic have appeared. However, stay open to considering journals outside your field. Editors today increasingly seem to be accepting papers on the basis of their importance to the journal's audience, rather than on the basis of narrowly defined academic fields.

Read through the rest of the *ITA*. Note that some journals with scientific society sponsorship may require that an author or coauthor be a society member. Additional factors that might influence your journal choice include costs such as page charges and Internet access fees. These vary widely.

Consider impact factors and related indices

So you have a tentative journal choice . . . Will your colleagues see your paper if you publish it there? One way to determine whether scientists in your field are reading a journal is to examine journal citation reports through various databases such as ISI Web of Knowledge or *Journal Citation Reports*. These reports indicate how often the average article of a journal appeared in citations in other journals during a calendar year. Thus, they can provide a rough indication as to which journals within a given field are being more widely read.

Do they also provide a way to assess the relative importance of a journal? This claim is subject to continuing debate. There is little doubt that the scientific community views journals as having various degrees of status. However, like beauty, much of this may lie in the eye of the beholder. Despite repeated efforts, prestige has been a difficult matter to assess reliably. Relative intellectual influence certainly is not simply a matter of circulation – some journals with a high reputation in the scientific community have relatively small circulation. Moreover, while ranking journals by their relative impact can be helpful when comparing journals within a particular field of research, it is of far less value for comparing one field with another.

Keep in mind, also, that these comparisons rank journals in their entirety, not individual papers. Regardless of where they appear, a few papers may become classics that are widely cited; others may seldom or never be cited despite publication in a supposedly prestigious journal. (In passing, we'll note that in response, subscription-based websites have arisen that purport to rate individual scientific papers according to their perceived merit as assessed by a very large team of clinical researchers and academic scientists. For an example, search the Faculty of 1000.)

Most of us would like to think that the best choice for each of our publications would be a prestigious large-circulation journal. We pretty well know which these are, and we would love to build our reputation by publishing in them. This is natural. However, remember that the match of topic, journal, and audience is the critical issue. Because high-profile journals often receive thousands of typescripts per year, their rejection rates can run as high as 90%. Subjecting a paper to these lottery-like odds means a fairly sizable risk of living in limbo for weeks (and probably months), before ultimately receiving a rejection notice.

If, after conscientiously going through all these steps, you still feel unsure whether you have picked the right journal and the right format, it is acceptable to email, write, or call the editor. Frame your query diplomatically. Don't ask, "Will you publish my . . .?" or "Will you publish a review of the diagnosis and treatment of . . .?" Instead, ask "Are you willing to consider for publication a 50-page detailed review of the diagnosis and treatment of . . .?" You may learn that the editor has just accepted such a review, or that the journal never publishes reviews that long – a disappointment for the moment, but an answer that can save you time and work.

If information regarding publication time is not indicated in *Instructions to Authors* or on the journal's website, it is also appropriate to query the editor politely about this matter, requesting average and range of time from submission to publication. Most editors take pride in their continued efforts to try to reduce the time from submission to publication.

Gold or green: open-access publishing

"Open access" is an idealistic concept that views scholarly scientific information as something that should be available online to readers without any financial, legal, or technical barriers other than those that are inseparable from gaining access to the Internet itself. There are two general methods for providing open access: open-access journals – sometimes called the gold road – and self-archiving articles – sometimes called the green road. (It is an interesting distinction, but the two methods are not totally independent, because some open-access journals permit self-archiving of articles.)

Open-access journals are relative newcomers on the scientific publishing field. The first digital-only, free journals were published on the Internet in the late 1980s, but the concept did not really blossom until after the turn of the century. Today, many types exist. Of course, nothing is ever entirely without cost, and without traditional subscriptions, publication costs must come from somewhere. Some open-access journals are subsidized, either by a sponsoring institution or through revenue from related activities such as advertising, membership dues, or reprint fees. Others require payment, in essence transferring the costs of publication from readers to authors. A few rely heavily on volunteerism. Some use combinations of these measures.

The obvious advantages and disadvantages of open-access journals have been subject to much discussion among scientists, academicians, and publishers. Free access to scientific papers, regardless of affiliation with a subscribing library, lowers the cost of research, improves access for both scientists and the general public, and generally leads to high citation rates for the authors. At the same time, questions have arisen about the impact of this system upon the gate-keeping nature of paid publication and upon the peer-review system as well. These concerns have been backed by some disturbing examples, such as the incident in which a grammatically correct but nonsensical computer-generated paper was accepted, apparently without review, by a major author-subsidized open-access journal (Gilbert, 2009).

Many open-access journals are clearly professional and of high quality, such as the Public Library of Medicine's publications, *PloS Biology*, *PLoS Medicine*, and *PloS One*. However, a rash of newer open-access journals lack the reputation of their subscription counterparts, and questions have arisen as to the integrity of some of them. In the decades from its humble and idealistic birth, open-access publication has grown into a global industry fed by author publication fees. For most working scientists today, hardly a day goes by without receiving at least one emailed manuscript solicitation from one purported new online journal or another with glowing promises of prompt turn-around time and rapid peer-reviewed publication.

Alas, when something seems to be much too good to be true, it often is. Recently, a spoof medical paper filled with easily detectable flaws was accepted by 157 of the 304 open-access journals to which it was submitted. Most of these acceptances (in one case accompanied by an invoice for over $3000!)

were made apparently without peer review and required no revisions, despite serious errors in scientific content. Tracing Internet Protocol (IP) addresses made it apparent that many of the journals were concealing their geographic location despite names that sounded North American, and invoices revealed a network of bank accounts based mostly in the developing world. Summing up his results, the investigator, John Bohannon (2013) bluntly states, "The data from this sting operation reveal the contours of an emerging Wild West in academic publishing."

Open-access publishing is here to stay. If it appeals to you, take care. Examine the journal's credentials. For example, the Directory of Open Access Journals (DOAJ) provides a rapidly growing list of credible open-access journals; it already contains over 8000 journals, with abundant metadata for each one. Another gatekeeper is Open J-Gate. Also check whether the journal's articles appear in standard bibliographic databases such as PubMed. Qualified open-access journals that have been established long enough to have an impact factor also appear in Web of Science and Scopus.

Avoid salami-slicing science

One final caveat – as your search begins to uncover a variety of specialized journals, each may seem perfectly suited for reporting a different part of your data. Some studies do justify more than one report, particularly when different portions have given rise to differing messages of interest to different audiences. However, given the importance of publication in academic circles, one often can be tempted to carve clearly related aspects of a study somewhat arbitrarily into more documents than is really sensible. When all the findings together yield a single message that can be presented in a paper of normal length for the intended journal, they belong together. There is no reasonable justification for what one writer (Lawrence, 1981) has called salami science. (We would add that salami science tends to produce baloney!)

2 Conduct a comprehensive literature search

The only place success comes before work is in the dictionary.

VIDAL SASSOON

To most people, the word "research" brings to mind a white-coated scientist actively carrying out a laboratory experiment, conducting a survey, or sifting through statistical data. "Literature search," on the other hand, summons an image of second-hand involvement, a desk-based worker compiling studies done by others. In reality, however, search and research are conjoined twins – a powerful duo, equally active and equally vital to one another's vitality and success.

As is true for other siblings, one or the other of these twins may grow and develop more rapidly than the other at various stages. The first substantial writing that many beginning scientists produce is either a prospectus or progress report on their thesis or dissertation research, or a short journal article written jointly with their supervisor or major professor. Increasingly, a detailed prospectus that includes a literature review is being requested before research projects can begin. Likewise, in business and industry, a written proposal often must precede approval for research projects, and its worth can influence promotion and pay. In fact, one would be hard pressed to find any scientific profession that would not require checking published sources of information about a specific subject, integrating this information with one's own ideas, and presenting one's thoughts, findings, and conclusions effectively in a wider context. For these reasons and more, scientific writing really begins when you first reach past your own knowledge and experience to seek out, investigate, and use materials beyond your personal resources.

A book like this one is not the place for a detailed procedural catalog of all the productive ways of doing research. Conducting a research study is undeniably a big job. Presumably various other mentors are guiding you through that task. (A good published handbook is Ridley, 2012.) However, because our goal is to see you through to publication in a timely and successful manner, we think some recommendations may be useful, even if only as reminders.

Adapt to new ways

The ways in which we obtain information are changing rapidly. Whether you consider this to be a blessing or a curse depends on your approach to the task and your knowledge of available resources. A few decades ago, most literature searching was done manually. Computerized literature databases were searchable only through a mainframe, searching software was difficult to use, and online searching was expensive and limited in scope. Specially trained librarians did most of the searching, and researchers paid telecommunication charges for reaching the mainframe and were charged for each record received. However, articles and journals were being published at a slower rate that made such search techniques basically manageable.

Today, in many fields, a literature search that once took 6 months to a year can often be done in less than a day, and with far more thorough results. The Internet offers direct access to both new and old sources of information. Thousands of specialized databases exist around the world. Their software has become increasingly user-friendly. Research libraries and even moderately sized community libraries buy site licenses to various indexes, and offer their clients free searching of indexes. However, at the same time, the number of articles and journals that are published is increasing at such a rate that

"Okay, I've had enough of the good
old days. You can bring back the
computers."

researchers can find it difficult or nearly impossible to keep up to date through manual searching, even on a relatively specialized topic.

Tracking down the published literature relevant to your research specialty within the biomedical sciences still may take some doing. Although computers have made the task easier in some ways, they have also raised the bar for expectations and made the process more complex. Done properly, the project will involve much more than merely searching with Google, copy–pasting Wikipedia links, or doing a keyword search in PubMed.

Become competent with search terms

Most literature retrieval services are really matchmakers. They have some provision for searching a subject by way of keywords – brief terms chosen (usually by a study's author) to describe the major topics included in the document. To find the document, one must specify the same keyword that the author has chosen.

Language gets much of its meaning through context, however. As a result, typing in keywords during an Internet search without specifying their context or relationships sometimes can lead to strange, frustrating, or humorous results. Major literature-mining programs are continuously improving their ability to identify relevant papers and recognize the biological entities mentioned in these papers.

To improve the outcome, most literature retrieval systems use a special system called Boolean logic to specify the relationships between search terms. Its history is rather interesting. Boolean logic is named for George Boole, a mathematician who lived in the middle 1800s. It really is just a highbrowed way of describing three logical choices:

- I want this one AND that one
- I want this one OR that one
- I want this one but NOT that one

Search tools let you apply Boolean logic in various ways. One simple system asks you to choose from a menu of options that describe the Boolean logic, such as "all of these words," "any of these words," and "must not contain."

Suppose you wish to undertake a comparative study of types of skin cancer. By specifying carcinoma AND melanoma, you would retrieve all the hits (entries computer-matched to your search) in which both types of cancers appear in the same document, but none that mention only one. For a comprehensive search on both kinds of skin cancer, you would specify carcinoma OR melanoma. Either or both terms would appear in each document that is retrieved. Alternatively, perhaps you want more information on skin cancers, but know that because of its potential deadliness, there will be hundreds of entries on malignant melanoma. To narrow the results, you could specify carcinoma NOT melanoma. Any document about skin cancer that mentioned melanoma would be omitted from the list of retrievals.

With another version called Implied Boolean, you use "logical operators" – a plus sign in place of AND, a minus sign in place of NOT. The signs abut the front of the word, with no space between them. Precede this with other search terms you want to have it coupled with. For example, type plastic facial +surgery to get results for facial surgery and plastic surgery but not for the words plastic or facial alone. (Note that some systems require grouped words like "plastic facial" to be set within quotation marks.) Use a minus sign in front of a word to ensure that a word does not appear in hits. For example, poisoning –food would yield information on poisoning without including entries on food poisoning.

With some systems you can use other punctuation marks to search simultaneously for more than one phrase or keyword in addition to the Boolean. For example, to search for any document mentioning either cancer, you might enter "skin cancer" (carcinoma/melanoma) to find the exact phrase *skin cancer* plus either of the words *carcinoma* or *melanoma*. Another useful capability of some online databases is the option of using an index tree or thesaurus. The vocabulary is arranged hierarchically, allowing you to scroll through the list and select topics to broaden or narrow search parameters as desired.

Because computerized searches use slightly different algorithms and have become automated or semi-automated to various degrees, taking a moment to learn the idiosyncrasies of a search engine or database in the beginning can save time and energy in the long run. For example, most databases will let you define a time period or subject area for your search; many general Internet searches still will not.

Whatever the system, the results that it returns to you will depend heavily on your ability to formulate precise queries using relevant terms. Run a computerized search using your initial set of terms, and look over a sample of the records it retrieves. Are they mostly relevant? If not, revise your search and use more, fewer, or different keywords. Scan the returns to identify additional terms that might have escaped your initial attention. Interestingly, when researchers examined PubMed queries from a medical teaching hospital, they found that most queries included three or fewer words; however, using four to five terms was most likely to result in retrievals that the physicians judged relevant enough to read (Hoogendam et al., 2008).

For practice with search terms, go to Exercise 2.

Practice literature mining and strategic reading

The ways in which scientists engage their literature is rapidly being transformed, thanks in large part to two factors. One is the increase in digital indexing, retrieval, and navigation resources (Jensen, Saric, and Bork, 2006). The second is the emergence of ontologies – structured vocabularies of semantically related terms that model a domain of knowledge in a standardized way to facilitate computational tasks. For example, the Medical Subject Headings (MeSH) terms in the PubMed document retrieval system form an ontology that is used for indexing and annotating PubMed documents. They can be arranged in a hierarchy in which the more general MeSH terms appear at the top and the more specific terms appear at the bottom. They also contain information about a paper that may not be inferred just from the title or abstract.

Recognizing the value of the convergence of these two trends, software developers are striving to produce increasingly more efficient ways to extract relevant information through automated or semi-automated text-mining tools (see Theodosiou *et al.*, 2011, and references therein). Do your best to stay abreast of these new digital support tools. Their promise is great, not only for locating and extracting what has already been published, but also for helping scientists generate novel hypotheses as a result of combining information from multiple papers in new ways.

Scientists have always been strategic readers, working with many articles simultaneously to extract, compare, and analyse fragments of content. Like all busy people, they also have always sought ways to speed up their searches and avoid extraneous reading. (That, after all, has been the reason behind developing the search strategies outlined in this chapter's next section.) Today's online environment clearly has accelerated the rate at which scientists can accomplish this. Some say it also has changed the way scientists work:

> Now, as scientists search and browse, they are making queries and selecting information in much tighter iterations and with many different kinds of objectives in mind, almost as if they were playing a fast-paced video game... Just as the aim of channel surfing is not to find a program to watch, the goal of literature surfing is not to find an article to read, but rather to find, assess, and exploit a range of information by scanning portions of many articles. (Renear and Palmer, 2009, p. 829)

Personally, we think this is just fine. Studies of the research process show that scientists work with information in many different ways (Palmer, 2001) and for many different purposes. Whether they study individual articles to identify key components, to assimilate information for an evolving area of interest, or to monitor the competitive progress of peers, all these aspects are part of strategic reading.

Master the ability to scan and read the literature with many purposes (and sometimes unapologetically none at all) in mind. Strategic reading is part of the daily work of scientists today, just as it always has been. Nothing has changed except that it has become vastly more efficient in the digital realm.

Evaluate Web entries carefully

This vast interconnected system of smaller public and private networks lets users communicate around the globe, finding and sharing information, offering commercial services, and opening vast information resources. The entire venture is mind-boggling in its scope, and offers the successful scientific researcher/writer unparalleled new search and research opportunities. Remember two things, however.

First, the Internet has no gatekeepers. Material can be, and is, posted by anyone who cares to do so. This form of publishing lets everyone have a voice, and it provides for a wealth of information. However, just because something appears – even on a really fantastically professional looking page – doesn't mean that the information necessarily is credible. You will need patience, time, and enough critical thinking skills to disbelieve anything you find until it is consistently and intelligently validated.

Second, the electronic robot "spiders" that continuously scan and catalog the World Wide Web are limited. They cannot see or index everything. As a result, the information that you can access directly through general search engines and directories is only an astonishingly small part (many estimates say 10–20%!) of the whole. Much of the massive remainder, often called the Invisible Web or the Deep Web, is publicly available. You do, however, have to know how and where to look for it.

As you gather and sift through your mountain of potentially useful material, you will be faced with what may seem to be the slowest step so far – filtering and validating which content is legitimate and trustworthy. Don't shortcut this process. Your resources must withstand close examination later. No less than your professional reputation is at stake.

Trust your intuition if something seems amiss about a site. Is the author an authority, or merely someone peddling a product? Does the page have its own domain name? Is it undated or unusually old? Are there spelling or grammar errors that might indicate the page is not what it seems to be? Be suspicious of scientific or medical pages that display blatant advertising for particular scientific or medical products. Likewise, be suspicious of overly positive or overly negative commentary.

It can be difficult to recognize a cleverly done fraudulent web page. Thankfully, an honest and reliable one is more easily identified. As Gurak (2000) pointed out years ago, one or more of the following characteristics still indicate a credible site:

- It is an online version of a reputable published source, such as a newspaper, major media source, or an academic or professional journal
- It includes a list of works cited
- It is affiliated with a reputable educational or research institution
- The authors of the site are identified, with information about how to contact them

If most or all of these characteristics are present, you can be fairly confident that the site is likely to be credible.

Search many information channels

A vast river of scientific information flows through this world. Some channels in this stream are informal and unmediated. Others are formal, with explicit rules that restrict the kind or quality of information that is admitted into their system. The Internet provides but a small part of this flow. For a comprehensive literature search, these other channels must be explored as well.

For efficient use of time and energy, try to delineate the potential scope of your literature review right at the beginning. How extensive do you want it to be? Do you want to get a broad list that includes records even slightly related to your topic, or just a few most relevant ones? To what extent do you need to rely upon informal channels versus formal ones?

Then, be prepared for a bit of trial and error. Identify a limited number of concepts that may be useful to describe the research question at hand, and choose terms and accompanying logic that seem to define them. Precision is imperative. Searching for instances of a broad term like ecology would be akin to drinking from a fire hose, summoning thousands of hits.

When you are satisfied with the records obtained from one information channel, but feel you do not have everything that you need or want, begin all over again with another. The results will probably be different.

Go wide, then deep

Trace information in all directions through time and space. Each search strategy has different strengths and weaknesses, and will uncover a somewhat different set of information. One common sense computer-based approach is to start with broad initial exploration through general gateway sites such as

© Randy Glasbergen
www.glasbergen.com

"Cloud computing is cool technology,
but every time it rains I lose my data!"

Google, Wikipedia, Clusty/Yippy, and Mahalo. Progressively narrow and deepen your pursuit with more specialized search engines as you discover which combinations of three to five keywords work well for you. Finally, dive into the vast expanse of Invisible Web pages, those sites that are not picked up by Google and other broad search engines; on the next few pages, we'll give you some suggestions to get you started.

Tap into formal and informal communications

Networking long pre-dates computer-based searches. For example, a time-honored search strategy called the Ancestry Approach starts by acquiring a research report and examining its references to find other relevant references. Through reiteration, researchers work their way back through the literature until either the important concepts disappear or the studies become so old they can be judged obsolete. A more recent set of searching tools employs the Descendency Approach. Citation indexes identify a publication's offspring – those more recent books and journal articles that reference the earlier work.

Tap into other informal and formal communication channels, too. Informal channels – often called "the invisible college" – are so common in our lives that you may not have even paused to consider their importance. A colleague down the hall passes along an article he feels would be of interest. A reviewer notes a relevant paper that the author has missed. A student reads a post on an Internet chat group that starts her thinking of a new interpretation for her research. In the past, the lines of communication occurred primarily one-on-one, but with the advent of the Internet, they now are also maintained through a newsgroup or a computerized mailing list management program (technically a "listserv" but often Anglicized to "listserve"). Anyone can join most such mailing lists or newsgroups. Special topic groups can be found in printed directories, in Internet directories, or by searching the Internet.

Formal channels are more restrictive, and involve third parties with an element of judgment. It has been said that if literature searching were court-ship, informal channels would be face-to-face dates, but formal channels would be blind dates arranged by friends (Cooper, 1998). The classic example of a formal communication channel is an article published in a refereed scientific journal. It must follow specific requirements, and both editors and reviewers judge its acceptability. (As a whole, electronic journals straddle the world between informal and formal communication channels. Some evaluate submitted articles; others do not. When assessing electronic articles, this can be important information to have.)

The conferences periodically held by professional societies are also formal communication. Although their selection criteria for presentations are some-times less strict than those required for journal publication, they accept only presentations structured to their topic area. For information to enter the system, the researcher must be a member of the society and be aware of the meeting, and the research generally must pass at least a weak peer review.

Consult subject directories and search engines

What if you don't know what information might be out there or where it might be located? In general, there have been two different approaches to searching for information on the World Wide Web – subject directories and search engines. Originally they differed in how their information was obtained. Subject directories were website lists compiled by humans and organized under broad subject headings. To get on such a list, a site owner would either visit the directory or use an automated submission tool to send information about the site to the directory. Search engines, on the other hand, used computer programs (variously called robots, bots, or spiders) to scan the web from one link to another, gathering information on the pages they visited. Thus, the search engine was most apt to find a site if it had many links connecting it to other sites. However, like everything else in the online universe, the clear-cut division between subject directories and search engines is changing. Many newer searching tools include both.

Keywords are used with both approaches, but in somewhat different ways. Reflecting the background in which it arose, each subject directory categorizes its materials in a slightly different way, and each directory covers only a small subset of the entire Internet. To use subject directories most effectively, choose broad, inclusive keywords because unique terms will often yield no results. Keep in mind, however, that failure to find information does not mean it does not exist. The directory simply may not have picked it up for indexing.

Search engine databases, on the other hand, are almost all created by computer software programs. One of the most popular of these, Google, is rapidly becoming a verb as well (as in, "google it"). However, there are many others. Currently popular examples include Ask (Ask Jeeves), Bing, Duck Duck Go, Dogpile, and Yippy (formerly Clusty). Their (nearly impossible) goal is to index every word of every visible Web page in their databases.

When you provide keywords to a search engine, so much information is available that the response will usually be overloaded with results that mix trivial or irrelevant results with the pertinent ones. Thus, to use search engines effectively, choose very specific keywords (and combine them in an appropriate syntax to take advantage of advanced search features). The more uncommon the word or phrase, the more manageable the number of retrievals will be, and (at least in theory) the fewer irrelevant documents that will appear. It also is a good idea to use several search engines, rather than relying on the results from only one. Search engines attempt to help with their retrieval overload problem by applying ranking algorithms or formulas that determine the order in which the results are displayed. Small differences in these algorithms can have a major effect on the results obtained, even when you use identical search terms.

Let compilations help

Research bibliographies, research registers, reference databases, and citation indexes are compilations constructed for the explicit purpose of providing relatively comprehensive lists of published information related to a topic. They can be some of your most valuable literature searching sources.

Each of these databases has limitations. Some contain only published research; others, only unpublished research. As with searching the Internet, one searches a database by specifying keywords; any mismatch between the seeker and the indexer is likely to result in missed articles. Furthermore, despite their claims, none of the online databases access all relevant journals on a topic. Use multiple sources.

Research bibliographies generally take the form of non-evaluative listings of books and articles relevant to a particular topic area, but it is even possible to find bibliographies of bibliographies. Prevalent in the medical sciences, research registers are databases of studies focusing on a common feature, such as subject matter, funding source, or design. Prospective research registers are unique in attempting to include not only completed research, but also research that is in the planning stage or is still under way. Some research registers are more comprehensive than others; whenever possible, determine how long a register has been in existence and how the research included in the register got to be there.

Locate reference databases and abstracting services

Reference databases (Table 2.1) are particularly fruitful sources of information. Maintained by both private and public organizations, these services focus on a specific kind of document (such as theses and dissertations) or field (such as agriculture or medicine). In the past, most included only titles and

Table 2.1 Examples of the many literature abstracting and indexing databases available to biological and medical researchers

Database	Focus
Agricola	All major areas of agricultural sciences
Agricultural and Environmental Biotechnology Abstracts	Genetic engineering and its agricultural implications
Bioengineering Abstracts	Biomedical and genetic engineering and related fields
BIOSIS (Biological Abstracts)	Biology, agriculture, and biomedicine. Includes five indexes – author, genus, biosystematic grouping, concept, and subject
Biological and Agricultural Index	Environmental and conservation sciences, agriculture, veterinary medicine, applied biology
CAB Abstracts	Agriculture, veterinary medicine, and biology
CINAHL (Cumulative Index to Nursing and Allied Health)	Nursing and allied health professions
Medical and Pharmaceutical Biotechnology Abstracts	Human health, molecular biology, and biotechnology
OmniMedicalSearch	Search engine for many specialized medical databases
PubMed (MEDLINE)	Medical and health sciences, preclinical and clinical medicine
U.S. National Library of Medicine	Wide range of resources, incl. over 140 medical databases
Web of Science (found within Web of Knowledge)	Sciences, social sciences, arts, humanities
Zoological Record	Animal biology and taxonomy

abstracts, but full-text databases are becoming more prevalent and probably will be the norm in the future.

All major research libraries subscribe to numerous reference databases and have reference librarians to help first-time users. Some databases are accessible only through licensed sites, such as a university library. Individual vendors and reference database publishers provide detailed and readily available instructions on database searching. Learn the shortcuts that can make your life easier. For example, database software usually has the capacity to format reference citations in a variety of ways, representative of the formats most commonly found in the scientific literature. Some database software programs also can be integrated with many word processing programs to format references automatically within a document and insert them during typescript preparation. Become familiar with the most widely used formats in your discipline and select the most up-to-date and versatile tools available. Take the time to master them.

Consult citation indexes and dissertation abstracts

Citation indexes are a unique kind of reference database that identifies and groups together all newly published articles that have cited the same earlier publication. They allow you to determine which scientific papers and authors have received the most attention from other scientists. The best known of these indexes is Science Citation Index Expanded, a huge endeavor that covers over 150 disciplines (subsets are also available). Citation indexes limit their entries to references in published research, both journals and books, but are quite exhaustive within these categories.

Academia also houses a great deal of potentially valuable but largely unpublished material in the form of doctoral dissertations and masters' theses. Although many reference databases contain abstracts of dissertations, *Dissertation Abstracts* focuses exclusively on them. Both the printed and the computerized versions include records dating back to 1861. Increasingly, the full text can be purchased and printed. Alternatively, you may need to use interlibrary loan services to obtain a photocopy from the university at which the dissertation research was conducted.

Keep track of your resources

Even with computer files, electronic dropboxes, and cloud-based storage, a comprehensive literature search still means you'll soon be handling a surprising avalanche of papers and files – at the very least, personal notes, photocopies, journal reprints, and both computer-based and printed copies of electronic publications (including, sooner or later, your own). It is essential to have some system in place to deal with all the information that will be converging upon you.

What system is most effective? There is no one-size-fits-all answer. The popular press is brimming with suggestions, often coupled with explicit or implicit promises of spectacular life results if one can only become properly organized (for examples, see Aslett, 1996, 2008; Bolker, 1998). Seek out such materials if you feel you need motivation, inspiration, or novel approaches, but maintain your perspective. The secret to effective and efficient scientific writing isn't simply in getting organized. It is in wanting to get the job done and committing oneself to do it. Nonetheless, any system is better than none, and having a system that you can consistently maintain will go a long way to keeping that commitment on track.

Bookmark and stockpile potentially relevant material

The Internet is an ever-changing entity. The secret to dealing with this vast, chaotically organized resource and its instability is learning to understand how it works and how to use specialized tools designed to facilitate your scientific writing efforts.

It is particularly easy to forget how one actually located online material. If the source is not printed somewhere on the page (it usually is), write the full journal source on each photocopy or computer printout. List the author, if available; title, document, file, or website; date of the material; name of the database or other online source; date you accessed the source; and the full electronic address or Uniform Resource Locator (URL). For locations you may want to revisit, consider establishing electronic bookmarks. Indexing databases such as Web of Science offer ways to establish customized folders to store materials in various ways.

Mind your Ps and Qs to avoid unintentional plagiarism

Whether you photocopy journal articles, request reprints, or print potentially helpful information from the Internet, you will soon amass a great many facts and ideas couched in the words of others. The old advice from typesetting days, "mind your Ps and Qs," is worth remembering in this new context. First, watch the *Ps* – print materials. It will be tempting to use these copies as a substitute for taking notes. However, because of the way that writing and thinking are related to each other, it is actually more effective if you can begin to digest these written materials as you go along. Adopt a good note-taking procedure right from the start. Take many more notes than you think you need and prune them later. Staple the notes to the print materials so they will remain together through the inevitable subsequent paper shuffling.

Second, watch the Qs – quoted material. To avoid unintentional plagiarism, always write notes in your own words. If you must quote directly (an uncommon situation in scientific writing), use extreme care to identify quoted material either with quotation marks or with the letter Q. Even when you have restated, rewritten, or summarized the author's words, you must still cite your source. No single universal standard has emerged yet for citing quotes from the Internet. However, the International Committee of Medical Journal Editors (ICMJE, 2013), the American Medical Association (AMA, 2007) and the American Psychological Association (APA, 2010) provide widely accepted citing methods.

Countries and cultures differ as to whether the tangible expressions of an author are "intellectual property" requiring permission and acknowledgments for the use of them. In Chapter 14, these issues are discussed more fully. Here, let us just note that if you are accustomed to using other sources freely without clear documentation or permission, you need to be very careful to adjust to the system of documentation used in the United States. Use of intellectual property by others can be considered theft. Such use is viewed as unethical and even illegal if it is not clearly documented or if permission is not obtained.

It is also unacceptable to use too much information from a single source, copy material directly from the Internet, or to use a great many of your own words (yes, even your own!) from an earlier paper without referencing that paper. These uses are also considered plagiarism.

A related word of caution here: No matter how tempting the idea may be, never add a bibliographic reference directly into your personal database from the literature cited section of a review article and other publication until you have personally viewed it yourself and have verified both its citation accuracy and its content appropriateness.

3 Prepare for the challenge

Failing to plan is planning to fail.

APHORISM

At this point, you have amassed quite a pile of research information – both your own, and that which you've gathered from your literature search. Gathering it probably has taken longer than you thought it would. Are you tempted to just grab something from the pile and start writing? Don't. To do so would be akin to leaving on a trip to unknown parts without a road map! Instead, take control of the journey with a bit of planning, combined with an approach that works with and around your natural inclinations and keeps the momentum going.

Take charge of the task

"How do you eat an elephant?"
"One bite at a time!"

TIME-WORN RIDDLE

Has this ever happened to you? Under pressure of a deadline, you must write a paper, but you just can't quite get started and aren't sure quite where to begin anyway. Days pass, and your guilt increases. Finally, a couple of days before the deadline, your adrenaline kicks in ... you throw words together in whatever way you can, writing into the wee hours of the morning, then print a copy and hurriedly send it off or turn it in. Not your best effort, you mutter, but considering how little time you had, not too bad, either!

This is an old, sad story. We all have fooled ourselves like this at times. We know in the back of our minds that time spent on revision would have improved that hastily written paper immensely. But ... it might take more work, and we're not even quite sure where to begin. What if fiddling around just made the paper worse? What if we ran out of time halfway through? What if? Maybe it would be easier to keep on making excuses.

There is a way to win control over your writing. It's called the Process Approach. It carries no promises of transforming scientific writing into an effortless endeavor, but it should make the journey more efficient, effective, satisfying, and perhaps even enjoyable, compared with your previous scientific writing efforts.

Understand the process

A "process" is a directed activity in which something changes. All work generally involves a process: Things go in, they are changed in some way, and they come back out, hopefully with value added. Something is always happening – work is being done, a product is being formed, an end of some kind is being achieved. To describe or organize a process, you must examine its stages.

In response to concerns about the lack of writing skills among U.S. public school graduates, the practice of applying a Process Approach to writing has been gathering momentum for over 30 years. Exact definitions for the approach often differ, but its underlying principles are that writing is a skill best approached by methodically breaking the task into discrete stages and tackling each stage in a systematic, efficient, and effective way. As Graham and Sandmel (2011) have succinctly summarized, Process Writing generally includes cycles of planning (setting goals, generating ideas, organizing ideas), translating (putting a writing plan into action), and reviewing (evaluating, editing, revising).

Table 3.1 presents a brief overview of the steps involved in a fairly typical scientific writing project. The early steps – search and research – involve planning, gathering, and organizing information. Next comes the "real" writing, a paper's first draft. We recommend that you write this preliminary version in a standard format and a fairly conversational style, working as continuously as possible, without stopping to fine-tune anything. Then set this first effort aside to "cool" for a bit, so that it can be revised more dispassionately. There is plenty to do during this interval. The development of visual aids such as tables, figures, graphs, and other artwork takes the stage early and plays a strong part in the Process Approach. The writing pause that occurs between the first and second draft is an excellent time to pay further attention to them. This is also a good time to deliver a strong visually supported oral presentation, thus inviting colleagues to help in the evaluation stages of the cycle.

Revision, an essential part of the process, follows. Although word processing has softened the distinction between writing and editing drafts, it still is helpful to think of the revision process as a series of tasks of successively smaller scale. The first revision concentrates entirely on organization, logic, and broad matters such as clarity, readability, and brevity. After these matters have been considered, the writer is free to pay attention to word choice and style, and then to the fine points of grammar, punctuation, and such.

At last, the typescript is ready to be sent to the journal editor or publisher. However, the paper is seldom quite finished at this point, because almost always it will return with comments attached from reviewers. Addressing these concerns can set the Process Writing cycle going for one or more additional spins before it comes to rest with a published paper.

Table 3.1 Writing a scientific publication by the Process Approach

Stage	Action steps
Plan the project	Identify research question.
	Develop specific hypotheses or aims.
	Design studies to test each one.
	Determine feasible timeline with checkpoints.
	Meet with potential collaborators.
	Begin using appropriate organizational and productivity tools.
Develop its framework	Review literature to develop research context.
	Determine authorship; assign contributions to research and writing.
	Identify or develop ways to test, analyse, and synthesize results.
	Choose a probable journal for submission.
Do the study	Obtain necessary permissions and submit required paperwork.
	Conduct the research.
	Evaluate outcomes and assess whether study is ready to publish.
Draft the paper	Write working title and preliminary topic headings.
	Write first draft in whatever order seems efficient.
	Prepare preliminary reference list.
	Design rough tables and figures.
Get input	Share draft with collaborators.
	Present study via seminar, poster or informal setting.
	Note comments, misunderstandings, or ambiguity.
Revise in progressively finer iterations	Revise first draft structure, style, word choice, grammar, and punctuation as needed.
	Write final title, running title, abstract, keywords.
Deal with details	Obtain permissions to reproduce any previously published materials.
	File any additional paperwork.
	Check conformity to journal's *Instructions to Authors*.
	Crosscheck all reference entries with text.
	Ensure that all coauthors have read and approved final version.
Submit paper	Send paper to editor with effective cover letter.
	Respond appropriately and constructively to each comment from editor and reviewers.
	Edit and resubmit as required.
	Submit data to databank.
	Celebrate publication!

Construct a timeline as an on-going reality check

There is a reason why business organizations, grant proposals, and thesis committees ask for timelines. Devising a simple organized timeline helps anyone appreciate the relationship between tasks and the time required for each part of a proposed project. A realistic framework shows that your project is feasible and builds confidence in your judgment.

List tasks and accomplishments, and include target dates or other schematics that make sense in the context of your work. A checklist based on Table 3.1 may help keep you from losing sight of the forest among the trees. Consider adding additional columns with target dates for finishing each step and for the dates of their actual completion.

Keep the timeline simple; a single page is usually enough. If you have doubts about your ability to set realistic deadlines, ask for help from colleagues who conduct the same general type of research as your own. Alternatively, make your best guess and then double it. (We're all optimists!)

Remember that these are estimates. No matter how carefully you plan your timeline, at some point "science and reality will meet" (Friedland and Folt, 2009). Don't beat yourself up over a missed deadline, but don't just shrug and give up, either. Try to get back on track.

Manage your message

For maximal efficiency later on, two important organizational tasks should be completed before you begin to actually write any paper, scientific or otherwise. One is to organize the building blocks that will compose your overall message, placing them into a structure that tells a story. The other is to compose a brief statement that succinctly summarizes your story. These steps are interconnected, of course; take them in whatever order works for you. Both have their advantages.

Summarize your story: the elevator pitch

Remember that we said a scientific paper should shape a persuasive critical argument? Another way to express this would be to say that is should tell a coherent story that has one or more strong take-home messages. In business, they call this the "elevator pitch." If you were accidentally to meet someone important in the elevator, could you summarize your project and its importance in the short span (usually 30 seconds to 2 minutes) of that elevator ride? Presumably a message that was both interesting and potentially valuable would lead to further contact and all sorts of future possibilities. Isn't that what you also are looking for when you publish?

To define your elevator pitch, a few questions can help. How would your mother describe your research? How would your department head explain it to a visitor? What would a reader remember about it after they closed the journal? If and when you are able to answer these questions, your writing task will become much easier.

Often, the most straightforward way to develop an elevator pitch is simply to focus on preparing the tables and figures first. Out of all the various things you might say about each one, list just one or two major messages. Draw arrows between the messages to connect the pieces of your story together, and rearrange (and renumber) the tables and figures to conform to that story line. Then write one or two sentences (yes, that's enough!) that will form your major take-home message.

If you have composed your elevator pitch before your story's long version, now is a good time to convene with your coauthors. In light of the elevator message, discuss which data should be included in the paper, which important points form the story, and what the take-home messages should be.

Organize the components of your story

Whenever the subject of organization comes up in the context of writing, people tend to picture an outline, the most widely used technique for placing ideas in linear sequence for a written document. However, organization has both thinking and writing stages, and half of any writing effort is taken by the thinking stage. At the thinking stage, outlining is actually less effective than a number of other lesser-known activities. Technical writers report that these other methods help minimize the edit–rewrite–edit–rewrite syndrome common in many commercial and academic situations. After capturing key points on a concept map, issue tree, or cluster diagram, these writers translate the points into an organized list rather than a complete sentence draft. Only after approval of this version by supervisors do they go on to produce a full-sentence version.

Test-drive the procedures mentioned below, and see which best suits your organizational style. If you find one of these techniques to be helpful, you will probably discover yourself using it freely and often.

Brainstorm to expose new possibilities

When you truly have no idea where to begin, try brainstorming. Brainstorming is a problem-solving technique in which one person or a group suggests as many ideas as possible about a given problem or situation, concentrating on quantity rather than quality; the result is a random topic list composed of brief notes compiled quickly without much concern for order. Ideas on a brainstorming list often overlap. Some are general and some are specific. Some may be important, others silly. This is necessary and desirable. Avoid making judgments during this stage. This powerful idea-generating technique works best when the brain functions in an unrestricted manner.

After an exhaustive set of brainstorming ideas has been listed on paper, evaluation and organization can begin. Add arrows or numbers to suggest an appropriate arrangement, such as chronological order or order of importance. Consider the points in light of the potential audience, desired outcome, and publication constraints. Now the list can be rearranged, edited, and structured into a functional outline, if desired or required.

Develop concept maps (clusters) to suggest relationships

When you know what ideas you want to include, but are unsure about how to put them together, consider the technique called "clustering." Midway in complexity between topic lists and outlining, this approach has been developed and refined more-or-less independently by various information-management experts in fields such as computer software development and data processing. As a result, the approach has many names and variations, but all involve a process that results in web-like charts called concept maps, pattern notes, idea wheels, or bubble charts. For the visually oriented person, these charts can be an extremely effective way to organize information.

To begin clustering, write the paper's main subject in the center of the page and circle it like the hub of a wheel. Think of major ways in which you could subdivide this subject, and write these ideas on the page at intervals around the circled main hub. Circle each of these second-level hubs (or bubbles, if you prefer that terminology), and draw lines or arrows connecting them to the central subject. Think about each of the second-level subjects. Near each one, add any details, examples, or further divisions. Circle these too, and draw lines connecting them to their respective subjects. Continue this process until you run out of ideas. When you see repetition, simply rearrange the pattern of spokes. If the pattern reaches the edge of the page, turn the spoke into another wheel hub, and start the process over to subdivide your ideas further.

After all your ideas are clustered on the page, you may wish to go back and add numbers and letters to show the logical order. The numbered arrangement of these linked clusters can be used as a guide in organizing your writing and your final document.

Develop an issue tree to assess presentation balance

An issue tree appears similar to an outline, and it looks more like the roots of a tree than its branches. These quibbles aside, an issue tree can help check the balance of your treatment of a subject (Flower, 2000). Because it is more flexible than a formal outline, an issue tree is easy to rework during the organizing process and for a visually oriented person, it can seem less intimidating than other choices.

To develop one, write the main point at the top of a page. List sub-points under this main point. They may be phrased in any way that is comfortable, from single words to sentences or fragments. Then list sub-points below these, in decreasing order of importance. Connect all these various levels with branching lines in a cascading manner.

As you explore topics, you may find that one branch begins to grow and spread across the page, almost excluding the others. Perhaps this material is an unnecessary digression. If so, this can be corrected at this early stage, before you have invested hours in drafting a narrative. Alternatively, the other branches may need more detail. Ask yourself questions about the subject of each branch: "How do I know this? Why is it important? Does it contribute to the whole picture? What evidence do I have for this?" Be as complete as you can.

Outline to develop the paper's framework

Outlines come in many types, from sketchy affairs that are little more than lists to full-blown formal documents. Constructing any of these is a fairly mechanical process, and standard grammar books usually present specifically prescribed heading styles and rules of indentation. If your outline must pass outside review and critique, careful attention to such outlining conventions will help you gain approval. Strive for consistency and balance. Use either complete sentences or just phrases or words, but never mix them. Each level also should always have two or more parts. If only one element appears, incorporate its information into the heading immediately above it.

Remember, however, that outlines serve two distinct purposes – to help organize one's thoughts, and to help organize one's written words. Writers who find them useful for one of these purposes may find them less helpful for the other.

> For practice with concept maps and issue trees, go to Exercise 3.

Work with (and around) your natural inclinations

> There ain't no rules around here! We're trying to accomplish something!
>
> THOMAS EDISON

Ready to begin "really" writing? Your first inclination may be to write a tentative title at the top of the first page and start charging along through one section after another. But is this really the way you usually tackle a job? Take a moment to consider some other approaches. It's time to work with – not against – your natural habits. The key to success is building up a head of steam with a steady sense of progress that propels you on toward completion.

Start in the place that makes sense for you

When it comes to writing style, are you basically a rabbit or a turtle? As Michael Alley explains:

> Rabbits hate first drafts. They despise juggling the constraints of writing with all the elements of style. So, in a first draft, they spring. They write down everything and anything. Rabbits strap themselves in front of their computers and finish their drafts as quickly as possible. Unfortunately, their first drafts are horrendous, sometimes not much better than their outlines. Still they've got something. They've put their ideas into a document, and they're in a position to revise.
>
> Turtles, on the other hand, are patient. Turtles accept the job before them and proceed methodically. A turtle won't write down a sentence unless it's perfect. In the first sitting, a turtle begins with one sentence and slowly builds on that sentence with another, and then another. In the second sitting, a turtle then goes back to the beginning and revises everything from the first sitting before adding on. It usually takes a turtle several sittings to finish a first draft, but the beginning and middle are smooth because they've been reworked so many times. Revision then entails looking at the document from an overall perspective and smoothing the ending. (Alley 1996, pp. 241–242)

Few writers are strictly one or the other, of course, but you'll be most efficient if you determine which approach fits your general style and personality the best. If you have turtle tendencies, ease into the first draft by starting with the section you feel is the most straightforward. (For many people, it is Materials and Methods.) If you are a rabbit type, begin with the Introduction and just jump right on, quickly getting as much information written as possible.

In this book, we've set apart the core of a paper – Introduction, Materials and Methods, Results and Discussion – so that it can be addressed before the more mechanical aspects such as title page and acknowledgments. However, start wherever you'd like, and proceed in any way that makes the job seem easier to you. If you are really dreading even getting started, getting the straightforward mechanical aspects down on paper may be just the approach you need!

Whatever approach you use, set a realistic goal for each sitting. Don't stop until you've reached it, even if you become pressed for time and must "cheat" by finishing the section in outline form. Reaching a goal is almost guaranteed to give you a feeling of accomplishment that will help keep your momentum going. But don't stop here. Before you finish, write a few sentences of the next section. Psychologically, this makes it easier to start writing next time. Some writers claim it even helps to stop in mid-sentence or mid-thought!

Minimize distractions

While you are writing, it is worth making the effort to remove or escape from as many distractions as possible. Because each sentence in a scientific paper depends so much upon those around it, losing momentum usually leads to losing one's train of thought. Try to find a time and place when you can be relatively undisturbed. ("Relatively" is really a key word here!)

Inevitably, from time to time your thoughts will tend to fly off in surprising directions while you are immersed in your work. Don't try to remember one set of ideas while working on another. They will either divert you, or flutter off and never be recaptured. Keep a notepad near your work. Pen unrelated ideas onto a list when they occur, and deal with them later.

Watch what you eat. This tip may seem frivolous to those who have never been involved in a really lengthy writing project. However, as Alley (1996) points out, writing makes people restless, and that often makes them hungry. The wrong choice of snacks can derail your writing momentum. If you must eat, choose foods that require only one hand, don't stain papers, and don't make you thirsty or (worse yet) sleepy.

© Randy Glasbergen
glasbergen.com

GLASBERGEN

**"Goofing off is harder than it looks.
After the fourth cup of coffee, it's very
difficult not to accomplish something!"**

Build momentum and keep it

> The words come out of you like toothpaste sometimes.
>
> GARRISON KEILLOR

Write as simply and conversationally as possible. Remember those readers who will not be specialists in your area of research, and may not be reading in their native language. Imagine that you are describing your work to an interested friend in another scientific discipline. At this stage, don't worry too much about details of style or grammar, however. These things can be fixed at the revision stage.

Readers need a story line that has a beginning, middle, and end, with clear links between each step. Insert headings to guide the way, especially if the paper is long. Follow your outline or other organizational aid, but treat it as a life jacket, not a straitjacket. As you write, new insights may come to mind and some previously identified topics may become irrelevant.

The reason for developing a timeline is to avoid a last-minute panicky scramble to finish, but sometimes life gets in the way. If your deadline is approaching only too quickly, be conservative. Spend more time on the first draft, not less. Make an extra effort to develop a first-draft structure that your coauthors or other readers can easily follow. Work steadily and quickly, and get the whole thing on paper in as rational an arrangement as you can. There may be no time to cut, paste, and rearrange. There may not even be time to polish. It's admittedly a horrible thought, but it would be even more horrible to have the paper in bits and pieces when the clock strikes!

Write around missing information

A common cause of lost momentum is the missing word. It's on the tip of your tongue, but after 5 minutes spent looking in the dictionary you still can't find it, and you've ground to a halt as a result. Write the name of your favorite sports team, your significant other, or simply "???" in its place, and keep on going. Your subconscious will bring it to the surface later. When that happens, use the "search and replace" command in your word processing program to find your space-holder and insert the word where it belongs.

If you can't find the sentence to express an idea, you may not have fully formed the idea yet. Again, leave a space-holder, and keep on writing. Think about it later, perhaps when you are exerting yourself physically; many writers and researchers feel that exercise sharpens their processing of ideas.

Recognize the signs of bogging down

At some point in the writing process, you may feel overwhelmed. It can be an intense emotion, but be reassured that most writers experience these feelings

FOR BETTER OR FOR WORSE © 2000 Lynn Johnston Productions. Dist. By Universal Uclick.
Reprinted with permission. All rights reserved.

as a very natural reaction to the magnitude of their task. Words rarely flow
effortlessly all the time for anyone. Professional writers struggle, just like you
do. Everyone also experiences times when their writing efficiency seems to
decline or die.

Instead of quitting altogether when such feelings strike, switch to writing a
different section. Alternatively, begin to write (or talk) about precisely why you
are bogged down – surprisingly, this exercise often will free you. If you stop
when you are stalled, it can become an excuse to avoid starting up again.

Deal constructively with writer's block

It's a writer's worst fear. The deadline is fast approaching. You sit down to
write and absolutely nothing useful happens . . . You chew your pencil or tap a
rhythm on the computer console, stare out the window, get up for a drink of
water, decide to run an errand or shop for groceries. . . The inspiration to write
has vanished. You have writer's block. Or do you?

Those who write about writing debate whether writer's block – particularly
in scientific writing – is a real phenomenon or just a bit of folklore used to
explain garden-variety distraction and provide an excuse to stop working.
Whatever may ultimately be decided, a great number of solutions fortunately
have been suggested over the years. Many of them sound like the ideas we've
already mentioned. Here are a few other imaginative suggestions:

- Alley (1996) suggests that writer's block can arise because many of us are
  inhibited by hidden voices, such as criticism from our eighth grade English
  teacher or our department manager. He proposes drowning them out with
  classical or jazz music.
- Even when you can't get a word down on paper, Shortland and Gregory
  (1991) point out that you might find that you could easily talk to friends

about your topic. Write down what you would say, much in the manner of a rambling letter to a close friend. (Or, as a colleague suggests, record your conversation, and listen to it for ideas.) It will become easier to keep going once you have words on paper instead of still in your mind, and you may even make your story more understandable to your audience than it would otherwise be.

- For particularly severe cases, Mack and Skjei (1979) recommend a technique called "kitchen-sinking it," in which one repeatedly sits down and writes nonstop for a fixed but short time (such as 15 minutes) about any aspect of the paper's topic. One ends up with "everything but the kitchen sink," but these bits can be revised and pieced together for a first draft. It may be crude but it is a start, and this is often enough to get the writing process flowing once again. Reading over this mixture helps promote a focus on ideas.

- In an interesting turnaround, Nelson (1993) suggests that, rather than treating the symptoms, an author should view writer's block as an asset – the creative mind's healthy response to an inner imbalance – and use it as a stepping stone to new levels of creativity and artistic growth. Presenting writer's block as a constellation of problems with different causes and treatments, Nelson offers ideas tailored to such situations as beginner's block, perfectionism, notes and plans that refuse to make a book, and obsessive rewriting.

- If you feel the need for the structure and directedness of an entire program with both short- and long-term solutions, see the Four-Step Plan and Nihil Nimus approach developed by Boice (1990, 2000), a psychologist who has spent most of his professional life coaching academic writers in moderate but productive ways of writing.

- If you're still feeling stuck, look to the experts for additional approaches. New books on overcoming writer's block appear every year (their authors must not have the problem!). Note that most of these are geared toward fiction writers; a helpful exception is *Speed Writing for Nonfiction Writers* (Healy, 2013).

Finally, look in the mirror and check your attitude. Because writer's block is most often a first-draft problem, the most important defense against writer's block may simply be to keep in mind that a first draft is just that. It will not go to the editor, the typescript consultants, the printer, your department head, or perhaps even the coauthors. You are the only one who ever needs to see it. So what if the first draft has intellectual faults and flaws in prose? You will have many chances to correct these later. Instead of worrying about its imperfections, congratulate yourself. With the first draft in hand, you will have successfully completed the hardest part of scientific writing! Now, if at all possible, set it aside to "cool" a bit, and go do something else.

Keep tasks in perspective – and know when to stop

Each chapter in this book presents suggestions and guidelines for dealing efficiently with another of the sequential stages involved in scientific writing. However, along the way, even a relatively brief handbook like this one presents what can seem like an overwhelming myriad of details.

Writing is only one part of a scientist's work, however. There comes a time when a writing project must be declared finished so that life can move on. Revision can be taken too far. We knew a successful artist who would occasionally become so possessed by the urge to "touch up flaws" that we learned to hide the brushes so she couldn't completely obliterate her artwork!

The same runaway obsession can happen with scientific papers. Consider this advice to be some anticipatory intervention. When in doubt, apply a cost–benefit analysis. A well-known maxim that seems to apply to a great many tasks, including revision, states that 20% of the effort is responsible for 80% of the results, and the remaining 80% of the effort only produces an additional 20% of the results.

We can't resist one final word of guidance ... Above all else, keep both your sense of perspective and your sense of humor. The mechanics of writing the paper are important, of course, but don't allow them to overwhelm the intellectual challenge of pursuing a question that truly interests you and analysing the science that forms the basis of your research. The excitement of pursuing, developing, and expressing ideas is one of the finest satisfactions of research and scholarship.

4 Begin well

Well begun is half done.

Writing is usually portrayed as hard, joyless work. Great authors, it is said, must suffer from a sort of "creative madness" and work in mindless binges under endless pressures of deadlines, exhaustion, and criticism. Writing often is said to be stressful, unpleasant, and disliked. Yet, people choose to write for a living. If suffering were really the sole route to successful writing, why would anyone choose it?

Yes, it is true that stress is associated with writing that is delayed and then forced under deadlines. However, there are more attractive and productive alternatives to writing in tedious, joyless ways. We've already walked you through some of the preliminaries. In this chapter we guide you along a bit further. We will offer guidelines for deciding when to begin actually writing. We'll help you deal promptly with matters of authorship, both to minimize the potential for misunderstandings and to guide collaboration and any division of responsibility. We'll remind you of ways to use word-processing tools that will help you write more proficiently, avoiding pitfalls while becoming adept at using efficiency-enhancing features. We'll show you how to ease the writing task by paying attention to standard format conventions. Then, in chapters that follow, we'll walk you through the what-goes-where to write each section of the most common types of scientific papers.

Assess whether your research is ready for publication

As your research proceeds, the specter of publication will loom ever nearer. To some, this can seem like such an important step that it can be tempting to rush to this phase prematurely – or to run from it in fear. But how will you know when a study is actually ready to be shared through formal publication? Or whether it should be published at all? And if it isn't ready yet, what can be done with it in the meanwhile?

A tried-and-true answer is to consider that your research will be ready to be written up for formal publication when the results and conclusions satisfy at least one of these requirements:

- They are reasonably consistent, reproducible, and complete
- They represent significant experimental, theoretical, or observational extensions of knowledge
- They represent advances in the practical application of known principles
- They take knowledge of the subject a step further

In other words, when you are fairly confident that the outcomes of your study are new, true, and meaningful, go for it! If none of this applies, delay publication efforts. Sometimes, a topic that originally looked worthwhile turns out to be a dud or simply unsuitable in its present form. Don't throw away the data – just defer writing a paper based on them until further work has been done.

If the data are fine but you still decide not to publish this work, don't hide it (or yourself) in a closet. Perhaps at the moment you simply need a different venue for sharing this information. It may be time to consider a poster or oral presentation.

Oral presentations are more than mere stations on the track to eventual publication of new information, of course. Whether or not you are ready to write a full-length study, you should seek opportunities to present your research orally or in poster form at a public forum. The comments and questions you receive will help you determine where more work might be needed to fill gaps in your arguments and observations.

In addition, these opportunities will help you gain valuable experience. Spoken presentations are overwhelmingly common in the scientific and technical professions. They take many forms, from conference presentations, departmental seminars, and job interviews to classroom presentations, brown-bag lunches, and public talks. Treat each opportunity with respect. Each has its own valuable role to play in a scientist's life.

Deal early with authorship

If you are working alone, authorship poses no issues. Count yourself among the lucky in this regard. Today, you are also rare. Despite the popular cartoon image of the "mad scientist" – generally a middle-aged white male, working alone in a beaker-filled laboratory – most of today's scientific research involves collaboration between individuals of differing genders, ages, and backgrounds, often across several disciplines. Each comes into the project with a different set of expectations, and each contributes in a different way and to a different extent. No one would disagree that each of these contributors should receive credit for their particular contributions to the research. However, when it comes to the nature and extent of that credit, and how it can and should be equitably assigned, there can be some devils in the details.

Confer before starting the first draft

Does it really matter who is listed among a paper's authors? You already know it does. On the purely intellectual level, authorship is a two-edged sword: It confers credit for the work and it implies responsibility and accountability for it. On a practical level, authorship (or lack thereof) can impact academic and social standing, and can have important financial implications. Thus it should come as no surprise that, except possibly for the issue of plagiarism, nothing in the world of scientific publication is more likely to breed hard feelings and wreck friendships than a disagreement over authorship. Get this matter settled (in a very polite way, of course) before you even begin to write.

Where can one go for authoritative guidance? An idealistic answer can be found in *Recommendations for the Conduct, Reporting, Editing, and Publication of Scholarly Work in Medical Journals*. This publication from the International Committee of Medical Journal Editors (ICMJE) has a long and respected history. It began in 1978 as a way of standardizing scientific manuscript format. In the process of going through several revisions, it has grown to encompass advice on topics ranging from author responsibilities and conflict of interest to clinical trial registration. Their recommendation on authorship (ICMJE, 2013) states clearly that authorship should be reserved to individuals meeting all four of these criteria:

- Substantial contributions to the conception or design of the work; or the acquisition, analysis, or interpretation of data for the work; AND
- Drafting the work or revising it critically for important intellectual content; AND
- Final approval of the version to be published; AND
- Agreement to be accountable for all aspects of the work in ensuring that questions related to the accuracy or integrity of any part of the work are appropriately investigated and resolved.

In other words, According to the ICMJE, decisions on authorship should be guided by a simple ethical principle – any author listed on the paper's title page should take public responsibility for its intellectual content. No one is likely to be able to take such responsibility unless they have taken part in the research *and* in writing the paper or revising it for accuracy of content. Those who have not done both should only be acknowledged, either solely or as a group. In response to the ICMJE recommendations, some journals now require an explicit statement, signed by all the coauthors, to the effect that each author has contributed significantly to the paper, understands it, and endorses it. Check the *Instructions to Authors*.

By this restrictive definition, participation solely in data collection or solely in the writing of the grant that funded the research does not necessarily justify authorship. Nor does general supervision of the laboratory group qualify one for authorship unless the supervisor contributed to the conception and design of the research or to the analysis and interpretation of the results. Don't lose your job over this issue, however! Many working scientists, supervisors, and administrators disagree with this idealized approach. In any team project, some people's contributions will tend to be more intellectual or creative, whereas others are more practical or skill based. In the real world of academic publication, a common answer is to simply list everyone as a coauthor.

The shortcoming in this inclusive approach is that a reader has no way of knowing the nature or actual extent of anyone's individual contribution. To clarify this, a number of leading journals are beginning to request (and publish) a statement listing each participant's contributions to the study. Usually this section appears near the end of the article's text, under the heading "Contributors."

Our personal feeling is that this is an idea whose time has come. Even if your intended journal does not yet require a Contributors section, consider including one in your manuscript.

Agree on the order of authors' names

Does it matter in what order names appear on the title page of a typescript or published paper? Yes, it does, and it is important to verify the conventions in your field of study. Although the use of contribution designations (see above) may make name order less important, at the moment it still strongly implies the authors' relative roles and input. There is no universal standard, however, and guidelines vary from one institution and discipline to another.

In most fields, the first name to appear – the "senior author" – is assumed to be the individual who played the largest part in the study. In some disciplines and institutions, the head of the laboratory, department, or research team is automatically included on any paper coming from the laboratory (often as either the first or the final author), whereas in others this practice is frowned upon.

Visibility is a second reason that name order matters. If several people have worked together on a project, and you are not one of the first three authors named, be prepared for your name to be invisible in other authors' articles.

In reference lists (and sometimes in text as well), journals typically print all the names up to some arbitrary number (three or six are common choices). Beyond this number, they usually include only the first one or three names, and use *et al.* for the rest.

Who should decide how to rank the names? Generally, the team leader (who generally also is the senior author) is assigned this task. For a thesis or dissertation, the student's name generally comes first, based on the assumption that he or she did the major portion of the research and writing. When many people all have contributed more or less equally to the research, alphabetical or reverse alphabetical name order is sometimes used. Alternatively, if more than one paper logically comes from a cooperative project, authors sometimes rotate as first author on successive publications.

Note that being named senior author is not all glory. The senior author is also usually designated as the corresponding author. This is most assuredly a working position. The corresponding author takes on the responsibility for communicating with the journal editor during manuscript submission, peer review, and whatever subsequent administrative details may be required. After the publication appears, the senior author must be available to provide additional information or access to data should questions arise, either from the journal editor or from readers.

Many research reports result from the efforts of large cooperative teams. Who should be cited as authors, and how? The greatest number of coauthors on a single scientific publication so far is one that listed 2,926 (alphabetized!) authors from 169 research institutions (Aad, Abat, Abdallah, *et al.*, 2008). Although authors understandably would like to see their individual names appear, editors may like to see such extensive authorship credited by group titles. Rather than listing the names of individuals, none of whom can really take responsibility for the whole, the group could coin a group designation. A footnote would list group members, and each could legitimately list the paper on their personal resumes. (The authors in the above example did call themselves "The Atlas Collaboration," but then went on to list all their names anyway.)

Precisely because authorship matters, expect occasional authorship disputes. It's human nature to overestimate one's own contributions, and feel entitled both to be listed as a coauthor and to be nearer to the top of the authorship ranking. For a general article published in *Science* over 30 years ago (Broad, 1981), participants listed as multiple authors for one research article were each asked to assess their own contribution – the total effort equaled 300%! There is little reason to think one would obtain different results today.

Let authorship guide collaborative writing

An early decision about authorship allows the work of writing to be divided accordingly. When several people are collaborating on a typescript, one's first temptation may be to simply assign a section to each and compile the sections. This poses potential problems – including illogical strategy, weak transitions, and inconsistencies in terminology and language use, to name a few of the more common. In the end, someone will almost certainly need to go through the entire paper carefully to correct these. The best scientific writing should read as though written by a single author, not a committee.

An alternative method of dividing responsibility is to designate as coordinator either the senior author or the person assumed to be the best writer in the group. This person should assume responsibility for the outline, Introduction, Summary or Abstract, and Conclusions. Divide responsibility for the other sections among the remaining authors. Set clear deadlines for each step of the writing. Communicate often and clearly. When the rough drafts are collected, give the coordinator the license to change any section in order to make it flow smoothly into the whole. Then give all contributors the opportunity to comment on the collated draft.

Before submitting the final version to a journal, require all coauthors to read and approve it. Some journals require a signed statement from each author testifying they have done so. This is the time to obtain it.

Master the practical mechanics of writing

> My computer is down.
> I hope it's something serious.
>
> GRAFFITO

We all love to snarl at our computers from time to time, but few in the academic world could work efficiently without them. The incredible capabilities of modern word-processing programs can have a profound psychological effect, particularly because changes are relatively easy to make, and mechanical aids save a lot of tedious effort. By all means, use the computer to compose your scientific paper, right from the beginning. While the typescript is on the screen, insert and delete words or passages and rearrange text without repetitious retyping. With a single command, change a word or a spelling throughout the manuscript. From the first draft to the last, word processing will save hours of time.

Much of modern day science is collaborative, resulting in typescripts that pass through many hands. Count your blessings that you live at a time when the ability to send even lengthy documents as attachments to email messages makes collaborative typescript preparation easier than it has ever been. You can correspond rapidly with colleagues around the globe, seek and give advice and suggestions, and work together more closely than has ever been possible. Even when you work on collaborative writing projects with the person across the hall, you can send drafts back and forth between team members for comment, and can receive and incorporate those comments electronically.

In addition, most journals are now accepting electronic submissions, either as disk copy, through an email attachment, or directly uploaded to a website. This too is a welcome development for everyone involved, saving time and money and decreasing the probability of errors creeping into the final publication.

But are you using all the features that could make your job simpler? And are you using them as effectively as possible? Human beings are creatures of habit, but new habits can be surprisingly difficult to cultivate. Each of us has our private glitches in this regard. You may know that almost nothing in a word-processed typescript need be numbered, alphabetized, or sorted manually – yet you persist in typing in the numbers manually in your lists. Or you may be aware that the software includes a thesaurus, but you've never bothered to use it. Stepping outside your comfort zone to master new techniques is a matter of attitude. In general, these features are included because a great many people have found them useful. Will you be one of those people? Or will you just find some of the features to be a nuisance that distracts you from the writing task at hand? You will never know unless you take the time to give them a fair trial.

Test-drive the electronic vehicles that can speed you along

Automatic formatting, styles, and templates comprise a potentially handy set of time-savers. Merrily type away and the computer will format the material, automatically handling such mundane details as paragraph indentation, hyphenation, pagination, and heading styles. Automatic formatting can save considerable time when used on lengthy reference lists, in particular. An additional advantage becomes evident if that format later must be modified. One simple change to the document style sheet will update all occurrences of text formatted with a given style.

Some journals require that lines of text be numbered in the left margin to allow editors to refer authors to specific passages. In the past, this required the use of special paper, and changes in text necessitated retyping the entire typescript. With the proper command, word-processing programs will number (and renumber) lines automatically, either page by page or from the beginning of the typescript to its end. Even if the final version of your document will not show line numbers, consider using this feature on your rough draft. Handwritten comments in the margins of a paper copy can be difficult to decipher; a separate page with comments referenced to the text by line number is easier.

Another option is to use hidden text, the equivalent of secret parenthetical notes throughout the typescript. Characters formatted as hidden text do not appear on the screen (or in print) without a specific command. The hidden text feature can be very useful for dialog between coauthors that does not affect the typescript itself. Hidden text also can use special commands to mark entries for a table of contents and index. This can be helpful when one wishes to index a concept rather than specific words. (An index also can be based directly on a search for the occurrences of specific words, a less powerful technique but one that is still faster than the old handwritten index-card method.)

You are probably already using the "search" or "find" feature to locate and change words or characters throughout the typescript with a single keystroke. Remember, you can also use this command to standardize format and to instantly locate and scroll to specific sections of the typescript.

"Search" or "find" is often combined with a "replace" option, which can be very handy but needs to be used with care. For example, suppose you wished to replace the word "one" with "two" throughout your typescript. Since such a short word often happens to be part of another word, you would find all sorts of interesting but nonsensical words peppered throughout the text. Questioned would now be *questitwod*; telephone, *telephtwo*; done, *dtwo*. This predicament can be largely avoided by specifying "whole words only" or by typing a space before and after the word in the "find" box. (However, with the spacing option, if the word begins a paragraph it might now be missed.)

If your word processor has a thesaurus feature, use it (conservatively!) to help make your prose more varied and interesting. Turn to it if you experience a mental block and can't come up with the right word. Try a possible synonym and let the thesaurus suggest and substitute alternative choices. Look up a likely candidate from among the list, and more choices will appear. If you are still uncertain, the dictionary feature should allow you to judge whether you have actually found the word that best expresses your meaning.

Several computer features offer ways to ease collaboration between authors. Each writer can work on the same draft concurrently, or each can write different sections and later circulate these for comments and revisions. Insist that each author save a backup copy of the original draft before sharing it among collaborators. (There may also be times when you will want to write-protect a document with a password so that permanent changes cannot be made. Even then, always save a backup copy of the original draft before sharing it among collaborators.)

By permission of Johnny Hart and Creators Syndicate, Inc.

At the revision stage, the coordinator should insist that everyone "track changes," a feature that will clearly mark suggestions and revisions, as well as identifying their author. When several individuals independently suggest revisions, it used to be necessary to manually transfer such changes from paper to computer. Word-processing programs now have the ability to merge hidden text annotations and revisions from different file copies of the manuscript onto a single master copy. This can be a tremendous time-saver, but the coordinator still must check the final result carefully for possible glitches.

Last but certainly not least, if your program has the option of saving your document automatically at specified intervals, learn about this feature. Computers do lose material – both during and after you've worked on it. You must take extra steps to safeguard yourself from this catastrophe. Save your document at frequent intervals while you are working on it. If a power failure or other problem causes the program to shut down while you are working, you can recover everything entered up through the last "save" command. Save an additional copy on a flash drive for additional peace of mind.

Use spellcheckers wisely

> I now can quickly spell hors d'oeuvres,
> which grates on many people's nerves.
>
> UNKNOWN

Don't ignore the suggestions from your spellchecker. The ability to check spelling is one of the strengths and blessings of word processing. Take advantage of it. More than that – make its use a regular habit. Professional writing requires perfect spelling. Many people view misspelled words and typographical errors as signs of carelessness, lack of professionalism, or limited intelligence – hardly the impression one wants to make on an editor, reviewer, or grant committee!

Most spellcheckers have several built-in dictionaries in various languages. In the United States, the main dictionary usually is called English Dictionary. However, there are many differences between American, Australian, and British spellings of English words. The customization feature will allow you to open one or more of these variant dictionaries, either singly or simultaneously.

Spellcheckers can be used for more than their name suggests. Faced with a word that is not in their dictionary, most spellcheckers will display a list of one or more potential choices. This feature can be a tremendous time-saver when one knows only approximately how to spell a word or when trying to think of a word one cannot quite remember. Make a best guess, and count on being able to recognize the word when it appears on the list.

At a command such as "change all," most spellcheckers will correct a word's spelling throughout the entire document without further need for

"GARFIELD, I THINK I KNOW WHY WE'VE
BEEN RECEIVING SO FEW COMMISSIONS."

© ScienceCartoonsPlus.com. Reprinted with permission.

confirmation. This feature can also be used like a "find and replace" command
to change one word to an entirely different one. (However, remember the
potential for problems will be the same.)

Use a spellchecker to catch repeated words or errors in spacing. The best
spellcheckers will do this automatically. This can be an important advantage,
for repeated words (such as *this this*) and run-on words (such as *thisandthis*)
are easy to overlook during proofreading.

At the same time, recognize a spellchecker's limitations. First, spellcheckers
don't really check spelling. Instead, they compare the words in a document
with correctly spelled words that are stored in the program's dictionaries.
If the computer cannot find a match, it flags the word as unknown or attempts
to autocorrect it with a word in its database, which may or may not be
the word you intended. Because it operates in this way, a spellchecker will
not catch correctly spelled words used in the wrong context, homonyms, or a
correctly spelled word with the wrong meaning or tense. One cannot expect

it to catch such errors as using *their* for *there*, nor can it catch misspellings that form other words. For example, omission of one letter will change *underserved* to *undeserved*, significantly changing the meaning. Nothing can substitute for a final human proofreading.

Second, a spellchecker is only as good as the words entered in its dictionary. Specialized terms, most names of people and places, and many commonly used scientific abbreviations and acronyms are generally absent. The words in the main dictionary of a spellchecker cannot be accessed; they are stored in a special, compressed file format. (Furthermore, if an incorrectly spelled word were added to this dictionary, the error could not easily be detected and repaired.)

Be sure the words are spelled correctly when you enter them. Consult an authoritative resource for specialized biomedical vocabulary such as *Stedman's Medical Dictionary* (2005), which also appears in several editions tailored to specific fields ranging from nursing to pharmacy to dentistry. Examples of other helpful resources that are updated regularly include *Dorland's Illustrated Medical Dictionary* (Dorland, 2011), *Saunders Comprehensive Veterinary Dictionary* (Studdert *et al.*, 2012), and *Henderson's Dictionary of Biology* (Lawrence, 2011). If you regularly write papers replete with specialized medical terminology, consider investing in medical dictionary software, which includes both definitions and specialized spellchecking.

For practice finding errors that a spellchecker would miss, see Exercise 4.

Let grammar and style checkers guide, not rule

Unlike a spellchecker, which is fairly mechanical and straightforward, grammar and style analysis programs can vary in what they flag, depending upon which rules were used to design them. Any of them can be helpful for picking up simple mechanical problems, such as a missing parenthesis or quotation mark or an incomplete sentence. Some of the best will alert you to commonly misused words such as *affect* and *effect*. They may identify redundant, over-worked, wordy, or trite phrases, and help you detect noun-heavy passages by counting prepositions. Some also can pick up writing quirks, such as too many short sentences or overuse of "to be" verbs.

Like spellcheckers, most style analysis programs tend not to be closely targeted to biomedical writing, however. They tend to flag a great many passages that do not need revision. For example, they may question every instance of the passive voice, even when it is used appropriately in scientific writing. Some programs allow you to disable the passive voice rule and certain

Ode to a Spell Checker

Eye halve a spelling chequer
It came with my pea sea
It plane lea marques four my revue
Miss steaks eye kin knot sea.

Eye strike a key and type a word
And weight four it two say
Weather eye am wrong oar write
It shows me strait a weigh.

As soon as a mist ache is maid
It nose bee fore two long
And eye can put the error rite
Its rare lea ever wrong.

Eye ran this poem threw it
Your shore reel pleased two no
Its letter perfect awl the weigh
My chequer tolled me sew.

ARTHUR ON GNOME
(Shamelessly hybridized from
several versions circulating online)

other rules, but many idiosyncrasies inherent to the topic of your scientific paper will probably be questioned over and over again. Because they flag only items that can be detected by matching patterns, errors such as subject-verb agreement – a particular problem in scientific writing – also sometimes slip by.

All in all, grammar checkers still require a great deal of personal judgment. Each word, phrase, or passage that is questioned must be considered individually to decide whether the program truly has flagged an error. Sometimes, this is more time-intensive than relying upon the grammar checker built into one's own neural anatomy.

For practice finding errors a grammar checker would miss, see Exercise 5.

Dodge premature perfection

Because it is so easy to make superficial changes, all these timesaving computerized writing tools breed the temptation to make each draft technically perfect, with every comma in its proper place, every word spelled correctly, every heading and margin perfectly aligned. However, a superficially beautiful paper with organizational problems can be compared to a beautifully painted house with termites – lovely outside but unsound within. Trust us – it's unlikely to fool editors and reviewers.

Because the manuscript looks so good, many people find it difficult to throw away unnecessary material. If you find you've strayed off course, and ended up with more verbiage or material than you really need, you will need to cut out the extra, no matter how hard you worked at it or how beautiful it has become. (If deleting it entirely seems too hard-hearted or cavalier, there are alternatives. Some writers save their trimmings in a separate "orphan" file. This can be a valuable approach if there is any chance that later you might change your mind about the deleted material.)

Spellcheck as you go. That's fine, and with autocorrect it's mostly automatic anyway. Recognize, however, that style analysis programs will accept without question a completely incomprehensible or nonsensical document, as long as it appears in a form that passes for Standard Written English. Organizing your narrative for logic, organization, and coherence must come first. Trying to use one of these programs too early in the writing process can waste time and promote writer's block. The most efficient time to pay attention to a grammar checking or style analysis program will be later, after the document has been shuffled into a reasonable organization and polished to a reasonable degree of coherency, style, and grace. At that point, a grammar checker can provide one more way to ferret out undetected mechanical errors.

Only one mechanical aspect of writing needs slavish adherence from Day One: Save work frequently and make backup copies! The more time and energy you have invested in a document, the more important it is to protect that investment. A bit of paranoia can be healthy. Remember to update the backup file each time you make significant changes, and to change the file titles so you can discern one version from the next.

For extra security, store the backup copy in a separate location, or consider emailing the file as an attachment to a colleague or yourself. Remember, there are only two types of computer users – those who have lost files, and those who will.

5   Compose the IMRAD core of a strong first draft

Planning to write is not writing.

Outlining, researching, talking to people about what you're doing, none of that is writing.

Writing is writing.

E.L. DOCTOROW

By this point in life, you've undoubtedly viewed enough scientific documents to recognize that almost all follow quite similar patterns, often expressed by the acronyms IMRAD – Introduction, Methods, Results And Discussion (Day and Gastel, 2011) – or AIMRaD – Abstract, Introduction, Materials and Methods, Results, and Discussion (Cargill and O'Connor, 2009). Research also is reported in other ways, of course, including such formats as case study reports, research notes, and letters. Adding to the variety, there are a few major journals that structure their articles in entirely different arrangements. However, if you examine any of these with an analytical eye, you generally will be able to find the same categories of information, even without conventional IMRAD headings to guide you.

Together, IMRAD forms the core of an effective scientific paper. Each IMRAD section is structured to address certain questions, and together they shape a critical persuasive argument. We'll present them in order here, but write them in whatever sequence works effectively for you. If you're a rabbit (see Chapter 3), you'll probably start with the Introduction. If you're a turtle, you might prefer to write it after the Methods and the Results because these two sections are generally more straightforward to compile. If you're an iconoclast, you'll wait to write the Introduction until after you've written everything else in the core and decided what everything should mean for your audience.

Tackle the Introduction

After they have glanced over your Title, Abstract, Tables, and Figures, your editor, referees, and ultimately your readers will probably start here. Several questions will be on their minds:

- Is this a field and a topic that I will be interested in reading about?

- What is the problem, and why should I care?
- Based on what I see so far, does it appear as though this paper will contribute anything new and significant?

In other words, why was this work done? Deal with these questions briefly, interestingly, and as simply as possible. A well-written Introduction should locate your research within an existing field of scientific enquiry and persuade colleagues and even non-specialists to begin reading the paper's text after their attention has been attracted by the Title, Abstract, Tables, and Figures.

Writing a three-part Introduction that addresses those three reader questions works well. Sports enthusiasts might think of the process as casting a hook, playing the line, and reeling the fish onto land.

Provide a hook to snare the reader's interest

A "hook" is the term many writers use for the first lines or first paragraphs of a book. A well-written opening provokes a reaction; it gets readers interested and oriented. Who comprises your intended audience? Try to choose words and concepts that will catch their attention.

A useful approach in scientific writing is to begin with a broad statement that most readers would agree to without questioning. Use the present tense to indicate a generally true statement, or the present perfect tense to indicate something has been found true for a long time. Whether you reference such a statement depends on your field of study, your paper's topic, and your audience. Here are two examples:

> The most conspicuous feature of bats, distinguishing them from all other mammalian species, is the capacity for sustained flight (Zhang, Cowled, Shi, *et al.*, 2013).

> A comprehensive explanation for the phenomenon of circadian rhythms has eluded researchers for decades.

Try to make your first sentence as broad as you can, but don't overreach. To continue the fishing analogy your chances for success are best if you use a good quality hook of the right size. These hooks are excessive (and made more so by the lack of citations to back them up):

> Honeybee species are as fundamental to biology as elements are to chemistry and particles to physics.
>
> More than 10 million Americans have osteoporosis, making it the most important health problem facing the country today.
>
> Poison ivy's growth and potency has already doubled since the 1960s, and without effective controls it will soon become North America's leading dermatological problem.

As you write, use the next several sentences in your hook to move on from one or more of these general statements to progressively narrower sub-areas until you arrive at your own particular topic. Don't jump into identifying the research problem yet. Rather, concentrate on continuing to orient the reader, who may be from outside your own area of expertise. Concisely present what is already known about the subject of your investigation, referencing the most important publications. Don't try to mention everything here. (The longer you drag a fish around, the more likely you'll lose it!)

One to three paragraphs of such orientation should be enough for most journal articles. (A review article, thesis, or dissertation might require more.) Here is one brief example. Scan your intended journal for others.

> On stabilized dunes, riverbanks, playgrounds, and other sandy areas across North America, an observant individual sometimes may spy large black and yellow wasps industriously digging burrows in the soil. The Bembicini, or sand wasps, prey upon various insect groups. Members of one genus, *Bembix*, provision their nests with flies. Because of their large size, gregarious habits, and relatively elaborate behavior, these insects have attracted considerable attention among entomologists over the past century. Two decades ago, much of what was known regarding the American *Bembix* species was summarized (Evans, 1995).

Reel in readers to the gap your study will fill

The reader assumes you must have identified a problem of some sort – something unknown, problematic, or apparently contradictory. Otherwise, you never would have undertaken this work. Now they want to know the specific nature of this problem, and how you propose to solve or answer it.

The second part of an effective Introduction usually addresses these aspects. This is the place to present others' findings that will be challenged or expanded. Explain why there is a need to extend or modify what is already known or believed. Construct a gap and contend persuasively but politely that your work is the best way to fill it. Continuing the example from above, you might write:

> The only identification keys to the North American species of *Bembix* were published almost a century ago (Parker, 1917, 1929). Since then, long series of many species have accumulated in museums, and many new data on their behavior (Evans, 1957; Fritz, 1963; Matthews, 1989, 1998), larval structure (Evans and Lin, 2001), and genetics (Rodeck and Hsu, 2004), have become available. With these advances, it has become increasingly evident that Parker's identification keys and his concepts of species are in much need of revision.

As in the example above, be sure to support each sentence with references where they are needed. At the subconscious level, readers are also trying to assess whether you seem to understand the problem well enough to address it effectively. This is where your careful and thorough literature search really begins to pay off. Emphasize the most relevant work in the area and the most recent studies. Cite your sources fully and take special care to avoid even unintentional plagiarism of others' ideas or words. By presenting the works of others in your field in a way that clearly establishes which ideas are yours and which are theirs, you present yourself as a knowledgeable researcher and a careful worker whose own ideas deserve to be taken seriously.

In reviewing the literature, don't try to cover everything. This doesn't mean you should ignore sources that disagree with your interpretation. In the Discussion, you should and will mention these. However, for now, concentrate on those sources that bolster your justification.

On a practical note, your intended publication undoubtedly has a preferred or required format for references. If that format is numerical, disregard it for now. Your paper's first draft will be going through various revisions, and numbered references can easily become error-ridden. Use a simple name and date system such as (Jones, 2005). During the final stages of manuscript preparation, when you are double-checking all the text and references against each other, it should be fairly straightforward to change reference citation format.

Introduce references in ways that help develop your case

Reading the published literature, you may have never considered the fact that reference citations may be written to emphasize the information being presented or to emphasize – either weakly or strongly – the name of the author presenting it (Table 5.1).

Each style helps develop your case in a slightly different way (Cargill and O'Connor, 2009). Safe and conventional, the information prominent style is the style most commonly seen in scientific publications, and the choice many writers automatically fall back on. The first sentence of this paragraph is an example. This style fits in well almost anywhere that you need to cite a source, but it is not your only choice.

The weak author prominent style commonly lists several sources that agree upon a particular point. This style is particularly useful when linking together paragraphs. It functions well as a topic sentence when you want to introduce a new subtopic or different line of argument.

The strong author prominent style involves verbs coupled directly with author names. Variations in this style allow you to signal comparisons and contrasts, and give readers a glimpse of how you feel about a given bit of

Table 5.1 Wording choices to introduce an in-text citation
(adapted from Cargill and O'Connor, 2009)

Citation introduction method	Example
Information prominent. Author cited only in parentheses.	Unconventional writing assignments in a science class have been shown to benefit non-science majors in a way that traditional formats do not (McDermott and Kuhn, 2011).
Strong author prominent. Author name coupled with a verb that indicates how the writer feels about the information.	Epidemiological studies suggest that pesticide exposure may increase risk of Parkinson's disease, but Kamel (2013) argues that lack of detailed exposure information prevents results from being definitive.
Weak author prominent. General neutral reference to authors in present perfect tense plus one or more author names in parentheses.	Several authors have reported that rising aridity leads to increased abundance of some species within ant assemblages (Whitford 1978, Marsh 1986, Sanders *et al* 2003, Gunawardene and Majer 2004).

information. It can be helpful as you begin to introduce the specifics of the gap your study will address.

State your purpose and plan of attack

The end of the Introduction sets up your readers' expectations for the rest of the paper. At this point, they are either with you – ready to learn what your research has discovered – or they have slipped from the line, and you've lost them.

Write a sentence that quite specifically summarizes the question your research intends to address. This sentence is often phrased in hypothesis form. The format for this final step varies considerably. Check recent issues of your intended journal to learn whether one particular approach is favored or required. If not, you have considerable latitude. You might indicate your experimental approach, point out what is new and important about your work, or when appropriate, briefly summarize the answer(s) you found. Here's one way our semi-fictitious sand wasp writer might wrap up the Introduction:

> This research on *Bembix* was undertaken to provide a more useful key, to indicate several new synonymies, to describe two forms presently without names, and to suggest natural groupings of species within the genus.

Write your recipe: Materials, Methods, and variants

> I refuse to believe that trading recipes is silly.
> Tuna fish casserole is at least as real as corporate stock.
>
> BARBARA G. HARRISON

This section may have any of several names. Materials and/or Methods, Experimental Design, Protocol, and Procedure are some of the common ones. Sometimes it is divided into separately titled subsections, as well. Here, for simplicity we'll just call it Methods. In essence, it answers a simple question: How was the evidence obtained?

Because it also will serve as a guide to others, the Methods section can be thought of as a recipe, adaptable to various audiences. Just as beginner cooks would need different directives than professional chefs, colleagues reading a peer-reviewed research article expect one level of detail but grant proposal reviewers would generally expect another.

Also like recipes in a given cookbook, Methods may be organized in any number of ways, but within a particular scientific publication, all will tend to be couched in a fairly similar format.

Know what to include

Begin by listing the supplies that were necessary for your work, including both animate materials such as experimental organisms and inanimate ones such as chemicals. Explicitly note that the care and treatment of animals and human subjects conformed to the ethical and legal requirements for the country or countries in which the research was conducted (see Chapter 14).

Next, specify what was done, and for what purpose. Conclude with a presentation of any statistical procedures employed (but not the tests' outcomes, which belong in Results).

The key to a successful Methods section is to include the right amount of detail – too much, and it begins to sound like a laboratory manual; too little, and no one can determine what you actually did. You will recall that "valid" publication is often briefly described as including enough detail that peers could repeat the research and test its conclusions. However, this really means not just any reader, but a trained investigator with considerable experience. Once again, it is important to know one's audience. As an additional guide, frequently refer to examples published in your chosen journal.

In reality, few readers will actually try to repeat your work by following your description, and those who wish to do so will probably contact you for more information. Referees will look this section over in some detail, but for another reason. As part of the review process, they are almost always asked to comment on the extent to which the Methods conform to acceptable scientific standards.

Increasingly, federally funded research in the United States is requiring studies to be conducted in accordance with Good Laboratory Practice (GLP) guidelines (Benson and Boege, 2002). The GLP guidelines require preparation of standard operating procedures for all aspects of a project. Referring back to these procedures can be very helpful, both when preparing Materials and Methods and when documenting the data that were collected. Even when GLP guidelines are not required for a project, using this research approach can facilitate the writing task.

If you have followed a widely known method, simply name the principles on which it is based and cite the original publication or recent textbooks or handbooks that give full details. If you made changes to a published procedure, describe only the changes and reference the rest. However, if the original reference is not readily available or is written in a language your readers cannot be expected to understand easily, it is common courtesy to give the methodological details in your own paper. Be sure to still cite the original source. If applicable, give the language of its publication in brackets in the reference list.

When you have employed an entirely new process or technique, you must describe it in full. Be as clear and concise as possible. Check that you haven't omitted any vital details. You may wish to test the adequacy of your description by asking a colleague to do an experiment while following the technique as your text describes it. After all, if your new way of doing things catches on, future workers may name the technique after you!

Orient readers often

Chronological order is a common way to proceed through the Methods section. Alternatively, parallel the sequence in which you will be presenting your results later. In either case, using identical or similar subheadings in the Methods and in the Results makes the paper's organizational logic much more evident.

Sentence structure helps make the logic apparent, too. Start each paragraph or section with a bridge – a phrase or sentence that carries the reader on to the unknown from something they already know. Orient your reader to the big picture before plunging into a myriad of details. This can be as simple as a reminder of what has just been done, coupled with a statement of what happened next and why.

> After the samples were collected, they were carried to the laboratory for analyses that included ...
>
> Next, we calculated the cross-correlation between the two color channels, using the methods outlined by Lewis and Bridgeman (1992) but with the following exceptions. First, we substituted ...

Starting the sentence with a statement of purpose is common. Using the infinitive form, "to this" and "to that," is so common, in fact, that it can become overused and annoying. An alternative, illustrated by the third sentence below, involves writing a sentence that implies the reason for the following steps.

> To determine the effectiveness of the Pollard walk, the numbers of species in these samples were compared with those collected earlier by the sweep-net procedure. To obtain a statistical measure of this comparison, the methods used included . . .

> To confirm that the periodic actin-spectrin structure exists in the brain, we performed STORM imaging of hippocampal tissue slices of adult mice. Our procedure was to . . .

> In the erythrocyte cytoskeleton, the network formed by short actin filaments contains other proteins such as adducin and ankyrin. Thus, we also probed the distributions of these molecules in axons by . . .

Notice that some of these statements use active verb forms – the grammatical subject actually does the action that the verb indicates. Other statements are couched in the passive voice – the grammatical subject does not do the action of the verb. Is one form to be preferred over the other? Writing experts tend to say yes. Sentences based on active verb forms tend to be more direct and less wordy. However, the active voice does tend to emphasize the person responsible for the action, rather than the action itself. In contrast, with a passive verb construction, the action stands out, and the agent of that action might not even appear. When describing an experimental procedure, this difference in emphasis can be quite appropriate and even useful.

Researchers often receive advice to improve their writing by using the active forms of verbs. More are doing so than in times past, but many scientists still prefer to use passive constructions. The Methods section is one place where we are willing to be quite flexible. Use whichever voice feels comfortable here, and even mix them up for variety, but read the discussion in Chapter 11 about avoiding common problems that can arise with either choice.

Marshal your results

Scientific journals vary in how they require researchers to format their results. Some put Results in one section, Discussion in another, and Conclusions in a third. Some have no formal sections at all. But no matter how they are organized, this part of the paper is where you present those data you have gathered that have a bearing upon your hypothesis or research question.

Report only pertinent outcomes

Start this section with a very brief summary of your main points, just one or two sentences. (Okay, we might allow three.) This will keep you (and your readers) from losing sight of the entire forest amidst the many trees.

If you have not already done so, now is the time to decide on a logical order for presenting your story (see Chapter 3). These sections generally parallel the organization used in the Methods section of the paper. If you are starting here, work backwards so that those sections will conform to the same order as this section.

Undoubtedly, you have a lot of information that potentially could be included. Most often, writing the Results section is both an exercise in what to include and in what to leave out. Almost invariably, a scientific study will gather more information than a given paper needs to include. Overall, what was found or seen? Deliver the results that have a bearing on the question you are examining. (However, do not interpret them here unless your journal combines Results and Discussion.)

Deciding what is pertinent is a judgment call, of course, and it can be difficult to leave out material that you worked hard to obtain. However, just because you have the data does not mean readers "need" to have it, too. Remember, you are trying to tell a story or present a unified, coherent message. (If you feel that additional data not essential to that story still might be valuable to others, check the *Instructions to Authors*. Many journals have provisions to make those data available through either appendices or supplementary online retrieval.)

If the Discussion section is separate from the Results section, as it usually is, confine your comments in Results to what the numbers, observations, or other results show. Don't refer to published background information; that belongs in the Introduction and the Discussion. Don't compare your findings with other research or suggest explanations, except in the unusual case in which a minor point is being made that relates to a facet that will not be mentioned in detail in the Discussion.

Include tables and figures

Tables and figures are almost always an integral part of this section. If you have started by determining your story and take-home message (Chapters 1 and 3) and have already prepared your tables and figures (Chapters 7 and 8), this section should almost write itself. Don't use the text to parrot the information in the tables and figures. Readers can see the data for themselves. Instead, point out salient features and note relationships between the various results.

Understanding scientific writing: a tongue-in-cheek key

What the scientists said	What they meant
It has long been known that …	We haven't bothered to look up the reference, but …
Of great theoretical and practical importance…	Interesting to me …
Typical results are shown …	The best results are shown …
It is suggested that; It is believed that; It may be that	We think …
It is generally believed that …	A couple of other folks think so, too.
It is clear that much additional work will be required before a complete understanding …	We don't understand it.
Unfortunately, a quantitative theory to account for these results has not been formulated.	We can't think of one, and neither can anyone else.
Correct within an order of magnitude …	Wrong.
Thanks are due to Joe Clotz for assistance with the experiments and to Boyton Fird for valuable discussion.	Clotz did the work, and Fird interpreted the data.

AUTHOR UNKNOWN

Data presentation styles vary with the discipline, the journal, one's personal preference, and even with trends through time. Start by checking the *ITA* for your intended journal. These instructions may or may not give much detail about data presentation. Check recent issues of the journal, particularly for articles in the same general subject area as your own. Note the format, the choice to use figures or tables, the choice of figure types, and the amount and type of data presented in the text, the titles, and the legends. If the journal has accepted a particular style for others, it probably will welcome that style from you as well.

One rule that always applies is that the figures and tables must "stand alone." Another way of saying this is that a reader should not have to refer to the text to figure out what a figure or table shows or what it means. This is a bow to reality. Most readers look at the title, figures, and tables (and perhaps the Abstract or Conclusions) before deciding whether to read an entire scientific article.

Develop the Discussion and Conclusions

What do your findings mean? Why are they important? Discussion and Conclusions sections exist to answer these questions. They are often combined with each other and sometimes with the Results as well. A quick look through some issues of your intended journal should show you what format is preferred.

Organize points logically

Again, make an effort to orient your readers. Begin with one or two introductory sentences that allude briefly to current knowledge and to your working hypothesis or the study's goal. Discuss each of your results in the same order as they were presented. If you used subheadings in the Results, use them here, with the same format and in the same order.

Place findings in context

Your task here is to interpret your results against a background of existing knowledge. The Discussion should summarize how each of your results led you to the conclusions that correspond to the title of your paper. Moreover, to be most effective, it should do this so convincingly that the reader inevitably reaches the same conclusions as you do.

Examine both the limitations and the implications of your results. Relate your observations to other relevant studies, but rein in any tendency toward sarcasm when pointing out the shortcomings of another investigator's report. Indicate what the next steps might be to resolve any apparent conflicts.

Never omit valid results that appear to contradict your hypothesis. Suppressing such data is unethical. However, you are allowed to explain why

you feel they are anomalous. Discuss any possible errors or limitations in your methods and assumptions.

Remember the elevator message (Chapter 3). Explain what is new in your work, and why it matters. State new hypotheses (clearly labeled as such) when they are warranted. Include recommendations when appropriate. However, your scientific paper is not a sales pitch! When writing this section, watch for symptoms of megalomania. Avoid exaggerated or extravagant claims for your work. Carefully distinguish between facts and speculation. Be wary about extrapolating your results to other species or conditions.

Know when enough is enough

Hailman and Strier (1997) state that as a general rule, the Discussion should never be the longest section in a paper. This is a rule that is often violated.

It's all too easy to over-analyse and over-interpret results. You don't need to cover every possibility by stacking up so many alternative hypotheses and explanations that readers become buried in the pile. As Körner (2008) drily comments, "Reviewers rarely complain that the Discussion section of a paper is too brief." In the rare case in which reviewers want more discourse, they will probably be very specific about what they want you to include when you return a revised edition of your paper.

In the Discussion, never introduce new results for the first time. Not only is it inappropriate, it may backfire. Reviewers may request that you take this new information into account, do additional experiments, and resubmit a completely revised and expanded edition of your current paper.

Conclude with a take-home message

Unless your journal's format includes a separately titled Conclusions section, the final paragraph of the Discussion is the place to present such major aspects of your take-home message as the potential present and future impact of your results, conclusions to be drawn from them, practical implications of your study, and ways that you or others might build upon your results.

6   Assemble the rest of the first draft

> Writing the last page of the first draft is the most enjoyable moment in writing.
> It's one of the most enjoyable moments in life, period.

NICHOLAS SPARKS

The task took vision, determination, and perhaps some figurative glue on the chair seat, but at last you've finished drafting IMRAD, the core of a scientific research paper. Now it's time to include the somewhat automatic details that will complete your first draft. Let's get started with the lengthiest section left to do – the reference list.

Compile a careful and complete reference list

> Forethought and care make accidents rare.

APHORISM

As you've been developing the basic storyline of your paper, you've come upon many places where you have explicitly relied upon the work of others to help develop your message. Text citations and reference lists exist to acknowledge that reliance. Notice that there are two places in a scientific paper where referenced citations are crucial – the Introduction and the Discussion, and two other places where they rarely appear – the Abstract and the Results.

In developing a Reference section for your paper, most of the challenge lies in maintaining a high and consistent level of attention to detail. When at last you feel ready to submit your paper, check the references and citations, one by one. Ensure that sources have been listed for every important idea that is not your own.

Verify each of your references against the original document (not someone else's list!), both to correct any inadvertent errors and to ensure that you have not misrepresented the authors' intent. Then check every entry one more time to make sure that its style and format are consistently correct for your intended publisher.

Match citations and references carefully and thoroughly

References do just what their name suggests – they refer readers to other published studies or other pertinent information. To do this, each source appears in two places. In the text, where it is known as a citation, it receives only brief mention, either by author's name and year (the Harvard system) or as a consecutive number (the Vancouver system). The citation directs readers to a second, more complete appearance at the end of the paper, where it is known as a reference. There, readers can find enough detail to track down the referenced study or other information.

Obviously, this dual appearance only works if the in-text citations and the listed references match perfectly. Every citation must have a reference; every reference must have a text citation. Surprisingly, citation–reference mismatches are one of the most common errors that reviewers encounter. Even with computerized reference tracking programs, errors can creep in.

Every rule has its exceptions, and in this case they involve those types of materials that are not available to the public. This generally includes categories such as meeting abstracts, conference proceedings, personal communications, and unpublished data. They still would be cited but only in the text, usually by giving the source information parenthetically. Because they are not widely available, as Hofmann (2010) cautions, it is prudent to be careful about using such sources to support any strong conclusions you might be tempted to draw. Instead, use them only to support findings.

A manuscript that has been submitted to a journal for consideration should be cited as "unpublished", and (if referenced at all – styles vary) should appear in the reference list with author name, year of the version, title, and the term "manuscript submitted for publication" without specifying the journal it was sent to. If it has been formally accepted before your current paper is published, change the wording to include the journal name (and volume, if known), and in parentheses, add the term "in press."

How many references are enough?

The story is told that long-limbed, gangly Abraham Lincoln once was asked rather snidely, "How long should a man's legs be?" Lincoln's swift reply was, "Long enough to reach the ground." A similar answer could be given here – the right number of references is whatever it takes to document the works you have mentioned during your writing.

This dismissive answer is a bit misleading, though, and not much help. First, an appropriate number depends on what you are writing and whom it is for. A review article generally has many references, because its purpose is to cover and summarize extensive information. A thesis or dissertation may have even more, because part of its purpose is to demonstrate the writer's skill in literature retrieval.

In contrast, a research paper is not intended to be an encyclopedia. Readers will be overwhelmed, not impressed, if you include many more references than are really needed to develop your story. In fact, some research-based journals formally limit the number of references you can cite; check the *Instructions to Authors*. A common restriction is 40 references for full articles and 10 for brief communications, but some journals specify even fewer.

Which references should be included?

Keeping the number of references within a specified range almost certainly will necessitate making some choices. How can a writer decide which might be removed? The first criterion obviously must be to retain the elements that are crucial to developing the paper's story and take-home message. These citations must be left in place, because it would never be proper to rely upon others' work without crediting it. However, if strings of references are being included to bolster an argument by their sheer weight, look askance at them. Perhaps you can prune the list or condense it by citing a secondary source (as in the example at the end of this section).

Often, writers of science also are advised that the most relevant references are those that are the most widely available and most recent. These criteria may be generally helpful when applied to your own reference list, but they are also quite relative. What is available to some researchers may be difficult for others to obtain, and recent is a judgment call. In some fast-moving biomedical specialties, writers routinely include only references within the last one or two years. In other areas, such as taxonomy and systematics, publications that are decades or even centuries old can be crucially important to one's story.

However, sometimes it can be helpful simply to recognize that there are different types of references, and each type plays a different role in developing your story and message. Your sources can generally be divided into three categories. Primary sources represent the original publication of data, results and theories; the best example would be the classic peer-reviewed scientific paper. Secondary sources build on, discuss, or generalize from these papers; review articles are examples of secondary sources. Tertiary sources such as textbooks use primary and secondary sources to generalize still further.

For a general overview, such as you might provide at the beginning of an Introduction or Discussion, secondary or tertiary sources are an excellent choice. Citing a review article in a format such as (Matthews and Matthews, 2010, and references therein) can be a space-saving alternative to listing a string of original sources. When you are attempting to support or validate a specific finding (in a Results and Discussion section, for example), always cite the primary source. Make sure you have seen it yourself. Never use a secondary or tertiary source as a shortcut, and never rely on a reviewer's interpretation of data while passing it off as your own.

Mimic the journal's style for details

There are literally hundreds of differences in literature reference styles. Journal names may appear in full or be abbreviated (usually according to the American National Standards Institute, PubMed, or some other database). Web citations may be allowed, or not, and when they are, their format can be extremely variable.

There is really no shortcut to checking – once again! – your intended journal's *Instructions to Authors*. Also check the style actually used in some recent issues. Sometimes the *ITA* will not have been revised to reflect current practices.

If no citation instructions appear in the *ITA* and you can't find a specific model to follow for a reference that has you puzzled, a generally safe approach is to follow one of the more commonly accepted styles (CSE, 2006; AMA, 2007; APA, 2010; ICMJE, 2013). Check to ensure you have found their latest edition. These associations and several others also provide online reference style guides.

For your first draft, we suggested beginning with the Harvard name-and-year system for citations. It is easier to compile (and double-check) a final reference list from names than from numbers, and the name-and-year system minimizes the chances that references and citations will become scrambled or uncoupled during reorganizations of the text. Once you have identified the appropriate format for your citations and references, some excellent computerized bibliographic programs (such as ENDNOTE®) are available to help you consistently apply it.

Generate a title and other front matter

From the moment when the first words are written, every document needs a rough working title for identification purposes. However, a working title is rarely suitable for the final paper. At some point, you'll need to pay some serious attention to what name this masterpiece will bear. This paper is your gift to the scientific community and beyond; it is time to give it the careful and appropriate gift-wrapping that shows them you care.

Draft a variety of potential titles, and share these with colleagues and friends. Get their judgment to add to your own. In choosing a final version, ask several questions:

- Is it interesting, concise, and informative?
- Is it descriptive, unambiguous, and accurate?
- Is it accurate enough for use in indexing systems and bibliographic databases?

- Will potential readers be able to judge your paper's relevance to their own interests on the basis of the title alone?
- Does it include the main key phrase for your topic?

Choose carefully. Together with the Abstract and Keywords and phrases, the Title will introduce your story to the world.

Capture readers' positive attention

The world is awash with scientific publications. For yours to stand out, your title must attract readers, clearly identify the main topic of your study, and separate your article from others in the field, After all the work you've done so far, it might sound a bit depressing to be told that so much of your paper's overall success after publication may hinge on just this one phrase or sentence fragment. This is reality, however. Indexing systems and bibliographic databases will rely on the information that the title contains. Most readers not only will find your paper through its title, they also will use that title to decide whether it appears to be sufficiently relevant to their interests to merit reading further.

Traditionally, the titles of scientific papers were written as neutral description of a study, mostly expressed by a cluster of nouns and prepositions. This is still the most conservative approach to take. However, it does carry the risks of wordiness, and does not always convey as much information as it might. If you choose the descriptive approach, place the most important words near the head of the sentence, and pay special attention to the tips on conciseness in the next section.

> *Wordy, with weak beginning*: Report upon incidence of DNA damage checkpoint as revealed by comparative analysis of bat genomes
>
> *Better for this style*: Bat genome analysis for DNA damage checkpoint incidence

The traditional descriptive approach is no longer a scientific writer's only "proper" choice, however. Fashions and trends occur in scientific writing just as they do everywhere in this world. The format of scientific journal titles has shifted considerably over the years, allowing much more variety and informality.

For journals in some fields, writers are being encouraged to use a declarative title written as a sentence or fragment that includes what the paper says, not just what it covers. In other fields, neutral descriptive titles remain the norm. Sometimes, they coexist. For example, in the international weekly journal, *Nature*, it is common to find both:

> *Declarative*: Selective elimination of messenger RNA prevents an incidence of untimely meiosis
>
> *Descriptive*: Mechanism of DNA translocation in a replicative hexameric helicase

Declarative statement titles can be a good choice when a study addresses a specific question and the answer is not complex. Because they include both a subject and a verb, they can be more explicit about what was actually found.

Another common technique is to employ a two-part title separated by a colon or dash. The first half of the title uses grand, attention-getting phrases, word play, or even puns. The second half explains the actual topic of the paper more specifically.

> Scared of spiders: A psychometric evaluation of the arachnophobia questionnaire
>
> No specimen left behind: Mass digitization of natural history collections

Proponents of this style note that it puts the most important words in the title into a position of power at the beginning of the sentence. When well done, a two-part title has undeniable potential to get readers' attention. However, this is a very informal style. Although it is widespread in science writing in the popular press, serious scientists may find it simply annoying in a specialized journal, particularly if the title becomes too cute or contrived. For the same reasons, most editors frown upon fanciful titles. Likewise, titles that end with a question mark are seldom acceptable, outside of journals that are writing for a broad audience that includes non-specialists.

> *Risky choices*:
>   German saxifrage pollens are superior to those in Austria.
>   Does *Saxifraga* pollen in Germany resemble that in Austria?
>   Pollen between a rock and a hard place: German and Austrian saxifrages
>
> *Generally accepted*:
>   Pollen morphology of German and Austrian *Saxifraga* species

Keep the title concise but clear and complete

Most journals frankly prefer short titles, typically not over 100 characters (and sometimes considerably fewer), including the spaces between the words. This usually works out to only 10–12 words. Make sure each of these words counts. Identify key phrases people might use to search for the information contained in your paper. Then be sure the most central and important of these phrases appear in your title.

Many scientific paper titles are wordy and overly long, but short titles usually have more impact than longer titles. A title can be shortened in several ways. One is simply to delete trivial phrases (such as "Notes on" or "A study of") and articles ("the" or "an") that clutter the beginning of the title. Sometimes, prepositions can be removed, but be very careful when stacking nouns and/or adjectives (see Chapter 10) because strange or ambiguous meanings can result. Also do not try to shorten the title by using uncommon abbreviations.

> *Poor*: A study of chipmunk muscle tissue ion channel amino acid activation parameters
>
> *Better*: Amino acid activation of ion channels in chipmunk muscle tissue

When writing a series of papers on a subject, title each separately. Numbered series with the same title and differing subtitles are a headache to everyone, especially if the papers have slightly different sets of coauthors. Editors are unhappy with the implication that acceptance of one paper obligates them to publish successive ones. Sending the parts of a numbered series to different journals can complicate the situation even further, especially if Part 4 is published before Part 2, or Part 3 is rejected entirely. If you feel it is vital that everyone knows the papers are a series, link them by mentioning the others in a footnote on the title page or by citing them in the Introduction. If the typescript you are sending to a journal is interdependent with another unpublished paper, remember to include copies of that other paper for reviewers.

> For practice with title choices, see Exercise 6.

Check first-page conventions, rules, and requirements

As you check your journal's *Instructions to Authors* and look over the publications in recent issues, notice the journal's preference regarding such stylistic matters as capitalization and punctuation, title length, and general form. Titles may appear in all capital letters, capitalized in sentence style (though without a period or full stop at the end), or in the style in which all words carry initial capital letters.

Most journals specify what information should appear on the first page below the title. Commonly, this will include authors' names, degrees, job titles, and the name and addresses (postal and electronic) of the corresponding author, that is, the person to whom correspondence, proofs, and reprint requests should be sent. Keywords and funding sources may be mandatory, and some journals request a text word count.

Some journals ask authors to supply a running title. In the published paper, this will become the short phrase that appears at the top or bottom of each page (or alternates with the authors' names on every other page). It helps readers find your article when they are thumbing through a journal issue. For

© Randy Glasbergen / glasbergen.com

Manifest excellence beyond a paradigm of betterment with magnitude for implementation of probity and cohesion with coalescence and diversity of purpose steadfast, bounded only by our prescience and predestination as we gloriously emanate eminence for the divine unified triumph toward quintessential destiny!

GLASBERGEN

"I'm not happy with the new mission statement. I can still understand parts of it."

this reason, make sure your running title clearly links to your full title. Even in the absence of a formal requirement to supply it, you still may want to suggest a running title. If it is short but well targeted, it will probably be used.

Develop a suitable Abstract or Summary

An Abstract is usually inserted right after the title page in the completed document. It can be easier to prepare when your document is finished, but writing a first draft of your Abstract now may help you stay focused. Its potential importance is quite out of proportion to its short length. Taken together, your Title, Abstract, and Keywords form both the elevator pitch that will tempt colleagues to read your paper (Chapter 3) and the information packet that will give search engines the data they need to find and rank your article.

Abstracts come in several varieties. Some journals use the term "Summary" to describe abstracts of their articles, but a summary is not really the same as an abstract. An abstract is an abbreviated version of the paper, written for people who may never read the complete version. A Summary restates the main findings and conclusions of a paper, and is written for people who have already read the paper. Include a summary only if the journal requires it.

Informative-style abstracts include some data, and are commonly used with documents that describe original research. They address the same questions as the body of the paper, but briefly and without supporting tables or figures. Indicative abstracts (also called descriptive or topical) contain general statements about the subjects covered. Often used for review articles or books, they usually can be created simply by turning the table of contents into sentences. Both informative and indicative abstracts are typically limited to between 100 and 250 words, and different points are emphasized in proportion to the emphasis they receive in the text itself. They are generally written as a single paragraph.

Structured-style abstracts are often longer, sometimes allowing as many as 400 words. These abstracts group series of points below headings such as Objective, Design, Setting, Patients, Treatment, Results, Conclusions, and Clinical Relevance. Writing specialists disagree whether structured abstracts are on the way to disappearance or are evolving into a new kind of publication, with the main text available only in electronic form.

Staying within an abstract's word count specifications is a challenge for almost every writer. Be as brief and specific as possible, but write complete sentences that logically follow one another. Use the third person, active verbs, and the past tense unless it becomes unacceptably awkward to do so. The Title and Abstract are always read together, so for your readers there is no reason to repeat words or paraphrase the title in the Abstract. However, a modest degree of repetition of key phrases may increase your paper's online ranking (see the next section on keywords).

Write the Abstract so that it can stand on its own merits, because many readers of your abstract will never see your entire text. If possible, avoid citing others' work here; in those rare situations when a citation is essential, include a short form of the bibliographic details. Likewise, avoid unfamiliar terms, acronyms, abbreviations, or symbols; if they absolutely must be used, define them at first mention in the Abstract, then again at first mention in the text. And finally, never introduce information in the Abstract that is not covered in the paper.

Identify effectual keywords

Many journals require authors to provide 3 to 10 keywords (sometimes spelled as two words) or phrases to help a paper be cross-indexed once it is published. These often are placed on a separate line just below the end of the Abstract, but sometimes are included with other title-page items. Again, check your intended journal's *Instructions to Authors*.

Beginning writers sometimes pick keywords in a careless, offhand manner, almost as an afterthought. Don't underestimate the importance of careful keyword choices! With the increasing importance of online searching, keywords have become the principal ways in which other scientists find an article. You undoubtedly did the same when you began your own literature search (Chapter 2). However, studies indicate that most people rarely investigate beyond the first 20 or so results that their search uncovers. If you want your publication to be noticed, maximize the chances that a search engine will find you and place you near the top of the entries that readers uncover.

To do this effectively requires taking some steps that are quite different from past advice. When printed articles were compiled solely by human hands, the standard recommendation was to choose important, specific terms that did not appear in the title because both were used concurrently as information sources. Repeating words from the paper's title as keywords served no purpose beyond reducing the number of other really useful words or phrases one might include.

This advice has been turned on its head by the way in which computerized search engines find, identify, and rank articles. In this highly competitive market, the exact nature of their mathematical algorithms is a closely guarded secret. However, it is quite clear that matching patterns of repeated phrases is a key component. This mode of action suggests that it is now preferable to repeat key phrases and keywords in the title, abstract, and keyword lists. Do this in a natural, unforced manner, however. If you go overboard with repetition, sites like Google will pick up on this and may un-index your article entirely.

Think of words or phrases that you would look up if you were trying to find your own paper and couldn't remember its title. This is a good opportunity for brainstorming (Chapter 3). Name the most important and most specific topics in your paper. Include your main three or four key phrases, and add in another three or four keywords. If the same thing is often described in more than one way, such as a drug name or a disease, try to include both variants.

Whenever possible and appropriate, choose two-word terms or short phrases instead of individual words. A single general keyword usually will apply to such a very large number of papers that it won't be of much practical use, and many people search on key phrases rather than single words. As one indication that you've chosen well, consult science databases (see Table 2.1) relevant to your research area, such as the MeSH list of *Index Medicus*, and see whether your terms appear.

Finally, compare your Keywords, Abstract, and Title. Check that key phrases have been repeated in all these places in a way that appears natural for your audience but also recognizes how search engines work.

Acknowledge the help of others

Everyone likes to be thanked for helping someone, and most scientific publications provide a place to do so. Acknowledgments usually appear between the Discussion and Reference sections. (Note that some journals spell the title of this section with two "e"s, others with three. Both "acknowledgments" and "acknowledgements" are correct; follow the journal's example.)

Be generous

As a guideline, identify anyone who went out of their way to help you succeed, whether they contributed ideas, information, advice, or writing and editing assistance. Include any substantial help received from organizations or individuals that provided grants, materials, or technical assistance. (Some journals specify that funding bodies be named on the title page instead.) Thank them and describe their contribution. At the same time, there is no need to list people who did not contribute directly to the reported work, did no more than they were paid to do, or contributed only routine laboratory, secretarial, or office duties.

Remain factual and concise

Fiction and trade books often include florid and fanciful dedications and acknowledgments and sometimes more than a bit of self-promotion. Avoid writing anything like the paraphrased examples below. Even if they were to make it through the review process, they probably would cause colleagues to raise their eyebrows and question your scientific professionalism.

> In writing this second edition of my best-selling book, once again I had more than the valuable benefit of my own 30 years of experience in this field. I appreciate the hundreds of you who wrote to me attesting to the value of my suggestions, and gratefully offer a special thank you to my office manager, Tobi "Taskmaster" Washburn, whose official duties included keeping me on task with frequent cups of black coffee.

> I wish to thank the entire staff at the Los Angeles City Morgue immensely for providing me with an endless source of autopsy materials that will certainly be sufficient to follow this paper with a dozen more.

> The author especially wishes to thank his ex-wife, who by her absence made this work possible.

Acknowledgments in a scientific paper generally take an "only the facts, ma'am" approach. Be succinct, and to the point.

Pay attention to format

Acknowledgments are almost always presented as one short paragraph. Typically, the listing follows the order in which most projects are done. Those individuals who provided intellectual support are listed first. Those who provided technical support, permits, or materials for the actual research come next. Next come those whose discussions about your results helped shape your presentation. The list concludes with the financial framework that allowed this work, including grants, fellowships, and any other sources of funding. If coauthors have been funded by different sources, parenthetically cite the authors' initials to clarify these relationships.

> We thank D. Finkelstein and R. Woo for laboratory assistance, S. Clouser for field assistance, and the Swiss National Science Foundation for support through innovation grant no. 12345.

> We thank R. Battacharya, L. LaFreire, and M. McDonald for surgical procedures, gut sample preparation, and data analyses, respectively; Harvard Clinical Science Award (LX1RRO12345) for the liquid chromatography; and Perkins Elmer for the Flexar ultra-high performance LC. Funding sources included (WB) the China Scholarship Council (54321012345) and (RB) NIH grant AZ67890.

After you've written the paragraph, look at it again. Cross out any effusive modifiers such as "immensely" and "incredibly valuable." Abbreviate first names, and omit titles. Shorten long-winded phrases. "The authors wish to acknowledge the able assistance of the following individuals" is unnecessary, when a simple "We thank" will do.

As a courtesy, always ask consent from anyone you name; some journals require signed permissions from everyone who is acknowledged.

Be transparent about potential conflicts

"Conflict of interest" (also called dual commitments, competing interests, or competing loyalties) is the term used to describe the situation in which a person or institution is involved in multiple interests, and one of these involvements has the potential to corrupt the motivation for an act in another. It does not mean that someone actually has acted inappropriately, only that the circumstances create a risk for decisions in one field of interest to be unduly influenced by interests in the other.

Conflicts of interest can occur for many reasons, from desire for personal gain to the simple wish to repay a favor for a friend (or skewer a known rival), but the potential for financial gain has received the most attention, perhaps because it is the easiest to identify and quantify. In recent years, for example, increasing attention has been paid to the possible conflicts inherent in the pharmaceutical industry's heavy sponsorship of continuing medical education. Likewise, there is potential for concern when scientists may benefit financially from patent applications or stock ownership related to their research or sit on the board of an institution that may profit from the paper's publication.

Any time that a situation arises in which an author (or his or her institution), a reviewer, or an editor has financial or personal relationships that could be viewed as a possible source of competing interests or competing loyalties, this should be disclosed. As Hofmann (2010) points out, such disclosure is particularly important for review articles and editorials because, she says, detecting bias can be more difficult in these types of publications than in reports of original research.

In response to all this attention, many journals now require a signed statement about conflict of interest, and some journals formally require authors to include a sentence about it, either at the very end of the Acknowledgments paragraph or in a separate section just before or after Acknowledgments. Whether these statements have any effect on the perceived problem is a matter of a great deal of debate (PLoS Medicine Editors, 2008, and references therein). Either way, they seem to be here to stay, and their numbers will undoubtedly increase over time. Here are two examples of the forms it may take:

> One of us (JRB) served as a consultant to Happy Dog Veterinary Pharmaceuticals in 1999, prior to the onset of this research. No other potential conflict of interest has been identified.

> The authors declare no conflicting financial interests relevant to this article.

Nonfinancial potential conflicts (sometimes called "private interests") can take many forms: academic ties, professional rivalries, nepotism, religious or political views, to name just a few. There has been less research on these aspects of potentially competing loyalties, and developing guidelines to handle them has proven difficult. For now, the recommendation of several policy-making groups seems to be to promote disclosure of nonfinancial conflicts as a standard of best practice rather than a formal requirement.

7 Compile tables to develop, clarify, and support your story

> It is a capital mistake to theorize before one has data.
>
> SIR ARTHUR CONAN DOYLE

Graphics come in many formats, but in the parlance of an editor, all illustrations in scientific writing are of just two types, tables and figures. Both types of visual data presentation have the potential to provide vital support for your scientific narrative, but each has its own strengths and limitations and they share few similarities in format.

Thus, a logical place to begin is by deciding whether a table is actually the best choice for presenting the data under consideration. Then we will move on to consider efficacious ways to develop and present tables for a traditional research paper. (Later, in Chapter 8, we will consider when and how to use figures, and in Chapter 15, ways to adapt both types of graphics for oral presentations or posters.)

Use tables appropriately

Everyone has seen scientific tables – not surprisingly, for they almost always are a scientist's first choice among visual aids. They range from short and informal in-text presentations to formal compilations spanning several pages. In scientific and technical communications, they are so common that beginner writers sometimes attempt to use them even when tables are not the most effective or appropriate way to tell their particular scientific story.

Choose the data display that tells your story best

The strengths of numerical tables include presenting exact values, raw data, or data which do not fit into any simple pattern. Word tables are particularly useful for classifying information or describing relationships. The overall goal of both is the same – not just to "present the data" but also to make either a trend or the overall picture more obvious. The most suitable form is the one that will make it easiest for readers to discern those elements that are essential to building your story.

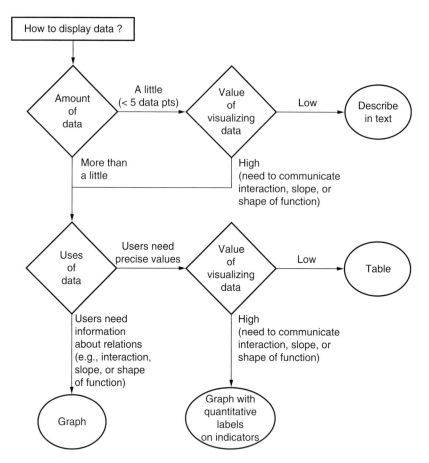

Fig. 7.1 The steps involved in deciding how to present data visually. In this flowchart, the diamonds indicate decision points. (Reproduced by permission from Gillan *et al.*, 1998.)

One's scientific discipline, particular dataset, and intended journal and audience will also influence this decision, of course. If you were delivering a fast-paced talk at a research meeting, simple tables showing small amounts of numerical data might be desirable, whereas numerically complex tables could be visually overwhelming. In a written document, however, those same small datasets might be summarized in the text or combined into larger, more complex tables because readers could examine the data in a more leisurely fashion.

Working through a multistage process (Fig. 7.1) can help a researcher decide how to present quantitative data (Gillan *et al.*, 1998). First, determine the amount of data you wish to present as a logical unit. Then consider the degree of numerical precision that readers are likely to need in order to follow your story. Finally, think of the different kinds of information that various readers might wish to have. For example, whereas readers with only a general interest in your topic might glance at your table or figure just to understand the main idea, specialists in your research area might examine the data in detail and perhaps even generate their own hypotheses about it.

Begin by constructing many rough tables in various formats

For many people, tables are the easiest graphic aid to compile, particularly now that they can easily be prepared electronically. In the process of conducting research, scientists often begin to construct rough tables to consolidate or summarize relevant information. This is an efficient approach that we heartily endorse. As early as is feasible, begin to organize your data into tables in various formats. By consolidating or summarizing information, the process will help you write your first draft more efficiently. Tabular format invites comparisons that would be lost or incomprehensible in narrative form. The results also can be serendipitous, suggesting new hypotheses and informing subsequent research efforts in unanticipated ways.

Consider word tables whenever you need to present parallel descriptions concisely. In medical writing, tables that appear in case-series analyses provide a good example of their appropriate use. In an oral presentation, a teaching article, or a review, small tables of text also may be useful to emphasize the main points or to serve as a convenient reference.

Number each table so you can keep track of them, and give each one a brief title. Beyond that, these tables can be crudely constructed, without much concern for details of style and presentation. Those worries can come later. (The Process Approach is at work again!)

For practice choosing between tables and figures, go to Exercise 7.

Revise tables thoughtfully

Almost every researcher has had the experience of puzzling over a scientific table. Regardless of what a table's nature, length, and complexity may be, thoughtful preparation makes the difference between a visual aid that confuses and one that informs the reader.

After you have decided which tables to include, it is time to revisit each one with an eye for details of composition. Tables are most effective when the data are arranged so that their significance is obvious at a glance. To achieve this result, pay attention to three factors – organization of the table itself, logical presentation of your findings, and visual simplicity.

Organize everything by apparent logic

In general, the independent variables in a table should be placed across the horizontal rows, and the items in columns should be the dependent variables. This rule is based on the simple precept that it is easier to compare like elements or work with numerical data when reading down, rather than across. (Try subtracting one number from another horizontally rather than in the usual vertical format, if you need first-hand proof.)

Some type of logic in presentation order of the research groups also should be immediately apparent, both within and between tables. Your readers will generally scan the table in the same way they would read text – across the column headings from left to right, and down the stub headings from top to bottom. Chronological order is a common organizer. Pre-treatment measurements, for example, might precede post-treatment ones; disease symptoms could be arranged from mildest to most severe. If there is no compelling reason for some other type of order, even listing material in rows or columns by the size of the numbers will help readers make mental comparisons.

The poorest sort of arrangement appears in analyses where data are arranged by arbitrary numbering of experimental subjects. Unless the numbers are truly relevant to understanding the results and some sort of explanatory code is included, experimental designations (A-307, D-10, and PC-2069) mean nothing to anyone but the investigator. In most cases, one can number the subjects by a conventional numeric system if they must be noted individually in the text. If they do not need individual mention in the text, omit subject numbers entirely in the accompanying table.

Some research on illustration effectiveness (Macdonald-Ross, 1977a, b) has suggested giving row and column averages as reference points. These averages can provide a visual focus that allows readers to inspect the data easily. This is a judgment call. Do not clutter up a table with columns of numbers that could easily be derived from other columns by simple arithmetic.

Format each table simply and efficiently

Word-processing software provides various table templates that greatly facilitate table formatting. Take the time to experiment with table shapes. Provide enough spacing between rows and columns to create a perceptual order to the data. The more visually simple a table appears (within reason), the easier it will be for viewers to comprehend.

REALITY CHECK © 2013 Dave Whamond. Reprinted by permission of UNIVERSAL UCLICK for UFS. All rights reserved.

It might seem that putting grid lines around everything would make a table easier to read. Actually the opposite is true. Unless your journal regularly publishes tables on lined grids, forego this option. Don't put a box around the table, either. A scientific table generally uses no vertical lines. Three horizontal lines run the full width of the table – one beneath the title, a second beneath the headings for the stub and the field, and a third below the field and before any footnotes.

Efficient use of space is a second goal worth pursuing. Most printed journal articles appear in either a one-column or two-column format. Whenever possible, design tables to fit the width of a single column of text. In printed scientific publications, narrow tables will stand a better chance of being printed close to the corresponding text.

The advice to list dependent variable data vertically not only facilitates comparisons; it generally makes tables more compact and reduces their width. For example, when a wide table is flipped so that the dependent variables are

Table 7.1 A wide table that would fit on a single-column page

MAb	A5969	F	6/85	tS-11	R	S	K503
	Assay scores (range 0–4) determined for various MG strains						
8F7/F	4	4	4	4	43	3	0
4G1/F	4	4	3	3	3	3	0

Table 7.2 Modification of Table 7.1 to fit one side of a double-column layout

MG strains	Assay scores (range 0–4)	
	MAb 8F7/F	MAb 4G1/F
A5969	4	4
F	4	4
6/85	4	3
tS-11	4	3
R	3	3
S6	3	3
K503	0	0

in columns, the result is visibly more compact. Compare the size of Tables 7.1 and 7.2. (In several ways, these two tables violate the guidelines in this chapter. When you have finished reading the chapter, see if you can identify them!)

Examine whether all the rows or columns are truly necessary. When all entries in a column or row are identical, it is nearly always advisable to drop that column or row. Instead, note the identical value in the text or in a table footnote.

Condense table headings to avoid multiple lines of text. Straightforward but often overlooked strategies for additional minor condensing include eliminating repeated words and economizing on heading lengths by judicious use of abbreviations. The key word is judicious, however. If abbreviations are overused, the table will no longer be understandable as a stand-alone product.

Steer clear of grossly oversized tables

Broadside tables – tables so wide that they must be printed at right angles to the text – are an annoying inconvenience to readers who must turn the journal sideways to read them. Likewise, lengthy tables that spill over from one printed page to another are difficult for printers to align and difficult for readers to use. Some journals flatly refuse to print such tables.

Large compilations of data often include information that is nonessential to the paper's real purpose. Before altering the table's format, ask (1) whether all the information in the table actually is necessary, and (2) whether it must be presented in its current form. Does the reader need to know individual test results, or might summary statistics (such as mean, standard deviation, range, or median) be sufficient?

If major condensing seems to be needed, reconsider whether the material in a complex table really must be presented as one unit. Two or more smaller tables might be easier to comprehend.

Decide how many tables are enough

When analysing your data and writing a rough draft, having a great many tables can be necessary and quite useful. A useful rule of thumb (Bjelland, 1990) is to use a table when putting data in the text would take at least three times as much page space as presenting it in tabular format. This usually occurs when four or more sets of data are to be presented.

When you move on to revising your rough draft, the urge may be over-whelming to keep all these tables in the final document. Resist that temptation. Instead, make a concerted effort to decide which tables might be combined, which tables would be better replaced by other illustrative materials, and which tables might be discarded in favor of summarizing the data in the text.

Because illustrations cost more to reproduce than text, some publications strictly regulate their number, size, and type; check *Instructions to Authors* and the format in recent issues of the journal. Reduce the odds of editorial requests for last-minute revision by not pushing any limits unnecessarily. An oft-stated general rule is that a scientific document should include no more than one table or illustration per 1,000 words of text. (Use the word count feature of your word-processing program to check.) Another general guideline says to use no more than one table or illustration per four pages of double-spaced typescript text.

Each time you consider including an element of data in your final paper, ruthlessly decide whether readers need that element in order to follow the logic of the story you are developing. Toss aside any tables that present tangential information, repeat information, or use a table when a line or two of text would convey the same information far more economically. Do not publish data solely because they were collected, no matter how much work was involved in that collection. Every study involves a certain amount of effort spent in gathering data that later turn out not to be needed. Careful planning can minimize this fact, but never eliminate it entirely.

Removing extraneous material from your manuscript does not mean throwing it in a trash bin or deleting the files, of course. Both legally and ethically, your responsibilities as a scientist and writer include retaining your sources.

Keep your data and be willing to share

The concept that observations can be repeated and verified by others is a keystone of the scientific method. Thus, researchers must keep the data that form the basis for their publication, and they must be willing to make it available to other qualified professionals upon request. This is required both during the publication process and for some period of time afterward.

How long is long enough? Conceptually, the length of this retention period depends on the type of data and the purposes for which it is (or potentially might be) used. Five to six years is a common recommendation, but in some fields it may be as short as two years whereas in others it can be essentially forever. Physically, cost and space considerations also enter the picture. There may be federal and state legal-regulatory requirements, fiscal factors such as tax laws, and operational needs of a particular organization.

As a result, literally thousands of specific data retention requirements have been put in place across many different fields, from government and business to education and the life sciences. Any time you have questions about the particular requirements that might apply to information under your control, it would be wise to contact your organization's designated legal counsel.

If you feel strongly that some subset of readers of your condensed table will be vitally interested in more details about your research long after you are able to provide them personally, consider placing your data in permanent storage at the time of its publication. Many journals now accept additional data as appendices or supplementary online files. The editor of the journal in which reference to the deposited material will be made can suggest arrangements for the deposit of such material. Within your published paper, give detailed information as to how to access this adjunct material; often this is included in the acknowledgments section or as a table footnote.

Watch the details

An effective table results from attention to a myriad of details. Study the format used by your journal. Consult *Instructions to Authors* and recent journal issues for table style, and mimic this style carefully. If the journal doesn't specify details of table style (and many do not), these details can usually be deduced from tables that have appeared in recent issues.

Note the style of table numbers and titles, box headings, subheadings, field entries, and footnotes. Check the use of horizontal and vertical rules. See where and how sample sizes ($n = 230$) are reported, and remember to include them. Without sample size information, your study may have little worth to others.

For numerical data, use decimals rather than fractions to express parts of a whole number. Do not switch units of measure within a column. Instead, restructure the table so that the second kind of unit and accompanying data appear in another column. Alternatively, change one of the units to an equivalent number of the other so that a single heading can apply to all.

Indicate units in column headings. If row headings designate numerical data, include the appropriate unit of measure immediately after or below the headings, either within parentheses or after a comma, depending on the journal's style.

Fill all cells in the field. This can be done in various ways. One system is to use ellipses (...) instead of dashes for a missing entry, *ND* for "not done," and *NA* for "not applicable" or "not available." For maximal clarity, some writers also append a footnote to the table to explain these abbreviations.

Remember that with the exception of certain camera-ready productions, print journals generally require that you double-space the entire table, including headings and entries in the text body. (Don't worry if this makes the table cover more than one page. The requirement to double-space originally arose to aid beleaguered typesetters; they will set the table back into a more concise format.)

Electronic journals, by contrast, often make you essentially become the typesetter. The published copy of the table that appears online will remain in whatever format you submit, complete with any errors.

Finally, notice that whereas legends and titles serve the same general purpose, they differ in length and in their location in your typescript. Table titles, usually the shorter of the two, appear at the top of the table itself just as they do in a published paper.

Mesh your graphics with your text

> Visuals must mesh with your text, like two gears that drive a machine.
>
> They must work in concert, each dependent on the other, to describe an object, a process, or a concept.
>
> H. BJELLAND (1990)

Table titles and figure legends are a vital part of every table and figure, not a tacked-on afterthought. When readers turn a page, they look first at illustrations, then at the legends and titles. Each one should orient readers toward that visual's meaning and enable them to identify its components. It should also differentiate that particular graphic aid from all other illustrations in the paper.

Make titles and legends stand alone but support each other

Consider the collection of tables and figures in your document as a sequence. Together, the entire set should tell your story and present the message of your paper. The first and most fundamental guideline is that they must stand alone. Each table or figure should be a complete unit of communication, containing enough information so that a reader can grasp its essential message without referring to the text. For this, the title or legend must be fully adequate. (In some journals, the "stand alone" requirement is taken to apply to the entire set of tables or figures, and abbreviated titles or legends are accepted after the first fully complete one.)

The task of table titles and figure legends is two-fold: first, to orient your readers as to what the data constitute, and second, to point out what these data mean to your story. Do not take chances on losing readers to frustration. Present your tables and figures, complete with their titles and legends but without the text of your paper, to someone who knows little or nothing about your research. Then listen, and be prepared to address the sometimes surprising questions your labeled illustrations may raise.

Paradoxically, while visual aids must be independent, they also must be indispensable. Good visual materials should spark reader interest, and interested readers will have questions. To be effective, use the text to answer these questions. The text, in turn, must refer specifically to each table and figure by number and clarify why the information is needed. The text statement that "Table 1 gives results" simply wastes space. Instead, use the text to summarize or explain, as in "Affected animals had significantly lower weights (Table 1)." However, avoid saying "as shown in the table above/below" both because it is verbose and because in a paper-based journal the position and page number of a table are not determined until typesetting.

Provide the information readers will need

Table headings must be complete and explanatory. All symbols and images within the table and figures should be explained in the titles or legends, in the table or figure itself, or in footnotes. If necessary for understanding, experimental details should be provided in the title or legend. If appropriate, matters such as degree of magnification and type of stain should be included. If possible, give statistical information.

An effective table title should include both the general subject and enough detail to make sense without the text. Many of the guidelines given for the titles of scientific papers (Chapter 6) also apply here.

Too vague: Deer deaths in Wisconsin

Better, classic style: Incidence of white-tailed deer fatalities in Wisconsin, 1995–2000

Better, declarative sentence style: White-tailed deer fatalities rose in Wisconsin, 1995–2000

Table title format varies considerably from one journal to another. Stating the point of the table, which items it compares, and perhaps the experimental design may be sufficient. However, some journals allow or require brief descriptions of methods, experimental design, or statistical analysis after the table title; others treat such information as a footnote below the table. In either case, keep them as brief as clarity and journal guidelines allow. They are generally printed in smaller text; lengthy titles, in particular, are difficult to read.

When including a number of tables in one document, use the same terminology and similar titles and headings. Sometimes, as in many clinical papers, the title of the first table can be used to identify the main component of the results for the sequence of tables, with shorter titles for the tables that follow. For example, the first table in your review of 25 cases of puncture wounds might be titled "Puncture wounds of the canine abdomen: clinical features." The second table could be titled simply "Operative findings and postoperative course."

8   Include figures for evidence, efficiency, or emphasis

> Art, like morality, consists of drawing the line somewhere.
>
> G. K. CHESTERTON

The general term "figures" encompasses all the graphics that are not tables. Whether or not one may be prepared to call them art, these visual aids can be vitally important in presenting a scientist's message. They summarize and emphasize key points and reduce narrative length. They simplify information and in this way enhance understanding. They improve the conciseness and clarity of the narrative. And finally, when carefully crafted, they add visual appeal.

Use figures when one will make your point more successfully than the text or a table would. Generally figures are necessary for one of three E's: evidence, efficiency, or emphasis. Evidence is easy. If something of visual interest occurs during a clinical trial or a case study, one naturally wants to document it with a photograph. During a taxonomic study, an unusual structure or notable range in a character's expression seems to beg for illustration.

Efficiency implies that the figure is the most succinct and effective way to make a particular point. In a scientific paper, for maximal efficiency one should generally combine material rather than presenting a repetitious series of similar figures. Draw several curves on a single graph. Combine diagrams to illustrate steps in a procedure, or cluster photographs to show morphological variation in a trait. Illustrations prepared for oral presentations generally present a relatively limited amount of information; they usually can and should be combined for publication.

Emphasis, the third E, is a major reason for using illustrations in a spoken talk, and often in popular science writing. However, journal editors may consider emphasis alone to be insufficient for a published research paper. Most editors will stringently assess each figure's usefulness in communicating the message of the paper.

In this chapter, we'll present guidelines for various types of figures for a traditional research paper. In Chapter 15, we'll discuss ways to adapt them for oral presentations and posters.

Match figure to function

Paradoxically, although figures in general are often overused, many specific types that could be used quite effectively seldom appear. Trends come and go, and the style preferred at any moment can vary with the scientific discipline and the personal and journalistic preferences of writers, editors, and reviewers. Even a quick search through the published scientific writing literature will reveal often-conflicting advice regarding the "do's and don'ts" each author judges essential for producing the most attractive visual aids. We suggest that you simply be aware of the different possibilities and keep in mind that each type of graphic aid has its own strengths and weaknesses (Table 8.1).

Table 8.1 Choose the most effective type of illustration for a given goal

To accomplish this	Choose one of these
To present exact values, raw data, or data which do not fit into any simple pattern	Table, list
To summarize trends, show interactions between two or more variables, relate data to constants, or emphasize an overall pattern rather than specific measurements	Line graph
To dramatize differences or draw comparisons	Bar graph
To illustrate complex relationships, spatial configurations, pathways, processes, or interactions	Diagram
To show sequential processes	Flowchart
To classify information	Table, list, pictograph
To describe parts or circuits	Schematic
To describe a process, organization, or model	Pictograph, flowchart, block diagram
To compare or contrast	Pictograph, pie chart, bar graph
To describe a change of state	Line graph, bar graph
To describe proportions	Pie chart, bar graph
To describe relationships	Table, line graph, block diagram
To describe causation	Flowchart, pictograph
To describe an entire object	Schematic, drawing, photograph
To show the vertical or horizontal hierarchy within an object, idea, or organization	Flowchart, drawing tree, block diagram

Many illustrations transform numerical data into other shapes. Graphs and histograms are examples. Developing these visual aids takes more conscious effort than tables do, but they are often the most powerful way to express relationships. Their best purpose is to illuminate ideas and trends that would be all but invisible to readers if the same data were presented as columns and rows of numbers in conventional table form.

Documentary illustrations such as instrument tracings, photographs, and micrographs offer primary evidence of the scientific observations presented in the text. Their most suitable purpose is to allow readers to see for themselves what you are basing your claims upon. When carefully chosen for clarity and relevance, these visual aids can be literally worth a thousand words.

Another category of illustrations includes explanatory materials such as maps, charts, and line drawings. Their primary purpose is to orient your readers. The less familiar with your work your potential audience is expected to be, the more strongly you should consider including these.

The most suitable figure format is the one that will make it easiest for readers to see the comparisons between those elements that are essential to building your story. One's scientific discipline, the particular dataset, and the intended journal and audience will also influence this decision. For a presentation to a group of specialists in your field, a logarithmic graph might be a perfectly appropriate way to back up your story, but showing the same figure as part of a talk to non-scientists could be confusing.

Prepare simple, honest figures

Even a cursory look through the scientific literature will reveal that published illustrations differ widely in their quality. Many details in format lettering and labeling call for careful attention, and seemingly small things can make the difference between a so-so illustration and an excellent one. The requirements for figures that will be printed are different from those for posters and oral presentations (see Chapters 15 and 16), and it is seldom that a single piece of artwork can serve a dual or triple purpose.

Perhaps because humans are so visually oriented, graphics are particularly prone to being misinterpreted unless special care is taken in their preparation. The suggestions in this chapter are only a brief introduction to the large research field called data visualization. To learn more, consider starting with one of the earliest books to discuss misleading graphs, *How to Lie with Statistics* (Huff, 1954, updated 1993). Accessible recent references include Tufte (2001) and Jones (2006).

Beware of glitziness and chartjunk

If professional graphic artists and photographers are available, count yourself among the lucky few. Increasingly, scientists are required to prepare their own graphic illustrations. Investigate the latest software and learn how to use a good graphics program. However, watch out for what Peterson (1993) calls "glitziness." It is easy to become seduced by the capabilities of sophisticated graphics software.

Edward Tufte, a well-known critic of scientific figure design, has coined the term "chartjunk" to describe the many sorts of unnecessary, distracting or misleading visual elements that sometimes appear in graphs and charts (Tufte, 2003). Some common examples might include overly heavy grid lines, ornamental shading, and unnecessary pictures or icons placed as decorations within data graphs. Chartjunk also encompasses any element that makes it more difficult for readers to understand the real nature of the data. This can include such distractions as items presented with different scales, inclusion of data irrelevant to the point of the graphic, or anything that artificially makes data appear more precise than they actually are.

Pay attention to size and scale

Even when there is no overt attempt to deceive, it is possible to present a compelling visualization that through choice of perspective can obscure or distort data. For example, reducing the size of artwork for publication can do strange things to scale. Reduction minimizes some flaws, but accentuates others. Use computer software capabilities or a photocopier with reduction abilities to check what a figure will look like after reduction.

A rectangle, with a longer horizontal than vertical axis, will usually fit within the layout of a journal's page. (A ratio of 2 vertical units to 3 horizontal units is considered especially pleasing.) Vertical rectangles often need reduction. Whenever possible, reformat them to a square or horizontal rectangle.

After reduction of the illustration for publication, experts suggest that the capital letters in written material on the illustration should be about 2.0 mm in height. Lines for the x- and y-axes and trend lines in graphs should be no wider than the width of the lines making up the letters. Points on curves in graphs should not be so large as to merge upon reduction.

If the size of the subject of a photograph is important, include a short scale line to indicate dimensions. If possible, lay a metric ruler in the field so that it will be visible in the finished photograph. Apply a scale to a photomicrograph.

Keep figures visually honest

Never distort the importance of a trend. Graphs can pose a particular temptation in this regard. Never finagle line fits, delete data points that do not fit the curve, or make data points so large that almost any curve would pass through them.

Begin at zero for the scales used for the axes of a graph whenever possible; choose these scales carefully and mark them clearly. Sometimes, a valid trend would disappear on a scale with a zero axis, and all the data points would bunch up at the top. In this case, signal readers that the graph's axis is not at zero, either with a statement in the text or with a break in the axis.

If a point represents the mean of a number of observations, indicate the magnitude of the variability by a vertical line centered at each point. State whether standard error (SE) or standard deviation (SD) is used and specify number of observations or sample sizes. Again, learning the capabilities of your graphing software ultimately will simplify the task. Most programs have the ability to insert such information automatically with a few keystrokes.

When two or more graphs or other figures are to be compared, draw them to the same scale. Then, if possible, group them into a single illustration. To minimize reduction during printing, place them one above the other rather than one beside the other.

Remember the limitations of your data. The extrapolation of a line or a curve beyond the points shown on a graph may mislead both the writer and the reader. As Winston Churchill is said to have remarked in another context, "It is wise to look ahead but foolish to look further than you can see."

Illustrate relationships with graphs

Tables present results; graphs promote understanding of results and suggest interpretations of their meaning and relationships. Most graphs are based on a set of numbers, just as most tables are. But, because graphs are fundamentally pictures rather than a set of numbers, information generally is easier for the reader to grasp than if it were printed in columns.

Consider graphing data when you feel that the relationships are more vital to your message than the actual numerical values themselves. Thus, you might use a graph to present trends dealing with two related variables, one or more variables changing through time, or data interesting for the magnitudes of differences that might be related to unknown factors or experimental manipulations.

A graph always shows how one parameter varies relative to changes in another. One factor may be controlled and varied (temperature, for example) while some effect of this change is measured. Alternatively, the effect of changes in some uncontrollable factor such as time may be measured. Temperature and time in these examples are independent variables, which are usually plotted in relation to the horizontal (x)-axis. The effect these changes have on something else (the dependent variable) is normally plotted in relation to the vertical (y)-axis.

Software programs can produce sophisticated graphs with the touch of a finger. Use them initially to construct various graphic presentations of the data and consider the alternatives. Then modify such aspects as fonts, type size, shadings, and symbols to produce visually dynamic illustrations. Remember, however, that legibility and comprehensibility should remain the most important criteria. For further help, see Robbins (2005).

Keep line graphs simple

Line graphs show continuous variables, such as movements over time. Perhaps the most popular of all graph styles in scientific writing, line graphs range from straightforward visual representations of trends to depictions of complex advanced statistical analyses. Unfortunately, many studies over the years consistently have demonstrated that readers often have trouble interpreting them accurately. Often, this is because the presenter has filled the graph with more information than readers need, forcing them to filter and search to grasp the fundamental point (Kosslyn, 2006).

If you decide to use line graphs, keep them as simple as possible. Limit the number of lines in any one graph. Visually distinguish different lines by using different symbols, and label each line carefully. To avoid giving a false impression, do not connect graph points for discontinuous data. Instead, present such information as a bar graph or leave the points on the graph without connecting lines.

Reveal general relationships with bar graphs

Bar graphs, also sometimes called column graphs, are used to present discrete variables in a visually forceful way. They are a single axis graph used to compare size and magnitude of discontinuous data. They are superior to circle and line graphs for showing relationships, magnitudes, and distributions (Macdonald-Ross, 1977b). On the negative side, bar graphs generally provide a relatively small amount of information while taking up a fairly large amount of space.

The bars may run either vertically or horizontally, but are most effective when they run in the direction in which people expect to see them. Thus, vertical bars are usually used for such data as temperature and weight,

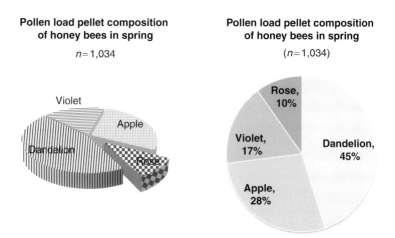

Fig. 8.1 Two versions of a divided-circle graph of the same data. Poor choice of visual elements in the graph on the left obscures text and may mislead viewers into judging the relative quantities of rose and violet pollen pellets to be almost equal.

horizontal bars for distance, time, and speed. Whatever type of bar graph you choose, make the bars the same width, and the space between bars or bar groups about one-half of a bar width.

Illustrate the relationship of parts to a whole with divided-circle graphs

Divided-circle graphs (Fig. 8.1), also called pie charts, are well suited for showing the relationship of a number of parts to the whole. Although divided-circle graphs make a striking visual display, they present a fundamental problem – the impossibility of comparing areas. They are generally used best as attention-getting devices, and even then, only when comparing five or fewer items. Experts say that pie charts are most effective when the segments are arranged by size, with the largest slice beginning at 12 o'clock and progressively smaller segments arranged in a clockwise manner. (Note that by default, some graphics software programs generate counter-clockwise charts.) They also counsel combining or excluding slices smaller than about 5% (18 degrees).

When preparing a divided-circle graph, be careful with visual elements such as perspective, superfluous dimensions, shading, font size, word placement, and inclusion or absence of percentage figures. Carelessly applied, each of these can unintentionally mislead readers. Two divided circle graphs based on the same data (Fig. 8.1) provide an example. In the three-dimensional exploded pie slice at left, pollen pellets from roses appear almost as numerous as those from violets. In reality, the percentage of pollen petals from violets was almost twice that from roses, as the two-dimensional graph clearly shows.

Show numerical relationships symbolically with pictographs

Pictographs, which are essentially bar graphs composed of pictures, can be very visually effective. Pictographs are of two basic types. In one, each symbol corresponds to a specific quantity. In the other, uniformly sized symbols each represent a given quantity with a key provided that explains their meaning. Often the precise actual numbers are posted at the end of each row or column, since such graphs present an approximation.

Perhaps because their construction historically has fallen within the domain of graphic artists, pictographs rarely appear in scientific writing, though they might provide welcome variety. With the ease with which they can be constructed using computer graphics software and clip art, they deserve wider use. They are especially appropriate and effective for illustrating oral and poster presentations.

Pictographs are most effective when the symbols chosen represent the subject matter and are arranged in a way that presents a clear, organized message. Once again, take care to ensure that the artwork is not potentially misleading. The paired pictographs in Figure 8.2 show how this can occur. Increasing both width and length of the syringe icons leads to a distorted perception that exaggerates actual numerical differences. In addition, the distorted background image is distracting, and the font sizes are too small.

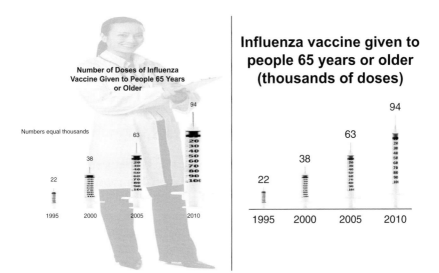

Fig. 8.2 Two pictographs based on the same data illustrate additional ways in which graphic depictions can be potentially misleading. Simultaneously increasing icon size in two dimensions distorts viewers' perception, making differences appear greater than they really were. Image of syringe: © iStockphoto.com/Alptraum. Background image of doctor: © iStockphoto.com/Neustockimages.

A more effective pictograph uses stretched syringes to depict bar equivalents. Increased font sizes enhance visual appeal and readability. In addition, moving the number designation to the legend reduces clutter and increases clarity.

Limit logarithmic and scatter graphs to professional audiences

Using a logarithmic scale can be desirable when doing so makes important variations easier to discriminate or when there is a large range of values on the axis and differences increase with larger values. A logarithmic graph has a series of open and grouped vertical lines in which the top and bottom of each group, called a cycle, is a decimal or multiple of ten.

Logarithmic graphs are commonly but not exclusively used to present data in which rate of change is more important than quantity of change. (An exception sometimes encountered in medical writing is the dose–response curve. Dose is logarithmically related to response in terms of number of receptors stimulated.) A logarithmic graph also is frequently used when the vertical range is so large that it is difficult to fit on a normal graph.

Scatter graphs, which sometimes are charted logarithmically, use single unconnected dots to plot instances where two variables (one on each axis) meet. The pattern of the dots expresses the relationship (a diagonal trend, which is sometimes approximated by a trend line on the chart) or lack of a relationship (random scatter) between the variables.

Interpreting logarithmic and scatter graphs can be difficult for many readers. If you choose to use either of these graphing techniques, explain their significance and discuss them clearly in the text. For more details on their use and presentation, see sources such as Cleveland (1994) and Kosslyn (2006).

Document with photographs and other illustrations

Image-based illustrations document discoveries. For most people, this is the first category that comes to mind when they hear that a paper has "figures." The photograph of a new organism, the print of gel banding patterns, the radiographic image of a patient's bone deformity ... all would belong here, and in traditional publishing, all would be submitted as photographic copy. Happily, electronic copy is now widely accepted, so all such illustrations usually can be scanned and submitted as digital files.

Check your journal's submission guidelines, however. Digital files usually must satisfy certain specified resolution levels and be submitted in one or more specified formats. Some print journals accept only tables and line drawings (such as diagrams and graphs). Others also accept black-and-white

photographs, which are then photographed again through a screen grid to produce dots that make up a printed image called a halftone. These images are usually of lesser quality than the originals because the printing process may transfer the image several times with some loss of clarity at each transfer.

When it comes to showing exactly what something looks like, nothing beats the realism of a photograph. Photographs usually only show surfaces, however, not the components or interior parts that a line drawing or diagrammatic exploded view can provide. Sometimes a traditional drawing is still a better choice. The realism of a photograph can be disadvantageous as well, of course. Your photograph may include clutter, extraneous information, or components you would rather not show. Happily, the ease by which digital images may be altered makes it possible to fix distracting components (and almost inexcusable not to do so) but it is unethical to alter or distort the basic substance of the illustration. Cropping a photograph requires no comment; any other alteration, such as "photoshopping" the background, should be mentioned in the figure legend.

Obtain the best photographic documentation possible

Take a number of photographs. Focus sharply. Whenever possible, provide a plain, uncluttered background that does not draw attention away from the object you're depicting. Be alert to the distracting presence of miscellaneous items. Try a variety of angles.

Electronic publications can easily include colored illustrations at no extra cost, so online journals often allow or even encourage authors to submit digital files in color. However, most printed journals still restrict photographs to black-and-white images unless color illustration is essential for reasons of evidence, efficiency, or emphasis. For example, color could be vital in illustrations of faint rashes, subtle histologic stain colors, or multicolor scan images.

If you feel a need to include full-color pictures or graphics, be sure to investigate your journal's policy. Few print journals will publish color illustrations without passing along at least part of the (often substantial) cost to the author. Note also that journals that still use non-digital images may ask that they be submitted as transparencies (slides) or negatives (negatives for color prints) rather than sending the prints themselves.

Compose the illustration to help the reader

After a photograph has passed the tests of quality and message, it should be tailored to give the reader as much help as possible. Crop the picture to a shape suitable for the journal's column dimensions without reduction in size while retaining the highest possible resolution. Select the center of the field to coincide with the center of interest. Affix letters and arrows identifying features of interest. Keep any lettering horizontal and consistent in size, font, and contrast for easy reading. In the legend, include a key to any symbols used. In the corner of the photograph, if appropriate, include a bar to represent a length suitable to the scale. Finally, consider grouping related figures into a single plate to fill an entire printed page, rather than scattering them throughout the publication.

Develop explanatory artwork when needed

Explanatory figures are those produced to communicate organization, illustrate basic principles, or otherwise clarify text materials. This figure type includes both drawings and diagrams – all those flowcharts, diagrams, maps, algorithms, and line art that some people characterize as "illustrations" as opposed to tables and photographs.

The effectiveness of explanatory artwork depends upon how well it focuses audience attention. This type of artwork must show the specific details of key features while omitting others to minimize the distraction caused by extraneous details. A common mistake in scientific writing is to present a figure that is much more complex than the accompanying prose. When this is done, illustrations confuse rather than inform readers. Anything that catches one's eye should be explained.

Guide readers through sequential processes with algorithms

An algorithm includes any logical sequence of steps or guidelines for solving a problem. Examples of biological and medical algorithms include such varied items as decision trees ("when conditions A, B, and C are present, do X"), taxonomic keys, look-up tables, and medical diagrams. The flow chart back in Figure 7.1 is another example.

Algorithms have been around for hundreds of years, reflecting the utility of this type of illustration. Once people become familiar with their use, they generally find algorithms much quicker and easier to follow than narrative instructions. In the current century, computerized algorithms are becoming increasingly important in biomedical communication, particularly in the areas of diagnostics, medical test selection, therapy and prognosis, and the automatic control of medical equipment.

If you feel an algorithm would be an appropriate way to present part of your story, examine algorithm use in your respective discipline and follow any style guidelines or examples you are able to find. Remember that an algorithm's strength lies in its clarity, so it must be kept free of clutter and extraneous detail.

Use traditional drawings to focus on essentials

Not surprisingly, pen-and-ink artwork has long been an integral part of technical communication, particularly in the biological and medical sciences. Carefully prepared two- or three-dimensional renderings of an object are often clearer than a photograph and thus preferable to it. The major advantage of drawings is that you can control the amount of precision while deleting extraneous details. Drawings also permit unique perspectives such as cutaway, blow-up, and exploded views.

Several computer graphics packages are now available. Some are very good, but there is a vast difference between creating artwork on a computer and creating it with pen and ink on paper. For some people, producing their own drawings is exhilarating. If you are not one of them and have the funds, employ a graphic designer or professional artist. For best results, communicate carefully and allow sufficient lead-time for the project. Remember that artists aren't technical experts. Sketch your ideas, explain your terms, provide correct spellings, and check everything carefully for errors during preparation of the artwork.

Employ symbols and notations with care

In many scientific professions, communication depends heavily upon specialized notations such as symbols, equations, and formulas. Use such notation judiciously, explaining specialized symbols as necessary and carefully following the recommendations in a comprehensive style manual for your field.

Short and simple equations, such as $x = 3y - 1$, can be set directly into the text as we have done here, but entering over-under fractions can be a formatting nightmare. Whenever possible, use a slant line or negative exponent to signify division. Change the format to a single line, like this: $(O–E)^2/E^2$. Fractional exponents ($X^{0.5}$) may also be used instead of square root and cube root signs (Swanson, O'Sean, and Schleyer, 1999).

If a document has a great many equations that are referred to repeatedly in the text, they can be displayed (set on a separate line) and identified with consecutive numbers placed in parentheses at the right margin. For clarity, equations set off from the text need to be surrounded by space. Triple-space between displayed equations and normal text. Double-space between one equation and another, and between the lines of multi-line equations. When a series of short equations appear in sequence, align them on their equal signs.

$$x(y) = (3y - 1) \tag{1}$$

$$p(x, y) = \sin(x + y) \tag{2}$$

If a really complex formula cannot be avoided, consider treating it like a figure. Furnish it in the form of a line drawing. Many specialized computer programs exist with the capability of creating these kinds of supplementary information. For example, chemical formulas can be created using software such as ChemSketch and ISIS/Draw. Newer versions of mainstream word-processing programs also now have equation editors that can handle mathematical formulas and equations. Alternatively, simple equations such as those shown above can easily be aligned with a standard word-processing program by placing each component in a separate cell of a table. Center them all. Then remove any grid lines.

Highlight your story with effective figure legends

When readers turn a page, they look first at illustrations, then at the legends. Each one should orient readers toward that visual's meaning and enable them to identify its components. It should also differentiate that particular graphic aid from all other illustrations in the paper.

The guidelines that apply to table titles (Chapter 7) apply to figure legends as well. Their length and location in the manuscript differ, however. Legends are often longer, and although they will be printed below or next to the figure in a published article, they almost always are placed in chronological order together on a separate page at the very end of the typescript.

Figure legends often are composed of a series of separate parts. The requirement to include these parts can vary; if your journal gives explicit instructions or if you can discern patterns in figure legend format in its published papers, follow them as completely as you are able to do. Otherwise, include only enough detail for readers to understand the illustration, and consign the necessary minutiae to the text.

Even long legends generally begin with a brief title that summarizes the figure's topic. This may be followed by details about the contents of the figure itself – such topics as figure components, methods, or how the figure contributes to the paper's story. Symbols, line, or bar patterns that appear in the figure are described next, using a telegraph style. Any other units, abbreviations, or statistical notations are described next. Finally, any other symbols or notation may be explained, if such explanation has not been interspersed in the details section. Remembering the fundamental guideline to make the figure stand alone, never include the phrase "see text for explanation."

The figure's brief title is generally written as an incomplete sentence without any abbreviations. The terms in it should be the same ones used in the text and (if they appear) in the illustration. Check to be certain that any abbreviations and symbols used are consistent between the figure content, the text of the paper, and both within and between figure legends. Keep the brief title short – 8 to 12 words, as a rule of thumb. Do not repeat figure headings.

> *Too vague:* Fig. 1 Graph of relevant data
>
> *Over-specified:* Fig. 1 Outcome of multifactorial analysis of relationship between symptoms, chronology of appearance, diagnostic signs, blood work constants from the literature, health outcome, and other parameters for a selected group of fifteen adult ostriches
>
> *Better:* Fig. 1 Multifactorial analysis of health records of fifteen adult ostriches

For a classic research paper, the legend for a figure is never included within the body of the figure itself. In the final version of the typescript, list the figure legends (double-spaced) on a separate page at the end of the text. (However, on visual aids for a verbal presentation, place the legend directly on each figure.)

9   Report numbers clearly and responsibly

> When you have mastered numbers, you will in fact no longer be reading numbers, any more than you read words when reading books.
> You will be reading meanings.
>
> W. E. B. DUBOIS

Numbers are the heart and soul of most scientific research. If they are not reported clearly, a paper's value can be compromised or lost entirely. But whereas few dispute their importance, many are willing to debate fine points of how they best should be expressed. Let's start with the simplest case – how to write simple numbers in the body of the manuscript. Then we'll turn to some more intricate cases – reporting percentages, statistics, and probabilities.

Determine how to express numbers in the text

Should the number ten be written out or expressed as a numeral? Should large numbers be given scientific notation? What should be done with a series that includes numbers of very different magnitude?

Numbers can be expressed by so many different systems that it should come as no surprise to learn that many publications simply handle the situation by decree. Check the *Instructions to Authors* for your intended journal, and follow their lead. In the absence of a clear edict, however, the following guidelines may help.

Choose an approach

The most conservative (some will say antiquated) system has been to use numerals to express numbers 10 and above and to write words to express numbers below 10 except when they are used as page numbers, as figure and table numbers, or with units of measurement. Several exceptions and instances of special usage expand on this rule (Table 9.1).

Table 9.2 summarizes the most conservative approach to the opposite situation – places where numbers should be expressed as words. In general, the numbers below 10 would be written, once again subject to a number of modifications. Ordinal numbers, which express degree or sequence, may

Table 9.1 Use numerals (conservative rules)

General guideline	Examples
All numbers 10 and above	trial 14; 35 animals; 16 legume genera
Numbers that immediately precede a unit of measurement	10 cm long; 35 mg of drug; 21 days
Numbers with decimals; fractions that include whole numbers	7.38 mm; 4 1/2 hours
Numbers that represent statistical or mathematical functions or results; percentages; ratios	multiply by 5; fewer than 6%; 3.75 times as many; the 2nd quartile
Numbers that represent exact times or dates; ages; size of samples, subsamples or populations; specific numbers of subjects in an experiment; scores and points on a scale; exact sums of money; numerals as numerals	About 3 weeks ago, at 1:00 a.m. on January 25, 2014, the 25-year-old patients with IQ scores above 125 all awoke in the nursing home at 125 Oak Street. They were paid $25 apiece to go back to sleep.
Numbers below 10 that are grouped for comparison with numbers 10 and above in the same paragraph	4 of 16 analyses; the 1st and 15th of the 25 responses; lines 2 and 21
Numbers that denote a specific place in a numbered series; parts of books and tables; each number in a list of four or more numbers.	Trial 6; Grade 9 (but the ninth grade); the groups consisted of 5, 9, 1, and 4 animals, respectively

follow the same rules (third, 15th). Alternatively they may be expressed as numerals whatever their size unless they are single words (fourth, nineteenth, 44th).

In today's increasingly international world, many grammatical rules in English are being relaxed or simplified. Number usage is following the same trend. Given the complexities of this conservative approach, it is no surprise that many if not most of the newer scientific journals now use Arabic numerals in preference to words in almost every situation.

Whichever style of expressing numbers you adopt, remember to be consistent. Apply that style throughout the entire text. When several numbers appear in the same sentence or paragraph, express them all in the same way, regardless of other rules and guidelines.

Even if you have chosen to follow a conservative numbering system, Arabic numerals would be used whenever you have three or more numbers in a series, even if each of the numbers were below 10. For example,

Table 9.2 When numbers should be written as words (conservative rules)

Use words for:	Examples
Any number that begins a sentence, title, or heading (but reword to avoid this whenever possible)	Five patients improved, and 15 did not. Sixty-nine percent of the sample was contaminated.
Common fractions (those without whole numbers)	One quarter; reduced by half; a three-quarters majority
Zero and one when words would be easier to grasp than figures, or words do not appear with numbers 10 and above	A one-line computer code; zero-based budgeting; one animal gave birth (*but* only 1 in 18 gave birth)
Numbers below 10 that do not represent precise measurements; numbers used in an indefinite, approximate, or general manner	Five conditions; trials were repeated four times; a one-tailed *t* test; a three-way interaction; about thirty years old; eight chapters
Numbers below 10 that are grouped for comparison with numbers below 10	The second of four stimuli; five of eight animals; in six cases, the disease lasted five times as long as in any of the other four

The 7 dogs, 8 cats, 9 mice, and 6 gerbils were exposed to applications of flea powder.

The analysis revealed 22 complete answers, 4 incomplete responses, and 7 illegible ones.

Know how to express back-to-back numbers

When numerals or number-related words appear side by side, confusion can result, regardless of the number system in use. A few general rules are needed to handle these situations:

- Use a combination of figures and words to express rounded large numbers, starting with millions. For example, one would write of a grant budget of $1.5 million.
- Numerals and words are also combined when they appear as back-to-back modifiers (two 13-ml aliquots). Generally it is best to keep the numeric form with units of measurement, and write out the other number.
- Sometimes, hyphenation will minimize potential confusion (twenty 6-year-old patients vs. twenty-six year-old patients). If more than two numbers appear back-to-back in a string (six 3–5 day intervals), however, it is usually better to rewrite the phrase (six intervals of 3–5 days each).

Beyond these general guidelines, you may spell out whichever number can more easily be expressed in words. Sometimes these combinations are awkward to read; in these cases, consider spelling out both numbers.

> *Awkward:* The 1st three animals; the first 3 animals
> *Better:* The first three animals

Begin sentences with full words

When a number and unit begin a sentence, you must write both of them as words, even if they would otherwise be written as figures with abbreviated measurements. This is part of a much larger writing rule that sentences should always begin with words and never with numerals, abbreviations, acronyms, or any other shortened form. Applying this rule to numbers often yields sentences that are awkward to read, however. Thus, a still better rule is to revise the word order of these difficult sentences. Usually, switching the verb from a passive construction to an active or direct one will solve the problem.

> *Incorrect:* 550 ml of hydrochloric acid should be added.
>
> *Correct but difficult to read:* Five hundred and fifty milliliters of hydrochloric acid should be added.
>
> *Revised:* Add 550 ml of hydrochloric acid.

Prefer Arabic numerals to Roman numerals

Arabic numerals are widely used, and are relatively easy to read and interpret. Roman numerals generally are not. Thus, the former are almost always preferred.

Use Arabic numerals to designate experimental research groups, organisms, virus types, and volume numbers in bibliographic material (even though Roman numerals may have been used in the original).

> group 3, echovirus 30
>
> case 3 in experiment 5
>
> *Creative Acupuncture* 9: 6–35

The same is true for units such as weights, percentages, and degrees of temperature. For example, write 3.2 m or 72°F, regardless of the way other numerical expressions may be treated.

Unless a journal specifies otherwise, do not follow written numbers with a figure in parentheses or brackets representing the same number (such as "send three [3] copies to the editor"). However, it is both acceptable and desirable to include parenthetical material that amplifies understanding of other numerical data.

> He was given 2 mg of tetracycline on each of three occasions.
>
> A 10% mortality rate is common.
>
> Necrosis occurred in almost 20% (50/247) of the cases.

Roman numerals should be used only in certain stylized situations, such as the numbering of preliminary pages of a book or the tables in some journals, blood-clotting factors, or cranial nerves. Likewise, when Roman numerals are part of an established terminology do not change them to Arabic numerals.

> See the author's note in the preface (p. xiv).
>
> Blood-clotting factor VIII
>
> We considered the possibility of a Type II error.

Use the SI metric system for measurements and weights

There actually are several metric systems, including the centimeter–gram–second system and the meter–kilogram–second system. However, these systems are gradually being replaced by a modernized metric system called SI, for Système International d'Unités. It provides unambiguous symbols that are standard in all languages. Most scientific journals use the SI system and also permit some widely used units outside the SI system, such as liter, hour, bar, and angstrom.

The SI system is built from seven base units plus two supplementary ones (Table 9.3). Other units for physiochemical quantities are derived from these SI base units, though they may have special names and their own symbols. For example, the widely used liter is non-SI; its equivalent is one cubic decimeter. (Note that in the United States the symbol "L" is generally preferred, because lower case "l" can be confused with 1.)

Prefixes join base units to express multiples. Because kilogram, the base unit for mass, already has a prefix, it is an exception. In this case attach the prefix to the unit stem "gram" rather than adding it to kilogram.

For quantities much larger or smaller than a given base unit, standard prefixes are used (Table 9.4). The usual practice is to choose the prefix in such a way that the number accompanying the unit is less than 1000. Only one prefix may be used for most symbols, and a prefix is never used alone. Both the prefix and the unit it modifies are either abbreviated or spelled out. When using SI, employ exponents for such expressions as 2 m^2 (rather than 2 sq. m).

Table 9.3 Fundamental SI units of measurement

Quantity	Name	Symbol
Base units:		
length	meter (metre)	m
mass	kilogram	kg
time	second	s
amount of substance	mole	mol
thermodynamic temperature	kelvin	K
electric current	ampere	A
luminous intensity	candela	cd
Supplementary units:		
plane angle	radian	rad
solid angle	steradian	sr

Table 9.4 Standard SI prefixes common in biomedical writing

Factor (power of ten)	SI prefix	Symbol
18	exa	E
15	peta	P
12	tera	T
9	giga	G
6	mega	M
3	kilo	k
−3	milli	m
−6	micro	μ
−9	nano	n
−12	pico	p
−15	femto	f
−18	atto	a

Incorrect: Add 6 mμg of insecticide per sq. m.
Correct: Add 6 ng [or six nanograms] of insecticide/m^2.

If you need help converting measurements from traditional units to their SI equivalents, charts readily can be found online. Young and Huth (1998) provide a useful manual that includes both conversion factors and reference ranges for a variety of clinical applications.

Communicate very large and very small quantities carefully

Very large or very small numbers can be expressed in different ways. One is to use SI prefixes. Another is to use scientific notation. Check the *Instructions to Authors* and be consistent throughout the document.

> *SI prefixes:* 8,000,000 N/m^2 (force of newtons per square meter) becomes 8 MN/m^2 (not 8 N/mm^2 because the acceptable prefix should be attached to the numerator)
>
> *Scientific notation:* 8 $\times$ 10^6 N/m^2

Often, a number can be rounded off without losing meaning. For example, 6,234,275 could be expressed as 6.2 million for most practical purposes. If a quantity must be converted to SI units, multiply the quantity by the exact conversion factor, then round it off appropriately.

The format for reporting very large round numbers depends somewhat on the journal. In the absence of other specific instructions, substitute a word for part of the number (such as 1.5 million for 1,500,000). Because of usage differences between Europe and the United States, it is better to avoid the words billion, trillion, and quadrillion.

When reporting large but exact numbers, U.S. journals use commas between groups of three digits (695,446) in most figures of 1,000 or more. (Exceptions include page numbers, binary digits, serial numbers, degrees of temperature, degrees of freedom, and numbers to the right of a decimal point.) For an international audience, do not break up numbers above 999 into groups of three digits with commas. In some countries, a comma indicates a decimal point. Instead, international journals often leave spaces (695 446).

Guard against false precision

The number of places to which a large decimal value is carried reflects the precision with which the quantity was measured. Omit statistically non-significant decimal places in tabular data. One useful rule of thumb is to report summary statistics to two digits more than are in the raw data. For example, if scores on a test are whole numbers, report descriptive statistics to two decimal places.

Similar entries in a table row or column should be measured to the same level of accuracy, and the number of significant digits must be commensurate with the precision of your experimental method. The best level of precision for numerical data will vary, but rounded-off values often display patterns and exceptions more clearly than precise values.

Handle percentages properly

Three similar-sounding words confuse this subject. The term "percent" (sometimes written as two words) means in, to, or for every hundred; the symbol % can take its place. Always place a number before this word or symbol. On the other hand, "percentage" means a number or amount stated in a percent. Seen less often, percentile is a statistical term for the value in a distribution of frequencies divided into 100 equal groups.

Use the symbol % and Arabic numbers for percentages, unless one begins a sentence, in which case it should be spelled out. Repeat the symbol for each number in a series or range, including zeroes.

> These values were compared with the percentages for 2012.
>
> Ten percent of our students scored at the 99th percentile.
>
> The incidence of mononucleosis ranged from 0% to 24%.
>
> The bacteria were found in 15%, 28%, and 0% of the animals in groups 1, 2, and 3, respectively.

Include the numbers from which percentages were derived

For purposes of comparison, percentages are often much more useful than an array of raw data. However, handling percentages properly can be tricky. Whenever percentages (or other proportional figures) are employed, the finite number (n) from which the percentages are derived must be given somewhere – no exceptions! If percentages are given in a table, the n values are usually presented in a separate column.

Some authorities also recommend that the text include the actual number of subjects for each percentage if the cited series includes fewer than 100 subjects. They also recommend using decimals in percentages in series only when the percentages are based on more than 1,000 subjects.

> *Instead of:* Pulmonary disease was present in 50% of the dogs
> *Write:* … in 50% (16) of the dogs, in 16 (50%) of the dogs, *or* in 50% (16/32) of the dogs

Whenever there might be a possibility of misunderstanding, state the basis for the percentages. For example, in reporting certain analyses, it may be essential to specify whether moisture-free ("dry") weight, fresh ("wet") weight, or volume was used.

Avoid percentages based on small samples

Journals differ in what denominator magnitude (value of n) they will accept as adequate basis for a percentage. Some clinical journals allow percentages only

Table 9.5 An example of misleading use of percentages

Animal group	*n*	Mating success (%)
Experienced	55	50%
Naïve, drug-treated	5	60%
Experienced, drug-treated	5	80%
Naïve controls	25	41%

for fractions with denominators greater than 50. Thus, percentages would be given for the reader's convenience for 31/75 (41%) but not for 12/25. When some fractions would appear with percentages and others without them, it might be stylistically better to omit the percentages entirely.

If differences in compared fractions are assessed statistically, the assessment must be based on the absolute numbers, not the percentages.

These rules and guidelines exist because percentages given for compared fractions with small denominators are likely to imply statistically significant differences when none in fact exist. In the example in Table 9.5, the percentages of drug-treated naïve animals and drug-treated experienced animals look very different (60% vs. 80%), but in fact because of the small sample sizes, the real difference was only due to the differing behavior of a single animal.

Report statistics correctly

Statistical inference is an orderly means for drawing conclusions about a large number of events on the basis of observations collected on a sample of them. As such, it forms an important part of scientific inquiry. Experts can help you plan and carry out whatever statistical analyses your paper requires. They can also help you avoid common errors in choosing and using these analyses.

When it comes to reporting the results of these analyses, equal care should be taken, but often it does not seem as though this has happened. Poor statistical reporting is a widespread, potentially serious problem. Across a range of scientific disciplines over the years, as many as one-quarter to one-half of all published reports – including those from high-ranking journals – have been found to contain errors in the ways in which their statistics are reported (Bakker and Wicherts, 2011).

With the growth of the evidence-based medicine movement, this problem has emerged from the shadows to justify the development of several sets of published recommendations for reporting statistics for different types of

GLASBERGEN

"You call it 'lying'. I call it 'perfecting the truth'!"

medical trials (see for example, Lang and Secic, 1997; Altman *et al.*, 2001; APA, 2010). Perhaps because human lives and survival are less often at stake, other biological fields have been slower to develop guidelines for their particular specialties. However, the same problems seem to occur in almost all biomedical research reporting, so applying good advice across specialties shouldn't be difficult. Most of the common errors concern quite basic statistical concepts, and others simply reflect a failure to be complete.

Determine the nature of your data

This might seem fairly elementary, but failure to recognize and properly describe the nature of data is the root cause of many common problems. For example, data may be nominal, meaning that they have been measured along a scale in which interval measurements have meaningful distances between them but the zero value is arbitrary; temperature is an example. Ratio measurements are similar, but have both a meaningful zero value and defined distances between measurements. Both of these are quantitative variables, which can be either discrete or continuous, depending upon their numerical nature.

If you choose to place quantitative data into categories (such as light and heavy, or day and night) that have a meaningful order but imprecise differences between consecutive values, they become "ordinal." This change can simplify statistical analyses, but it reduces both the variability and the precision of the measurements, and the way boundaries of the ordinal categories are chosen can bias the results. Thus, if you have decided to use ordinal categories, you must explain why you selected an ordinal scale and how you determined those boundaries.

"Paired" data (measurements taken from the same organism or sample) should be reported together in addition to giving group means; reporting only one or the other can mislead readers by hiding possible conflicts between the two measures. Whenever reporting group means for paired data, report within-pair changes as well. At the same time, double-check that you have used a statistical test designed for paired data, not for independent samples.

A related problem may occur when the "unit of observation" is not the same as the entire organism. For example, in a study of treatments for lame hind legs in border collies, how many dogs were involved? And what does a 75% success rate actually mean? If 18 dogs out of 300 that were examined had the problem, the sample size was 18, not 300; if both back legs were lame and each leg was treated with a different topical medication, the sample size might be 36, but the data were definitely paired.

Avoid pseudoreplication, a common error that occurs when investigators apply inferential statistics to test for treatment effects with data from experiments where either the treatments are not replicated (though samples may be) or the replicates are not statistically independent. Carefully clarify what was actually studied, specify the actual sample size, and be sure you have used the appropriate statistical test for the situation.

Check for normality and linearity

Continuous data may be normal or non-normal (skewed) in distribution. In statistics, "normal" describes a very specific situation: about 68% of the values are within ±1 standard deviation of the mean, about 95% are within ±2 standard deviations, and about 99% are within ±3 standard deviations. Most biological data and many medical test results are not normally distributed (Lang, 2004), a fact that influences both statistical analysis and statistical reporting.

Hundreds of statistical tests are available to scientists, but their appropriate use hinges on meeting their assumptions, and normality in data distribution is a very basic one. Always check and report this. The need to do this will also help to protect you against another common statistical error, using a parametric test (such as Student's t test) when a nonparametric test (such as Wilcoxon rank-sum test) would be more appropriate.

Within the Methods section, include an explicit statement such as "the data were normally distributed and thus did not violate the assumptions of the chosen tests." Don't just say the data were "normal"; that word has at least five other definitions in medicine, depending on whether the word is being used in the context of diagnosis, therapy, risk factors, the frequency of values, or social values.

Linearity describes a special relationship between a response and an explanatory variable. Don't just look at a graph of your data and decide they look "close enough" to be suitable for a linear regression analysis. Take the time to graph the "residuals" (the difference between each data point and value predicted by the regression line). If the relationship is linear, the graphed line will be flat and close to zero. When you describe your use of linear regression analysis in the Methods, state that your data met the assumption of linearity.

Use descriptive statistics appropriately

All measures of variable biological parameters should be reported with statistical measures of this variability, but terms such as mean, median, standard deviation, standard error of the mean, and confidence interval can be confusing. Not surprisingly, their incorrect or inappropriate use is common.

Mean and standard deviation (often abbreviated as SD) are statistics that correctly describe a sample characteristic that has normal ("bell-shaped") distribution. The mean is the center, or "average"; the SD describes the variability or "spread" of the data. Because that distribution is so explicitly described by its definition, readers can interpret these statistics easily in this situation.

The problem arises when the data are not normally distributed, as is often the case in biology and medicine. Then, the mean and standard deviation are no longer the best values to give. Instead, report other measures such as the median and the range or interquartile range (usually reported by giving the 25th and the 75th percentiles).

Whereas the standard deviation describes the specific sample that you collected, the standard error of the mean (SEM) describes the uncertainty about how well the sample mean represents the mean of the actual population from which you obtained that sample. (For a normal distribution, one SEM on either side of the mean is essentially a 68% confidence level; that is, about two-thirds of the samples randomly drawn from that bigger population would be expected to give values between one SEM above and one SEM below the sample mean you obtained.)

Because the standard error of the mean is always smaller than the standard deviation, it can be tempting to make measures look more precise by reporting the SEM rather than the SD. Even when there is no attempt to deceive, it is wrong to give SEM for a sample.

To address how well your sample represents the entire population, the preferred measure is to report the 95% confidence interval instead of the SEM. This would be expressed in the Results section with a statement such as "The mean value was 72 mm (95% CI = 70.4 to 73.6 mm)." Readers easily would be able to interpret this to mean that if you were to draw repeated samples randomly from your same population, about 95% of these samples would be expected to have mean values between 70.4 and 73.6.

One further note: avoid using the $\pm$ sign without explanation. A statement such as "the mean was 13.3$\pm$6.2" gives no indication whether the second number is a standard deviation, standard error of the mean, or something else entirely. Some journals do not even allow this construction. Instead, use a clearer presentation such as "the mean was 13.3 (SD 6.2)."

Account for all the data and all the subjects

Check that your numbers are complete, and that totals agree with their parts. Readers can add, and often they will. Missing data will raise issues in their minds about the quality of the entire study. If the totals don't match, why should they believe you were careful during the rest of the research?

Account for all the patients in the study, all the animals that were observed, all the samples that were tested. A flow chart can be a helpful way to provide this information. In human medicine, the CONSORT Statement (Altman et al., 2001) recommends this type of schematic summary for reporting randomized clinical trials.

Describe statistical results in a standard manner

Whenever you are reporting quantitative differences that are not due to chance alone, provide statistical statements that are the result of appropriate statistical tests you have described in the Methods section. In the text, statistical results are usually presented in a concise style consistent with standard statistics books. In a table, these often are placed in a footnote.

Statistical methods do not need elaborate presentation, nor do the mathematics of the test results need to be detailed. A simple statement of the chosen test and probability level is usually sufficient. Reference a basic text detailing the procedure if you feel readers might need it.

Poor: To determine whether the two species differed in their egg cannibalism rate (Table 1), we used the Fisher Exact Probability Test, in which $P = (A + B)!(C + D)!(A + C)!(B + D)!/N!A!B!C! D!$, to obtain a $P = 0.56$ which was not significant.

Better: The differences in the egg cannibalism rates of the two species (Table 1) were not statistically significant (Fisher Exact Probability Test, $P > 0.05$).

Present probabilities clearly and fairly

If a fishing expedition catches a boot, the fishermen should throw it back, not claim that they were fishing for boots.

J. L. MILLS

Probability statements are nearly universal in research articles that include statistical analyses, but the prevalence of errors of several types suggests neither the conceptual appropriateness of their use nor the mechanics of their presentation are necessarily well understood.

Probability ≠ truth

One misunderstanding about reporting statistics seems to be that a probability of 0.05, 0.01, or 0.001 indicates some sort of magical line separating a publishable truth from a non-publishable waste of time. However, these so-called significance boundaries mostly reflect tradition and convention. In truth, P values of 0.04 or 0.06 are not much different than 0.05, and really should lead to similar interpretations rather than radically different ones. Recognizing this, many journals now ask that exact P values be given when they fall above 0.001.

Still another misunderstanding seems to be that P values alone are sufficient to support a research finding. They are not. Instead of or in addition to P values, report the absolute (not relative or percentage) differences between groups and the 95% confidence interval for the difference. With all this information at hand, readers will be able to infer the precision and usefulness of the information more easily. As Lang (2004) points out in the context of a medical drug study:

> When a study produces a confidence interval in which *all* the values are clinically important, the intervention is much more likely to be clinically effective. If *none* of the values in the interval are clinically important, the intervention is likely to be ineffective. If only some of the values are clinically important, the study probably did not enroll enough patients.

(LANG, 2004, P. 363)

Absence of proof $\neq$ proof of absence

Scientists sometimes mistakenly describe their non-positive statistical results as negative when in actuality there are merely inconclusive. Statistical "power" is the ability to detect a difference of a given size if such a difference really exists in the population. If a test is underpowered, it will not yield a statistically significant result even when there actually is a difference. This result is of little value because it does not provide a conclusive answer, but it is not negative.

Statistical significance $\neq$ clinical importance

Consider a seemingly odd (but nevertheless true) pair of observations about statistics. First, small differences between large groups can be statistically significant but clinically quite meaningless. For example, a long-term study of 4,081 Finnish men with high cholesterol (Brett, 1989, cited in Lang, 2004) treated one group with gemfibrozil and gave the other group a placebo. After 5 years, the men in the treated group had statistically fewer heart attacks ($P < 0.02$), but because total mortality from cardiac events was only six in the treated group and ten in the control group, the absolute risk reduction was a mere 0.2%.

The reverse is also true – large differences between small groups can be clinically important but not statistically significant. In a study of five patients with spinal cord injuries, if two were able to walk again after receiving a new medication, the results would be clinically outstanding although the sample was too small for the results to be statistically different.

Similar confusion can arise when a study concurrently tries to be both explanatory and pragmatic. These two approaches seldom coexist well, because they have different aims and necessitate different conditions. Explanatory or efficacy studies are usually conducted in the laboratory with tight controls; pragmatic or effectiveness studies are performed under more natural but less controlled circumstances. Once again, the solution is to go back to the beginning, and remind oneself what the actual message of the paper was to be.

The results of a study should always be interpreted in the light of the nature of the questions the study was designed to investigate.

These and related problems have their basis in unfortunate word choice, namely the fact that the English word "significant" carries meanings and implications that stretch way beyond the field of statistics. Guard against statements that seem to imply value judgments about the results of statistical analyses with phrases like "nearly reached significance." Do not describe differences that are not statistically significant as *insignificant*! Likewise, avoid using the term "significant" to describe results when no statistical tests were run and you merely mean "important."

Adjust for multiple hypothesis tests and subgroup effects

When statistical analysis was a tedious, largely hand-calculated affair, many scientists shunned it entirely. Now, with the popularity of statistical analysis software, scientists face a strong temptation to overuse statistics, reporting strings of similar analyses or "massaging" data to an unreasonable degree. Almost nothing is more transparent than reliance upon packaged analyses without a corresponding understanding of their meaning.

One situation where this is particularly evident is when tests of numerous subsets have been run in an attempt to unearth all possible correlations from a data set, a process sometimes called "data mining" or "data dredging." Multiple testing and exploratory analyses (which should be reported as such) are not wrong, and can even be desirable in some situations. In fact, many fundamental breakthroughs have come from such unexpected findings. However, it is considered poor research to dredge wantonly through one's data in hopes of finding something statistically significant so it can be reported!

A related situation occurs with subgroup effects. It is reasonable to carry out a small number of subgroup analyses that have been specified in advance, but using the computer to search through every type of subgroup you can devise is not. Over-interpretation of this sort is almost certain to uncover some spurious effects. In one example (cited in Collins *et al.*, 1987), subgroup analyses of data from a study of 16,000 patients with suspected acute myocardial infarction turned up the supposed finding that the benefit of treatment was four-fold greater for patients born under the astrological sign of Scorpio than for patients born under all other signs combined.

A major reason why data dredging is inadvisable is that the more P values obtained, the greater the risk of making a type I error and saying that a treatment is effective when chance is a more likely explanation for the results. Defining a significant result by the usual probability threshold of 0.05, there already is a 1 in 20 risk of finding an apparently significant difference when comparing two groups that are actually alike. Suppose, however, that you were to conduct pair-wise comparisons of six groups. This would result in 15 P values, and without an adjustment, the chances of making a type I error would rise from 5% to 55%.

Some ways to address this problem are outlined in statistics books (see the Bonferroni method, for example). However, a simple, practical alternative is to decide in the planning stage which statistical comparison will be of major interest. Focus your attention on this variable, both in the research and in the current paper. Analyse the other data if you wish, but save those interesting findings for further research and a subsequent publication.

For practice with number use and interpretation, go to Exercise 8.

> Put it before them briefly so they will read it, clearly so they will appreciate it, picturesquely so they will remember it and, above all, accurately so they will be guided by its light.
>
> JOSEPH PULITZER

Written communication has two aspects. The first is your choice of words to express your thoughts. The second, which takes place in the mind of the reader, is interpretation – the conversion of your written words into their thoughts. The essential difficulty is in trying to ensure that these aspects are congruent. Studies have shown that readers base many of their most important interpretations about what they are reading on clues they receive from its structure (Gopen and Swan, 1990).

Revising is the process by which you try to optimize writer–reader congruence. Undertaken by the Process Approach, it entails a series of nested steps, each concentrating on successively finer points. The first and broadest step concentrates on the document's structure and basic style. It includes matters such as organization, logic, accuracy, brevity, and clarity. Coherence is the desired result.

Start with organization and logic

> The single biggest problem in communication is the illusion that it has taken place.
>
> GEORGE BERNARD SHAW

During the process of writing a first draft, most of us include things in one place that should be in another location. We think of additional things as we write. We use words as they come to mind, even though our first thoughts are not necessarily the best and they may not be arranged in the most effective order. This step in the revision begins the process of bringing it all together into an orderly, coherent final product.

Examine the big picture first

Return to your first draft and examine the order of presentation. Check whether all your lines of reasoning hold up. Correct any misquotations. Evaluate your inclusion of literature citations. Watch for padding – a common temptation is to include references that merely relate to the same complex of ideas rather than having a true bearing on the argument. Combine or simplify tables where necessary.

In short, do any and all of your major cut-and-paste work. Thank your lucky stars that you no longer need actual scissors and glue. This all can and should be accomplished on your computer screen. Remember to turn on "track changes" right from the beginning.

Always revise on a copy

Never make changes directly on the original document, either on the screen or on paper. As you move things about, change wording, or add and delete paragraphs, there is always the chance that you might decide you liked the original or an earlier version of the document better. Save a copy of your paper with a new name and date, and revise this copy instead.

If you are working on a really involved project, you may find yourself needing to work with fresh copy several times. To save your sanity, be super-careful to apply distinguishing labels to each version. Place previous versions in separate electronic or paper folders and archive them in a location where you won't be able to work on the wrong one accidentally.

Switch to paper copy at some point

You will almost always see different things when shuffling papers and making handwritten corrections than you do when scrolling through screen copy. The computer screen shows only a small part of the typescript at a time. Some problems – such as scrambled organization, omissions, or redundancy – simply aren't very noticeable unless several pages of the typescript are spread out in front of you.

Whatever the eventual format of your typescript will be, save a copy with double-spaced lines and wide margins for paper-based revision. An inch of margin on each side, with at least an inch on the top and bottom, is not excessive. Use a standard font in a reasonable size, such as 12-point Arial, Helvetica, Times New Roman, or New York. Number the pages automatically in a header or footer. Include a brief identifying title for the typescript and (especially in collaborative writing situations) your own last name or initials.

Include a date and/or time into the header or footer, as well. These fields also are particularly useful when more than one person is working on a document, or when a document goes through several revisions. Dates and times can either be frozen, or can reflect the current date and time each time a document is opened or printed.

Rework for clarity of style

> The beautiful part of writing is that you don't have to get it right the first time, unlike, say, a brain surgeon. You can always do it better, find the exact word, the apt phrase, the leaping simile.
>
> ROBERT CORMIER

Clarity includes what some call "grace of expression." People have grace when they go beyond politeness and act with an eye to the needs and comfort of others. Graceful prose is much the same. It does not offend readers or divert their minds from the message. It does not try to impress readers with its erudition, or force them into side issues. It serves readers without imposing upon them. "Good prose is like a window pane," wrote George Orwell, the English essayist – it is transparent in the sense that it puts no visible obstacle between the reader and the message.

Two independent but closely related aspects of style need decisions at the outset of a revision for clarity. One is formality. The other is point of view. Although the content of a document is more likely to determine whether it is accepted for publication than is its prose style, gracefully written text gives readers a sense that the author has mastered his or her subject. The first of those readers will be the editor and the document reviewers.

Consider formality of style

Most scientific papers are written in a formal style. This shows in their methodical approach, limited range of emotion (no exclamation points or emoticons), absence of contractions (no "you're," no "didn't"), and longer sentence structure.

An informal style is more common in science writing for the general public. It often takes on the characteristics of a spoken conversation, including slang, figures of speech, and broken syntax. It also takes on a personal tone, seeming to speak directly to readers using second person pronouns (you, your, we). The decision is not solely between personal informality and impersonal formality, however. Though unusual, a personal point of view can accompany a very formal writing style and vice versa.

Choose a point of view

As a writer, you can choose to present a subject in a personal or impersonal manner. In a personal point of view, you play the role of writer and reporter openly, using *I*, *me*, and *my*, or *we*, *us*, and *our*. The impersonal point of

THE BORN LOSER © 2014 Art and Chip Sansom. Reprinted by permission of Universal Uclick for UFS. All rights reserved.

view, on the other hand, requires that you avoid all explicit reference to yourself.

On many occasions one point of view or the other is preferable, but sometimes – as in this book – both may be appropriate. When we are offering tips and suggestions, we've taken an openly personal point of view, feeling that it is a friendly approach to a very personal subject – your efforts at scientific writing. When we have had to present stern pronouncements or inflexible dictums, a more impersonal and formal style has often been used.

In their professional publications, scientists almost always maintain an impersonal writing style, which the scientific culture generally views as somehow having more prestige and objectivity. Usually, it is coupled with passive constructions and avoidance of the first person.

Total avoidance of the first person in scientific text is neither necessary nor desirable, however, as increasing numbers of journal editors are realizing. Some scientists believe that journals do not allow the use of personal pronouns, but our informal survey of over 200 of them located none that formally specified this in their *Instructions to Authors*. We suspect that scientific writing's heavy reliance on the passive voice is more a matter of tradition than a formal requirement.

Using the first person is often shorter, simpler, and less pompous than avoiding it. For example, "the authors are prepared to argue" can be shortened to "we contend." "The authors wish to thank" can be shortened to "we thank." An added benefit is that active verb forms can replace passive ones, making it more difficult to construct dangling participles.

When referring to published results and then giving one's own, directly claim the latter. Narratives such as the one below are a common source of confusion. Whose results are whose? And who found which inconsistencies? Phrases such as "it was found that" leave readers wondering who made the discovery. They are best avoided.

Speed Bump. By permission of Dave Coverly and Creators Syndicate, Inc.

Confusing: This result was elucidated by Smith (1990) and Jones (1991). In these studies the authors found inconsistencies in the results. It was found that the data differed slightly.

Better: Smith (1990) was first to explain this result; Jones (1991) expanded upon the idea. Our research uncovered minor inconsistencies in the data given in both of their studies.

When using the first person, employ it consistently and correctly. Sudden and illogical shifts in point of view make a document difficult to read.

Inconsistent: We have reached the point where one should do further experiments. *[Does this mean we intend to do them? Or are we suggesting someone else should do it?]*

Better: We have reached the point where we should do further experiments.

Unclear: The authors established the gene-splicing service in 1976, and we have expanded it ever since. *[Are we and the authors one and the same?]*

> *Better:* We established the gene-splicing service in 1976 and have expanded it ever since.

One further point on correct use of the first person: When you are the sole author, do not refer to yourself as *we*. You must use *I* – unless you are a monarch or pregnant!

For practice with person and point of view, go to Exercise 9.

Improve readability

A common complaint about scientific documents is that they are difficult to read because of the complexity and length of their words, sentences, and paragraphs. To present ideas effectively, minimize the combined weight of these factors. As the complexity and length of words increase, reduce the complexity and length of sentences and paragraphs to compensate.

To reading experts, "readability" refers to aspects that can be measured and subjected to a formula. Systems such as FOG, SMOG, Fry, Flesch, and many others are widely available on computer software and online. They are generally based on relationships between average word length (or number of syllables) and average sentence length, and rank readability by difficulty or by grade level.

To scientists writing for other scientists, these scores can be helpful in tailoring material to a particular audience or in maintaining uniformity in multi-authored compilations. However, they generally do not adequately address three important elements of scientific writing: content difficulty, the recognition factor, and document design. Even general readers easily recognize some multi-syllable biomedical terms. Conversely, highly technical material may use short words, but still be difficult for any but specialists to comprehend. However, verbose words and phrases should not be included in a vain attempt to impress the reader with the writer's intellect, professional status, or mastery of scientific jargon. Sentence structure should not have to be puzzled over. Paragraphs should not ramble on and on.

Strive for sentences of about 20 words

For maximal readability, most sentences should be between 15 and 20 words. More than 40 words generally is too many. If your sentences consistently include fewer than 12 words – rare in scientific writing – consider linking and expanding some. As a bonus, constructing a set of sentences 15–20 words long often will express an idea in somewhat fewer words overall than a set of overly long or short sentences does.

Too long: Two canine cadavers with orthopedic abnormalities were identified which included a first dog that had an unusual deformity secondary to premature closure of the distal ulnar physis and a second dog that had a hypertrophic nonunion of the femur, and the radius and femur of both dogs were harvested and cleaned of soft tissues. *[54 words in 1 sentence]*

Too short: Two canine cadavers with orthopedic abnormalities were identified. The first dog had an unusual deformity. It was secondary to premature closure of the distal ulnar physis. The second dog had a hypertrophic nonunion of the femur. The radius and femur of both dogs were harvested. They were cleaned of soft tissues. *[51 words in 6 sentences; average, 8.5 words per sentence]*

A readable balance: Two canine cadavers with orthopedic abnormalities were identified. The first dog had an unusual deformity secondary to premature closure of the distal ulnar physis; the second, a hypertrophic nonunion of the femur. The radius and femur of both dogs were harvested and cleaned of soft tissues. *[46 words in 3 sentences; average, 15.3 words per sentence]*

Guidelines refer to averages, however. Variation in sentence length and complexity helps sustain reader interest. A publication crammed with overly long sentences is difficult to follow, but a sustained string of extremely short sentences can be choppy and annoying.

Prefer independent sentences

Children commonly string together a web of sentences connected by *and* or *but*, hardly stopping to draw a breath lest they lose their audience. Writers often unconsciously practice a similar approach, unnecessarily linking loosely related thoughts. (Researchers are particularly prone to doing this in the Methods section, giving their prose a decidedly singsong cadence.)

When faced with overly long sentences in your own writing, locate the connecting words and punctuation. Separate the conjoined thoughts into independent sentences.

An overly long sentence with weak connections: Exposed poults developed enteric disease and exhibited 21% mortality during the first 3 weeks but controls had no enteric disease and exhibited no mortality; 20-week-old exposed turkeys weighed 0.6 kg less than controls and had a higher incidence of angular limb deformities and also had a greater incidence of rotated tibias and showed bowed tibias, whereas controls had a significantly higher measurement for tibial shear strength. *[69 words in 1 sentence]*

Separated at weak connections, then edited for wordiness: Exposed poults developed enteric disease with 21% mortality during the first

3 weeks. Controls exhibited neither enteric disease nor mortality. When compared to controls at 20 weeks, exposed turkeys weighed 0.6 kg less, had more rotated and bowed tibias and angular limb deformities, and showed significantly less tibial shear strength. *[49 words in 3 sentences; average, 16.3 words per sentence]*

Limit average paragraph length

Paragraph length and complexity also influence readability. A paragraph length of about 150 words has been judged to be optimal for a scientific article. A paragraph that covers more than two-thirds of a page when typed double-spaced usually should be shortened. Select a few representative paragraphs, and use the word-processing program to check their word count.

A paragraph that is too long and complicated is tedious to read. Check to see whether it includes more than one idea. Often it will. Divide the paragraph between ideas. If paragraphs in a scientific publication consistently include fewer than 50 words (five average typewritten lines), they may seem scrappy and annoying to readers. Look over such text to see which paragraphs could be combined.

Present ideas in expected word order

In the English language, changing the word order clearly changes the meaning:

> Hunter kills bear.
>
> Bear kills hunter.

Proper word order is obviously needed to provide the intended meaning. In addition, studies have shown that people's ease in reading and understanding sentences depends to a surprising degree upon the grammatical order in which words appear.

The use of standard and expected word order – in English, this is subject, verb, object, or SVO – makes ideas easy to follow because the words appear in the sequence in which things happen. When one writes "The cow swallowed a magnet," the reader mentally follows the action, seeing the cow, then the swallowing motion, and then the magnet, the object being swallowed. If instead, one writes "A magnet was swallowed by the cow," the reader unconsciously unscrambles the backward construction, converting it back into SVO order before grasping it fully. This takes extra mental energy and always interferes to some degree with effective communication.

This is one of the reasons why overuse of the passive tense makes scientific documents difficult to read. Studying the works of 20 top writers (10 fiction and 10 nonfiction), Bjelland (1990) found that over 75% of their sentences used standard SVO order. However, in scientific writing, heavy reliance upon

Table 10.1 Hedging words commonly used by biologists and medical researchers.

Nouns	Adverbs	Verbs
supposition	presumably	appear
idea	probably	postulate
speculation	possibly	suggest
conjecture	apparently	seem
possibility	not unlikely	may be
inference	seemingly	speculate

passive constructions results in an overwhelming number of inverted sentences. Change sentences back to SVO order whenever possible, although simultaneously keeping other aspects of readability under control.

Remove unnecessary hedging

To "hedge" is to protect one's arguments or statements with qualifications that allow for unknown contingencies or withdrawal from commitment. It also means to allow for escape or retreat. Whether from timidity, awe at the complexity of natural phenomena, or a misunderstanding of scientific "objectivity," scientists love to hedge (Table 10.1).

In fact, double and triple hedges are common. However, each additional qualifier drains more force from the sentence. Sometimes the result is a sentence that says nothing at all.

> The cause of the degenerative changes is unknown but *possibly* one
> cause *may* be infection by a *presumed* parasite.

One way of saying "I'm not sure" is usually enough in a sentence. When one hedging word is already in a sentence, prune away all the rest. However, if qualifying clauses must be used in a statement for accuracy, by all means include them. If there are many, consider itemizing them.

For practice with readability, go to Exercise 10.

Condense for brevity

Editing for conciseness is both a matter of choosing the shorter, simpler alternative to express each word, phrase, and idea and a matter of eliminating redundancy. Wordiness is a common problem both within and outside the scientific community. Manuscripts are regularly returned to authors with the

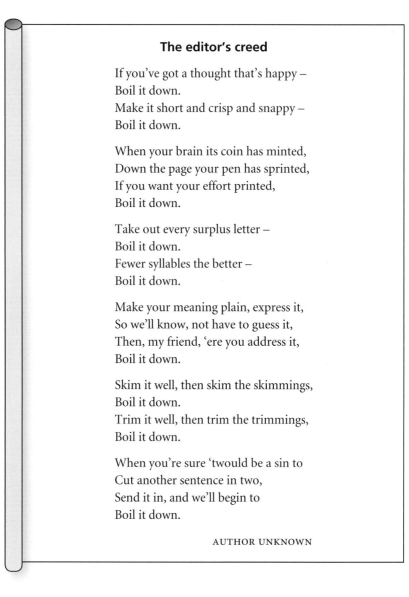

The editor's creed

If you've got a thought that's happy –
Boil it down.
Make it short and crisp and snappy –
Boil it down.

When your brain its coin has minted,
Down the page your pen has sprinted,
If you want your effort printed,
Boil it down.

Take out every surplus letter –
Boil it down.
Fewer syllables the better –
Boil it down.

Make your meaning plain, express it,
So we'll know, not have to guess it,
Then, my friend, 'ere you address it,
Boil it down.

Skim it well, then skim the skimmings,
Boil it down.
Trim it well, then trim the trimmings,
Boil it down.

When you're sure 'twould be a sin to
Cut another sentence in two,
Send it in, and we'll begin to
Boil it down.

AUTHOR UNKNOWN

instructions, "Shorten this considerably before resubmitting it." Do not despair if this happens. A wide range of methods is available to edit for conciseness without having to remove significant material from the text. However, by attending to these matters before submitting the typescript, you may avoid that dreaded editorial directive entirely.

Beware of verbiage

Verbiage, which coincidentally rhymes with garbage, means the use of many unnecessary words. Often it leads to a sort of ritualistic, pompous writing style like this:

> Following termination of avian exposure, there was a substantial incrementation in lung volume and at this moment in time, it would appear that there has been a marginal degree of improvement in diffusing capacity. *[34 words]*

Even the most diehard among us would welcome with relief a shorter and more specific rewrite such as:

> After the man stopped keeping birds, his lung volume increased and diffusing capacity apparently improved slightly. *[16 words]*

Work on this point is not just an altruistic act directed toward readers. Practice directed toward simplifying expressions sharpens a writer's vocabulary and thinking skills.

Remove empty fillers

In spoken English, many words and phrases act as "fillers." They have little more meaning than *and-um* or clearing one's throat. Unless they are used to excess, neither the speaker nor his audience is even aware of them.

In the lecture hall, a case for their utility can even be made – they pace a lecturer's talk to the slower pace of note-taking by listeners. In scientific writing, where each word should count, empty fillers have no place. Yet they sneak in, persistently and repeatedly. Certain of them are so common as to require special attention (Table 10.2). Most "it ... that" phrases, such as "it is interesting to note that," are pointless fillers. Strike such phrases entirely. Particularly avoid those that contain thinly disguised double negatives.

Omit "hiccups" and other needless repetition

Short words (often prepositions) that unnecessarily accompany verbs or other parts of speech are sometimes termed "hiccups." Omitting the italicized words in the first column of Table 10.3 does not change the meaning, a sure sign that the hiccup is unnecessary. A longer sort of hiccup occurs with roundabout, indirect constructions such as "There is a cure available. It consists of ..." This can be rewritten simply as "The available cure consists of ..."

Tautology, a closely related problem, is defined as needless repetition of an idea in a different word, phrase, or sentence. Poor scientific writing often includes many phrases in which one of the terms implies the other or in which

Table 10.2 Examples of "it … that" phrases to remove or replace

Phrase with empty fillers	Shorter equivalent
It would thus appear that	Apparently
It is considered that	We think
It is this that	This
It is possible that the cause is	The cause may be
In light of the fact that	Because
It is often the case that	Often
It is interesting to note that	*omit*
It is not impossible that	*omit*
A not unlikely cause could be that	*omit*
It seems that there can be little doubt that	*omit*

Table 10.3 Examples of tautology and hiccups; omit the italicized words

Hiccups	Tautology	
continue *on*	1 a.m. *in the morning*	*positive* benefits
refer *back*	at this point *in time*	*true* facts
check *up on*	collaborate *together*	large *in size*
all *of*	circulate *around*	many *in number*
true facts	*end* result	red *in color*
enter *into*	*mandatory* requirement	repeat *again*
face *up to*	*new* beginning	*past* history
	optional choice	*complete* stop
	five *in number*	prioritize *in order of importance*

one term in a phrase is in the general category to which the other term belongs (Table 10.3, columns 2 and 3). For example, a *consensus* is defined as an agreement in opinion, so *consensus of opinion* is redundant. A variation of tautology is phrases that contain two words which both mean the same thing. Common examples include *basic and fundamental*; *final and conclusive*; *null and void*; *each and every*; *first and foremost*; and *visible and observable*. Omit one word in each pair; the meaning is unchanged.

A similar sort of wordiness occurs when words that are absolute are mistakenly modified. There is no difference between *absolutely complete* and *complete*, for example. Other absolute words that resist modifiers include *dead, extinct, fatal, final, honest, horizontal, impossible, inferior, libelous, lifeless, matchless, moral, mortal, obvious, peerless, perfect, permanent, rare, safe, straight, unique, universal,* and *vertical.*

Shorten modifying phrases and clauses

Restrictive ("that") and nonrestrictive ("which") clauses have a valuable place in scientific writing (see Chapter 12), but they are often overused. These types of phrases have shorter equivalents. Replace "that" and "which" phrases with participles or other verb forms:

> *Wordy:* The organism that Chu (1993) found was a guppy that laid eggs.
>
> *Better:* Chu (1993) found an egg-laying guppy.

Prepositional phrases are also often overused. Scrutinize all prepositional constructions, especially those introduced by *of*. To reduce the length of wordy passages, substitute the adjective form of the nouns that are the object of these prepositional phrases. Alternatively, place nouns or noun substitutes in apposition.

> *Unnecessary prepositional phrases:* The dog with dyspnea was referred to a clinic in the neighborhood.
>
> *Better:* The dyspneic dog was referred to a neighborhood clinic.
>
> *Wordy prepositional phrase:* Group One includes a number of plants of the genus *Coleus*.
>
> *Nouns placed in apposition:* Group One includes *Coleus* plants.

Redundancy and verbosity are often coupled with jargon (see Chapter 12) and worn phrases so familiar that they pass unnoticed.

> *Verbose:* Due to the fact that breeder flocks in most cases are being subjected to periodical vaccination programs ...
>
> *Better:* Because breeder flocks usually are vaccinated periodically ...

When all these various kinds of changes are taken together, substantially shorter text can result:

> *Wordy:* The genera of the group of fungi that was studied by Fitzpatrick at this time are placed in the group of genera that are called the order Hypocreales because of the work of Miller (1941). *[35words]*
>
> *Shorter:* The fungal genera studied by Fitzpatrick are now placed in the order Hypocreales because of Miller's (1941) work. *[17 words]*
>
> *Wordy:* The kitten that was the sole offspring of the calico was devoid of hair that was orange in color. *[19 words]*
>
> *Shorter:* The calico's sole offspring was a kitten without orange hair. *[10 words]*

Condense figure legends

Many journals prefer a clipped, sentence-fragment style of writing in figure captions; examine recent issues. Usually, articles (*a*, *an*, *the*) can be omitted and prepositional phrases can be treated as above, shortened, or omitted.

> *Full sentences:* Figure 1 The chromosome characteristics of the unknown strain of *Tetrahymena* are illustrated; notice the large and heavily stained object in the center of the photograph, which is the macronucleus. *[28 words]*
>
> *Clipped form:* Fig. 1. Chromosome characteristics of unknown *Tetrahymena* strain; note large, heavily stained macronucleus (center). *[12 words]*

For practice with clarity and brevity, go to Exercise 11.

Recognize when short might be too short

When equivalent alternatives exist, choose the one that takes the least space. This rule is the single idea behind all more specific hints. A corollary, however, is that when clarity and brevity conflict, clarity is the more important of the two. Two situations in scientific writing are particularly prone to this conflict: nouns clustered with a string of modifiers, and words shortened into abbreviations and their kin.

Minimize noun clusters and strings of pearls

In English, a noun can be used to modify or describe another noun. Such noun clusters are common in our language, adding variety and flexibility to writing. For example, *liver disease* (a two-noun cluster) and *hepatic disease* (an adjective and a noun) have the same meaning, and may be used interchangeably.

Two-noun clusters are acceptable, sometimes even desirable, and usually cause no problems. However, scientists have a tendency to take clustering to extremes, running together whole series of nouns (and adjectives) that modify one another and the final noun in a chain of words so long that the reader becomes lost. This construction – several modifiers stacked up in front of a noun – has been dubbed a "string of pearls" (Table 10.4). Consider this excellent example that was actually published:

> Five two week old single comb white leghorn specific pathogen free chickens were inoculated with approximately 105 tissue culture infected doses of duck adenovirus. *[Which nouns are substantive and which are modifiers?]*

Table 10.4 Strings of pearls: revising noun phrases that have too many modifiers

Sentence fragment with string of pearls	How it might be revised for clarity
A system necessitated automated motor starting circuit	An automated motor-starting circuit required by the system
A 4 month secretory cell produced mucosal accumulation history	A 4-month history of accumulation of mucosa produced by secretory cells
The negative penicillin skin test result group	The group with negative results on the penicillin skin test
Blue absorbing pigment spectral curve	Spectral curve for blue-absorbing pigment
Climate controlled gene cluster phenotype variation	Climatically controlled variation in gene-cluster phenotype
Two dimensional real time ultrasonographic blood flow detection techniques	Ultrasonography techniques that detect blood flow in two-dimensional real time
A calibrated transit time ultrasonic blood flow probe cable end	The cable end from an ultrasonic blood-flow probe calibrated to measure transit time ultrasonically

Strings of pearls often arise from an overly zealous attempt to be brief, but additional words and punctuation are preferable to barely comprehensible meanings. Suppose you encounter the phrase *aged dog meat samples*. It might have at least five meanings: samples of aged meat used for dogs, samples of aged meat from dogs, aged samples of meat from dogs, aged samples of meat used for dogs, and samples of meat from aged dogs. Although this example may seem silly and extreme, similar examples are common in scientific writing. How would you interpret *brown egg laying flocks?* (It turned out that the eggs, not the flocks, were brown.)

Disconnecting strings of pearls is tedious but straightforward. Working methodically through the typescript, circle every batch of more than two nouns. The goal should be to reduce these strings to simple pairs. As a memory trick, recall that "two is company, but three's a crowd." Because hyphenation links two words to reduce a three-word cluster to two, it often bends this rule a bit. However, any cluster beyond two or three words usually needs attention.

Strings of pearls can be revised in many ways. Decide the precise relationship of one word to another, and express this relationship by inserting necessary words. Start with prepositions, commas, and hyphens. Watch for unintentional changes in meaning. Noun and adjectival forms often have subtly different definitions (as in *paramedic training* vs. *paramedical training*). Do not add an adjectival ending if the noun more correctly expresses the thought.

Use abbreviations sensibly

In scientific and technical writing, abbreviations, initialisms, acronyms, and symbols are on the increase. You undoubtedly are already well steeped in their use in your own research field. Here we offer an appeal for restraint. Shortened forms should serve as an aid to readers, not simply a convenience to the author. In particular, avoid using a string of them. This sort of shorthand is fine in a researcher's notebook, but not in a publication:

> Use of IV 2-PAM and ATR lessened 1.5 LD50 OP toxicity at 3 h PO.

Many authorities decree that one should eliminate any abbreviation that is not used at least eight times in the text (including tables and figure legends). When a cumbersome name or phrase must be used frequently in the body of the typescript, first try replacing it with a pronoun or shortened version ("the drug," "the substrate"). Then go back and substitute abbreviations only where the text seems really to require it. Whatever abbreviations you use, make sure they remain uniform throughout your paper. Inconsistent abbreviations, more common than one would assume, are exceedingly annoying to readers.

Check for approved format

Some technical, scientific, and industrial groups have adopted specific forms of abbreviations. Internal and terminal punctuation marks are often omitted. Carefully note such matters as punctuation, spacing, capitalization, and spelling. Many journals include a list of permitted abbreviations under *Instructions to Authors*. Commonly accepted lists appear in many places; a well-regarded example is *Stedman's Medical Abbreviations, Acronyms and Symbols* (2012). See also Baron (1994), Leigh (1998), and Jablonski (2008).

The form and acceptability of abbreviations for dimensions, distances, time, degree, measures, and weights are particularly apt to vary somewhat from one publisher to another. Abbreviate these terms only when they follow numerals. (Note that SI metric measures are nearly always preferred and usually required.)

When they stand alone, names of geopolitical entities should be spelled in full. The abbreviation U.S. (which sometimes appears without spaces or periods) is an adjective, as in U.S. Fish and Wildlife Service. As a noun, spell it out ("wildlife conservation in the United States").

In the reference list, abbreviate the journal names by the system used by your intended publisher. Examine recent issues, and check the journal's *Instructions to Authors*. Most biological and medical journals follow the abbreviations in the BIOSIS List of Serials (*Biological Abstracts*) or PubMed/ MEDLINE (*Index Medicus*). These generally are available in the reference section of science libraries and online. The systems differ slightly from one another in both spelling and capitalization, but single-word titles (such as *Nature* or *Science*) are always spelled out in full.

Define shortened forms at first mention

The first time it appears, spell out any term you want to shorten, then give its abbreviation, acronym, or initialism in parentheses. Thereafter use the shortened form. If the abbreviation appears in the Abstract (not generally recommended), define it again, since this may be published separately.

> The whooping crane (WC) differs from a lattice boom crane. Observers of the WC must watch that they don't become confused.

> For a partial list, consult the International Union of Pure and Applied Chemistry (IUPAC). The IUPAC list includes only those . . .

> Cultures were grown in trypticase soy broth (TSB). After TSB was added to the flask, the cultures were incubated.

Pluralize short forms correctly

When dealing with units of measure, use the same abbreviations for singular and plural forms (*50 mg, 25 IU, 100 ml*). For all-capital abbreviations, form the plural by adding *s* without punctuation (*EKGs, IQs*).

An apostrophe normally indicates the possessive case (*the animal's bones*). It may also be used correctly to indicate the plural of words or lower case letters when adding an *s* alone would be confusing ("mind your *p*'s and *q*'s"). Omit the apostrophe when pluralizing all-capital abbreviations and numerals, including years.

> *Incorrect:* In the early 1960's, RCB's . . .

> *Correct:* In the early 1960s, RCBs . . .

The words *page* and *species* have special plural forms that when abbreviated sometimes cause confusion in scientific writing. One page is "p." (not "pg.") and many are "pp." (not "pgs."). One species is "sp." and many are "spp."

> To determine the identity of *Xanthoxylon* spp. consult Smith (1999, pp. 10–48).

> As the author states, "Infection by *Amblyomma* sp. is a serious matter" (Jones, 1998, p. 5).

When in doubt, spell it out

Unless an abbreviation is internationally accepted *(DNA, RNA)*, avoid using it in the Title or Abstract. Titles and Abstracts are often translated into foreign languages, where readers may find the abbreviations perplexing.

Do not begin a sentence with an abbreviation. Do not abbreviate generic names when they are used alone. (*Drosophila melanogaster* or *D. melanogaster* is acceptable, but never simply *D.* or *D. m.*) Do not abbreviate units of measurement when they are used without numerals. (Never write "Several ml were added.")

Finally, do not abbreviate when confusion might result from doing so. If two words would have the same abbreviation, both should be spelled out.

For practice with abbreviations and other shortened forms,
go to Exercise 12.

> On the whole, I think the pain which my father took over the literary part of the work was very remarkable.
>
> He often laughed or grumbled at himself for the difficulty which he found in writing English, saying, for instance, that if a bad arrangement of a sentence was possible, he would be sure to adopt it . . . When a sentence got hopelessly involved, he would ask himself
>
> "Now what do you want to say?"
>
> and his answer written down, would often disentangle the confusion.
>
> CHARLES DARWIN'S SON, FRANCIS

Like Charles Darwin, most of us need to go over our writing to disentangle confusion, particularly in syntax, style, and word choice. (Syntax refers to the relationships between the words and other elements in a sentence. Style means the way something is done, or its basic "personality." Thus we speak of a scientific writing style characterized by clarity and organization, an editorial style that presents written material in a certain way, or a typographic style with various artistic elements.)

The importance of these three aspects of scientific writing springs from the precision which science requires. More than one interpretation of a sentence or phrase is unacceptable, so careful attention must be paid to both word choice and word arrangement.

This step may have been what you have been expecting – and perhaps dreading – from the start. Admittedly, it can be hard work, but stick with us through the next few chapters as we work our way through this writing phase together. Mastering the fundamentals of scientific style demands no special inspiration or genius that stamps a person as different from all others. It is simply a skill akin to doing crossword puzzles or solving logic puzzles. It is a word game in which the winning combination is a sort of functional beauty that arises from barrier-free communication.

Don't get so close to the supposed difficulties that you lose sight of the pleasure in it –for there is pleasure to be derived from any effort of creative activity, including this one. Like the hand-turned table you might build or the picture you might paint, each article you write is an original vehicle of self-expression. The material you choose to include, the arrangement of your

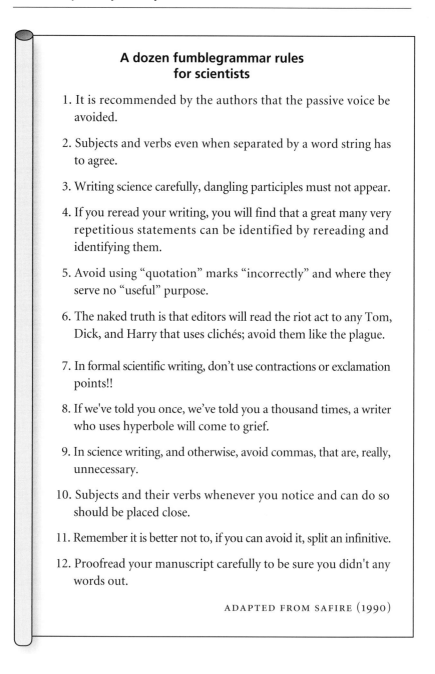

**A dozen fumblegrammar rules
for scientists**

1. It is recommended by the authors that the passive voice be avoided.

2. Subjects and verbs even when separated by a word string has to agree.

3. Writing science carefully, dangling participles must not appear.

4. If you reread your writing, you will find that a great many very repetitious statements can be identified by rereading and identifying them.

5. Avoid using "quotation" marks "incorrectly" and where they serve no "useful" purpose.

6. The naked truth is that editors will read the riot act to any Tom, Dick, and Harry that uses clichés; avoid them like the plague.

7. In formal scientific writing, don't use contractions or exclamation points!!

8. If we've told you once, we've told you a thousand times, a writer who uses hyperbole will come to grief.

9. In science writing, and otherwise, avoid commas, that are, really, unnecessary.

10. Subjects and their verbs whenever you notice and can do so should be placed close.

11. Remember it is better not to, if you can avoid it, split an infinitive.

12. Proofread your manuscript carefully to be sure you didn't any words out.

ADAPTED FROM SAFIRE (1990)

arguments, the criticisms you raise, and the conclusions you reach, all reflect your own personality and intellect.

Use verb tense rules to show the status of work

Read a scientific paper carefully for its grammar rather than its science, and at first the verb forms may seem puzzling. However, they are not arbitrary. The use of present or past forms of verbs has a very special meaning in scientific papers. Proper tense use derives from scientific ethics. It is a way of indicating both the status of the scientific work being reported and respect for those who discovered and reported it. In brief, present tense indicates that a fact has been published, is generalizable, or is otherwise considered part of the body of established scientific knowledge. Past tense indicates information that is not yet published or cannot be generalized. Here's how it most often works in practice.

Use present tense for established knowledge

Generalizations, references to stable conditions, and general "truths" should be given in the present tense. When scientific information has been validly published in a primary journal, it likewise becomes established knowledge. Similarly, when previously published work is mentioned, and the author is cited parenthetically or by footnote number, the sentence usually should be written in the present tense.

> Serological tests commonly *are used* for the diagnosis of *T. cruzi* infections.
>
> Several recent reports (2, 3, 6) *describe* similar findings.
>
> This phenomenon *determines* the absorption coefficient of the tissue (Christensen *et al.*, 1978).

In giving the author's name non-parenthetically as a source of the information, one can use either past or present tense for the verb that is linked to the author. However, the part of the sentence that refers to the scientific work itself is still given in the present tense.

> Smith (1975) *showed* that streptomycin *inhibits* growth of the disease organism.
>
> The investigations of Graff (1932) *show* that the structure *is* a true perithecium.
>
> Jones (2013) *does* not *believe* that streptomycin *is* effective.
>
> Boice (1912) *did* not *believe* that *Diplococcus exists*.

A variation of this rule is to use the present perfect form of the verb for observations or events that have been repeated or continued from the past to the present.

> Nesting behavior *has been studied* under many environmental conditions.
>
> These drugs *have been shown* to produce significant elevations in blood pressure.

Use past tense when mentioning specific results and unpublished data

Results that cannot automatically be generalized include both unpublished results and those that have been obtained under such specialized conditions that they clearly pertain only to the particular study being reported. Numerical data sometimes fall into this category. (Sometimes both rules will be at work in the same sentence. Whatever you may do with other verbs in the sentence, use the simple past tense for the verb that refers to the scientific work.)

> According to Barber (1980), 28% of the 396 wasps in his study *displayed* signs of parasitism.
>
> Hirano and colleagues (2013) *report* that significant accumulation of hemagglutinin-tagged CRTC *occurred* after 16 hours of food deprivation.
>
> Many arachnophobes *cannot recall* when their condition originated (Vester, 2013), but parents in our study *reported* that their daughters first *feared* spiders at an average age of 4.7 years.

Your research in the paper you are writing is an unpublished study being reported for the first time. It would be a bit presumptuous to call it "established knowledge" now. Therefore, use past tense to describe what you have done.

> In the study presented here, the drug *killed* 95% of the *M. tuberculosis* bacilli.
>
> Our data *showed* that few monarch caterpillars survived.

After it is published, the paper will become established knowledge because it will be officially part of the scientific literature. Thus, in citing your own previously published work, use the present tense, just as you do for others' work. Once again, both rules can apply to the same sentence.

> Although earlier studies (Me, 2010, 2012) *emphasize* science as a theory-building social enterprise, trials reported here *ran* under a different conceptual model.
>
> Positive selection in the oxidative phosphorylation pathway *suggests* increased metabolic capacity (Jones, Zhang, and Me, 2003), yet our data (Fig. 1) *gave* conflicting results.

Use present tense when referring to the work you are currently reporting
Use the present tense to refer readers to the figures and tables in the paper you are writing. Even though these include new and unpublished material, they are explanatory aids, not research. Note that although directives such as "see" or "refer to" appear in the present tense, discussion of the research itself remains in past tense as always.

> Antibodies *occurred* in 11% of our mice, as Table 1 *indicates.*
>
> *See* Figure 3, which *illustrates* the six-fold increase in leukocytes that *was found* in the study population.
>
> When we *measured* the two transitions that *are depicted* in Figure 1, we *found* a discrepancy.

Because of these conventions regarding tense use, a scientific paper usually should seesaw back and forth between the past and present tenses. An Abstract or Summary refers primarily to the author's own unpublished results, and uses the past tense. Most of the Introduction section emphasizes previously established knowledge, given in the present tense. Both the Materials and Methods and the Results sections describe what the author did and found. They appear in the past tense. Finally, the Discussion emphasizes the relationship of the author's work to previously established knowledge. This section is the most difficult to write smoothly because it includes both past and present tenses.

A disclaimer is in order, though. Every decree in this world has exceptions, and scientists are a fairly independent bunch. A few subfields of science and a few journals (some of them major players) choose to disregard these grammatical conventions. Always examine articles from your intended journal and your own research area, and refine any guidelines we give in light of what you find.

> For practice with tense use, go to Exercise 13.

Know when to use active and passive voice

"Voice" is the form of transitive verbs that shows whether the subject acts or is acted upon. When the subject of a sentence performs the action expressed by the verb, the voice is said to be active. When the subject undergoes the action of the verb, the voice is passive. The phrase *it was carried* is passive; *we carried it* is active.

The passive voice usually consists of some form of the verb *to be* plus the past participle of another verb. Passive phrases include such common phrases as *were studied*, *is being considered*, and *will be examined*.

Who or what did the studying, considering, or examining? In the passive voice, the agent can be left unnamed. (It can, however, still be expressed with

Table 11.1 Sentences based on the active voice of verbs tend to be shorter, clearer, and more specific than those based on the passive voice

Vague, wordy passive phrasing	Precise, succinct active phrasing
It is recommended by the authors of the present study that these efforts be continued.	We recommend continuing.
The animal was observed to be situated in dorsal recumbence, which had the effect of rendering its legs useless.	Lying on its back, the animal could not use its legs.
The data which were obtained by Johnson were probably indicative of infection.	Johnson's data probably indicate infection.
The following results were obtained through electrophoresis.	We obtained these electrophoretic results.
It is suggested that a sustained coordinated effort should be undertaken by all of us.	We need to make a sustained coordinated effort.

by if desired.) When the agent performing the action is unknown or irrelevant in the context, the passive voice is appropriate.

> Darwin's most influential work *was published* in 1859.
>
> Twenty-five genera of Capnodiaceae *are recognized* in the tropics.

The passive voice can also be used to emphasize something or someone other than the agent that performed the action. You might write *Johnson caught a fresh specimen* to emphasize Johnson or *a fresh specimen was caught by Johnson* to emphasize the specimen.

Many scientists overuse the passive voice, however. They write as though it were somehow impolite or unscientific to name the agent of action in a sentence. They seem to feel that every sentence must be written in passive terms, and they undergo elaborate contortions to do so. However, in any type of writing, the active voice is more precise and less wordy than the passive voice. It is the natural voice in which most people speak and write. The active voice also adds energy to your writing, and forces you to decide *what* you want to say. The passive often obscures your true meaning and compounds your chances of producing pompous prose. Compare the alternatives in Table 11.1.

Use the active voice unless you have good reason to use the passive. To convert a sentence that is in the passive voice to one in the active voice, search for the true subject, and name it. (Often, it may be hidden in a prepositional phrase.) Then find the verb, and mentally drop the form of *to be*. Convert what is left of the verb to the active voice.

Passive: The genetic relationship was studied by Berger and Shanks (1981).

Active: Berger and Shanks (1981) studied the genetic relationship.

A more vigorous active verb also may be hidden in a noun ending in *-ion.* You can often exhume these buried verbs to convert the sentence into the active voice.

Verb buried in "-ion" noun: Antibody detection was accomplished by Team A.

Resurrected verb: Team A detected antibodies.

For practice with active and passive voice, go to Exercise 14.

Check for subject–verb agreement

Because of the writing style that they have adopted, scientists find it surprisingly difficult to use correct verb forms. Attention to subject–verb agreement is especially crucial because of the confusion introduced by this sort of error:

The effect of feeding rations containing concentrations of aflatoxin on the immune systems of young swine with lesions and enzymes were studied.

Were the effect and the enzymes studied? Or did the swine have both lesions and enzymes? Is "effect" the subject, in which case "were" is incorrect? Because of lack of subject–verb agreement, the reader cannot be sure.

Two common situations are responsible for most subject–verb clashes in scientific writing. The first is when writers have allowed the subject and verb to become separated by so many other words that they have lost track of them. It can be helpful to know that objects of prepositions are never the subjects of sentences. To find the true subject, temporarily omit all phrases that separate the subject and verb, including those that begin with such words as *together with, including, plus,* and *as well as.* This will give a sentence in which subject and verb are readily apparent. Both should be singular, or both should be plural. Correct the grammar, and move the subject and verb closer to one another to improve the sentence. For good measure, whenever possible also tighten the wording and recast the sentence in the active voice.

Incorrect grammar with separated subject and verb: A high concentration of sialic acids which are a group of substances principally composed of amino sugars attached to polysaccharides, lipids, or proteins are found in the mammalian epididymis.

Omit intervening phrases: A high concentration . . . are found in the mammalian epididymis.

Improved, grammatically correct sentence: The mammalian epididymis contains a high concentration of sialic acids, principally composed of amino sugars attached to polysaccharides, lipids, or proteins.

For practice with subject–verb agreement, go to Exercise 15.

Attend to the mischief of multiples

Hungry Joe collected lists of fatal diseases and arranged them in alphabetical order so that he could put his finger without delay on any one he wanted to worry about.

JOSEPH HELLER

A second situation in which subject–verb clashes are common occurs when quantities are involved. Whether a person is compiling disease lists, parenting twins, or writing a paper, handling more than one of anything takes extra attention and care. Collective nouns, comparisons, and lists require special attention.

Watch for collective nouns and noun phrases

Whereas most nouns are clearly either singular or plural in both sense and form, collective nouns can be singular or plural, depending on context and your emphasis as the writer. You must decide whether the action of the verb is on the group as a whole (and treat the noun as singular) or the action is on group members as individuals (and treat the noun as plural).

Collective terms denoting quantity are particularly tricky to handle. When regarded as a unit, these nouns take singular verbs, but when considered individually they take plural verbs. We say "ten liters *is* a good yield" but "ten liters *were* poured into carboys." The problem is that, even with careful attention and the help of a good stylebook, such sentences often sound illogical or clumsy. Many writers simply prefer to redo such sentences. Write the sentence in the active voice and/or reorder it so the collective noun or quality is no longer the subject. Alternatively, use parentheses for the quantity.

Instead of: Five milliliters of serum was added to the mixture.

Write: We added 5 ml of serum to the mixture.

Instead of: Two-tenths of a milligram per liter of mebendazole and 0.9 mg/L of trichlorfon effectively control freshwater *Gyrodactylus*.

Table 11.2 Examples of verb use with collective nouns and the pronoun "none"

Singular in context	Plural in context
A pair of dogs was housed in each cage.	A pair of dogs were watching.
All the protocol was carefully followed.	All the data were incorrect.
Statistics is a difficult subject.	The statistics are easily gathered.
The number of people in this study is dwindling.	A number of people who enrolled in this study have dropped out.
None of the information was used.	None of the trials were finished *or* Not one of the trials was finished.

> *Write:* A combination of mebendazole (0.2 mg/L) and trichlorfon (0.9 mg/L) effectively controls freshwater *Gyrodactylus*.

Phrases like *a total of* can be particularly troublesome. *Total* is singular, and should take a singular verb. Do not write "a total of 35 animals *were* examined." Even the correct phrasing, "a total of 35 animals *was* examined," will cause many readers to stumble. It just sounds wrong! Usually the phrase *a total of* should simply be omitted.

The pronoun *none* can also be singular or plural. When the object of the prepositional phrase that follows it is singular, use a singular verb; when the object is plural, use a plural verb. If you mean *not one*, use that phrase with a singular verb instead of *none*. Some examples appear in Table 11.2; consult a good dictionary if in doubt about the form of others.

Remember that although the word *data* is sometimes used as a singular noun (particularly in the popular press), it is still correctly considered plural. (A *datum* is one of the single facts or pieces of information that collectively constitute the data.) Thus, in a scientific publication the conservative approach is to write, "Additional data *are* available."

Consider proximity with strings of subjects or verbs

When the subject is composed of a singular and a plural noun joined by *or* or *nor*, the verb agrees with the noun that is closer.

> *Incorrect:* Neither the dogs nor the cat *were* in the cage when the assistant returned.

> *Correct:* Neither the dogs nor the cat *was* in the cage when the assistant returned. *OR* Neither the cat nor the dogs *were* in the cage when the assistant returned.

When a single subject is coupled with more than one verb, auxiliaries such as *was* and *were* can safely be omitted with verbs after the first. Many writers shorten sentences by doing so. However, a problem can easily arise when this condensing technique is used for a sentence with more than one subject.

> *Single subject, auxiliary verbs omitted:* Tissues were fixed in 10% buffered formalin, embedded in paraffin, cut, and stained with hematoxylin and eosin.
>
> *Two subjects, both plural, correct but confusing:* Samples were obtained from kidneys and sections cut and stained with lead citrate. *[Were samples taken from kidneys and sections?]*
>
> *Improved by removing one subject:* Kidney sections were cut, and then stained with lead citrate.

If the number of the subject in the sentence changes, keep the verb in each clause. When two or more verbs are used with two subjects, one singular and one plural, keep the auxiliary words such as *was* and *were* with their verbs.

> *Incorrect:* The positions of the tubes were reversed and the test repeated.
>
> *Correct:* The positions of the tubes were reversed and the test was repeated.

Beware the grammar of comparisons and lists

Most grammatical problems that occur with comparisons and lists arise from the omission of important words. When words are missing, the reader intuitively finds a parallelism among the words that are present. Strange, illogical comparisons sometimes result.

> *Nonparallel construction:* These results were in general agreement with others who found increased mortality. *[The Results and "others" cannot logically agree with one another.]*
>
> *Parallel construction:* These data and others' results generally agreed.

The need for clarity always outranks the need for brevity. When comparing two agents under two conditions, fully specify which items are being compared. In the second part of a parallel construction, include all the words necessary to complete the comparison.

When comparing one person or thing with the rest of its class, use a word such as *other* with the comparative. Do not compare one with *all*, for it could be misinterpreted as the sum of the others.

Incomplete comparisons: Solution A yielded more amino acids than protein. The trial was significantly longer. The animal's weight was greater than all the others.

Completed comparisons: Solution A produced a greater yield of amino acids than of protein. The trial was significantly longer than the other trials were. The animal weighed more than any of the other animals did.

When comparing only two things, use the comparative term (better, poorer, lesser, more) rather than the superlative (best, poorest, least, most).

Of the two medications, this is the *less* (not *least*) effective.

The brown dog was the *sicker* (not *sickest*) of the two.

Check to ensure that the words *as* and *than* are next to their comparing word, especially when you have set off a phrase by commas or parentheses in the middle of the comparison. Check your grammar by omitting the phrase. Does it still make sense? Moving "than" and adding another "as" will correct the problem.

Incorrect: Group A was as large, if not larger, than Group B. *[Does "Group A was as large ... than Group B" still make sense?]*

Correct: Group A was as large as, if not larger than, Group B.

Lists carry their own sets of grammatical pitfalls. If there is an introductory preposition or article, either use it with only the first item or phrase in your list, or include it with every one. When some items take "a" and others take "an," you must repeat the article with each item.

Group 1 included a salamander, an alligator, and a skink.

Do not categorize clients by sex, by age, or by birthplace on these forms.

The patient's skin exhibited a red rash, an itchy lump, and a scar.

If a list is not inclusive, introduce the series of words or phrases with *such as*. Alternatives *like* and *e.g.* are less desirable. *Et cetera (etc.)* is rapidly falling out of favor, and at any rate, should never be used with these phrases.

Incorrect: Laboratory animals, like rats, mice, gerbils, etc., were evaluated.

Correct: Laboratory animals such as rats, mice, and gerbils were evaluated.

For guidelines on punctuating lists, see Chapter 13.

For practice with collective nouns, comparisons, and lists, go to Exercise 16.

Watch for strange linkages

> Under extreme pressure, we observed lysis.
> Now almost 7 months old, the physician said his daughter was healthy.
>
> FROM ACTUAL MANUSCRIPTS

Sometimes, you may find that your words and phrases become linked together in strange and unanticipated ways. Confusion, ambiguity, or downright humor can result. Usually, the problem lies in unclear antecedents or poorly placed modifiers. An antecedent is a word or phrase that a subsequent word refers to. Modifiers are words, phrases, or clauses that expand, limit, or make more precise the meaning of other elements in a sentence. Because both antecedents and modifiers must be linked to another word or phrase in the sentence, they cause problems when they appear in the wrong location. Readers will try to link them to the nearest word, whether you intended this or not.

Correct ambiguous antecedents

Pronouns always have antecedents, so pronouns can be a major source of confusion. Ambiguous pronoun reference often takes the form of two-sentence clusters, in which the first sentence has two possible antecedents for the pronoun in the second sentence.

> *Ambiguous:* Inadequate training in PCR techniques resulted in incomplete data. This has been our most pervasive problem. *[Does "this" refer to poor training or incomplete data?]*
>
> *Specific:* Inadequate training in PCR techniques resulted in incomplete data. Training inadequacies have been our most pervasive problem.

Check such words as *it, its, this, that, their,* and other pronouns. Clarify their antecedents.

Move misplaced modifiers

Because modifiers provide detail and clarification, they are the darlings of the scientific writing world. Scientists stack them, fill them with jargon, and place them in strange locations that cause ambiguity and unintentionally shift their meaning. Most modifiers function as adjectives or adverbs. To correct a misplaced modifier, simply move it as close as possible to the word it modifies.

> *Unclear:* The researcher tested the women observing this schedule. *Who observed the schedule, the researcher or the women?]*
>
> *Better:* Observing this schedule, the researcher tested the women.

Rework dangling participles

Phrases that do not clearly and logically refer to the correct noun or pronoun are called dangling modifiers. Various parts of speech can dangle. However, participles are the undisputed champions. Many dangling participles are misleading, confusing, or unintentionally ludicrous.

> Being in poor condition, we were unable to save the animals.
>
> Lying over the heart, you will discern a large growth.

Most participles end in *-ing*, *-en*, or *-ed*. Examine the text for words with these endings. Those most apt to cause problems usually appear at the beginning of the sentence as an introductory phrase. To correct a dangling participle, either rewrite the sentence so that the subjects agree or turn the phrase into a dependent clause with an explicit subject.

> *Dangling:* While having a committee meeting, the spectrophotometer exploded.
>
> *Subjects agree:* While having a committee meeting, we heard the spectrophotometer explode.
>
> *Dependent clause:* While we were having a committee meeting, the spectrophotometer exploded.

Two common "-ing" words are especially troublesome. *Following* is a noun or adjective meaning "that which comes next", as in "check the *following* reference" or "animals were examined the *following* day." It causes problems because it sounds like a participle to the reader. "*Following* a fat meal, the animal collapsed" sounds as though the animal was trailing the meal when this happened. Substitute the word *after*, which is clearly a preposition.

The other "-ing" word to distrust is *using*. It often dangles. Even when correct, *using* is a dull word that appears too commonly in scientific writing. Substitute a richer, more interesting word whenever you can. If you cannot think of one, at least substitute the safer word *with*.

> *Dangling participle:* No mosquitoes were found using the standard bait traps.
>
> *Better:* No mosquitoes were caught with standard bait traps.

Dangling participles can be corrected in several ways. Perhaps the most straightforward method is to rewrite the phrase to include the true subject of the verb that was turned into a participle. Alternatively, omit the verb of the participle entirely.

Dangling participle: Using our inoculation procedures, infected hamsters developed granulomata.

True subject included, but wordy: When we used our inoculation procedures, infected hamsters developed granulomata.

Verb of the participle omitted: Our inoculation procedures produced granulomata in infected hamsters.

A third way to correct a dangling participle is to switch to a gerund phrase. A gerund looks superficially like a participle, because it also ends in *-ing*. However, a participle functions as an adjective, and a gerund functions as a noun.

Dangling participle: Flushing the flask, the impurities were removed.

Participle changed to gerund: Flushing the flask removed impurities.

Dangling participle: Drawing a diagram, the Kreb's cycle explained the situation.

Participle changed to gerund: He explained the Kreb's cycle by drawing a diagram.

For practice with misplaced modifiers, go to Exercise 17.

"When I use a word," said Humpty Dumpty, in rather a scornful tone, "it means just what I choose it to mean – neither more nor less."

LEWIS CARROLL

How nice it would be if word choice were as simple in our own world as in Wonderland. Instead, like the bugs that plague computer programs, word choice flaws creep into scientific writing unnoticed (Weiss, 1990; Dupré, 1998). Almost always, there is more than one way to get rid of them. Like computer programmers, writers and editors may do anything to eliminate a bug – except add a new bug.

Recognize and minimize jargon

Derived from a medieval French word for the chattering and twittering of birds, jargon consists of highly specialized technical slang arising from the overuse and misuse of obscure, pretentious, or technical words or phrases. Eventually, the changing English language may even fully embrace the word or phrase. Until that time, however, jargon can pose an insidious trap for a scientific writer because its familiarity makes it seem acceptable before conservative usage embraces it as being correct.

Like other slang, jargon follows cycles of popularity, and fads are common. With a little reflection, you can probably add new examples to the ones we've listed in Table 12.1. Many of these arise by back formation, with a legitimate word or grammatical construction that gives rise to illegitimate offspring. Modern dictionaries describe many of these words and phrases as "variants." This just means that many people are prone to the error.

When conventional words or phrases within a discipline are overused, the result is also jargon (Table 12.2). A list of these terms could go on and on. The basic idea is to substitute shorter, everyday terms for polysyllabic synonyms of Greek, Latin, or Romance language derivation.

Eliminating jargon does not mean removing all technical terms, of course. Although many of them are polysyllabic, technical terms are also concise because to convey their precise meaning in any other way would require many more words. Simply be sure they are used correctly. Avoid using scholarly words or

Table 12.1 Types of scientific jargon

Origin	Examples
Careless extension of language	The kidneys were ground and the grindate was chilled.
	The material was rechromatographed.
	The mass was biopsied.
Acceptable words used in grammatically unacceptable ways	The substance was reacted with acetic acid. *[An intransitive verb such as "react" does not take an object, and has no passive voice.]*
	The feline developed leukopenia. *[Words like feline, canine, or bovine are adjectives; when you mean cat, dog, or cow, say so.]*
	No histology was found in the liver. *[Histology is a medical discipline; it is jargon to use it as a synonym for abnormality.]*
Spoken fads	Inoculize, prioritize, verbalize, visualize, or any such attempt to make a verb by adding "-ize." *[We have even encountered "formalinized samples" as a description of samples placed in formalin.]*
	Reactionwise, stepwise, or any such "-wise" except likewise.
	Phrases with "experience" tacked on the end, as in "a learning experience."
Words or phrases formed by dropping parts of a word or phrase	Prepped *[prepared]*
	Jugular ligation *[jugular vein ligation]*
	Osteopath *[osteopathic physician]*
	Vet *[veterinarian]*

phrases in a pseudo-scholarly way. Such jargon results in statements that are inaccurate as well as verbose. Words such as *spectrum, strategy, parameter, significant,* and *approximated* have a meaning in the disciplines in which they arose. Used in a pseudo-scholarly way in other disciplines, they can be misleading.

Biomedical terms can pose a special hazard because some are used incorrectly in speech so often that the misleading ring of familiarity can lend them false authenticity. Some examples follow.

> biopsy – This is not a verb. (The mass was not biopsied, but a biopsy of the mass was performed.) Observations are made on a biopsy specimen, not on the biopsy itself.

Table 12.2 Suggestions to replace some commonly overused words and phrases

Instead of	Use
at this point in time	now
due to the fact that	because
employ, utilize	use
high degree of accuracy	accurate
implement	do
in the event that	if
method	way
neonate	newborn
oftentimes	often
plethora	excess
postoperatively	after surgery
prior to	before
retard	slow
sacrifice, euthanatize	humanely kill
subsequent to	after

die of, die from – Persons and animals die of, not from specific diseases.

euthanatized, euthanized – Which of these words, if either one, should be used is a debated but unresolved matter; neither term even appears in some unabridged dictionaries. Use humanely killed, if possible. Avoid the term sacrificed, which has shamanistic overtones.

parameter – Reserve this word for its specific statistical meaning of a potential variable to which a particular value can be assigned to determine the value of other variables. Do not use parameter to mean measurement, value, indicator, or number. When it means those other words, use those other words instead.

significant(ly) – Use only when statistical significance is meant, and include a probability (P) value. For other uses, change to important, substantial, meaningful, or notable.

Watch out for words that end with -ology. This suffix means the study of something. Thus, words with this ending become jargon when used in sentences such as these.

Jargon: No pathology was found.

Correct: No pathologic condition was found.

Jargon: Cytology was normal.

Correct: Cytological findings were normal.

Jargon: Serology was negative.

Correct: Serologic findings were negative.

For example, "the only pathology found" translates into "the only study of pathogens found." It does not mean what scientists intend, "the only pathogens found" or "the only tissue damage by a pathogen." Likewise, "etiology" is not a pompous synonym of "cause" to be used in phrases like "the etiology of the disease"; it is the study and description of causes.

Note that words ending in *-ical* need an editorial check. Some editors drop the *-al*, but others don't, as in *pathologic* versus *pathological*. Be consistent.

Computer-based words, acronyms, and abbreviations are proliferating with the digital age of electronic communication. Language is always changing, and we anticipate that with time many of these terms will become widely accepted. For now, be conservative. Used excessively, computer jargon can easily become annoying and appear pretentious.

An additional problem with computer jargon can be determining how to punctuate these newly minted compound words pertaining to technology, some of which have not yet found their way into standard dictionaries. The iconoclastic approach of those in the computer industry seems to be "when in doubt, close it up." Since they are the people introducing new terminology and coining new meanings, they seem to be the ones setting the rules as well. Thus these new compound words commonly appear without hyphenation. Examples include desktop, download, email, keyword, online, toolbar, website, wildcard, and workstation.

CALVIN AND HOBBES © 1993 Watterson. Reprinted with permission of UNIVERSAL UCLICK. All rights reserved.

Avoid coining unnecessary new words, phrases, or usage

Rarely, a new scientific discovery truly justifies adding a new word to the language; if this happens, define the word carefully at its first mention in the document. Usually a little thought and dictionary work will produce an equivalent word that already exists in the English language. The work of translating a scientific paper is difficult enough without putting these additional stumbling blocks in the path of the foreign reader.

New grammatical constructions that arise by back formation are particularly dubious. These include such "counterfeit coins" (Weiss, 1990) as *administrate* for *administer*, *preventative* for *preventive*, *remediate* for *remedy*, and *deselect* for *reject*. Sometimes they become slightly silly, as when the legitimate word *attend* gives rise to *attendee* rather than *attender*.

For practice recognizing and avoiding jargon, go to Exercise 18.

Use bias-free, inclusive language

> Words, like Nature, half reveal
> And half conceal the Soul within.
>
> ALFRED, LORD TENNYSON

To avoid charges of prejudice and insensitivity, language and visual aids must be accurate, clear, and free from bias. Just as you have learned to check what you write for spelling and grammar, practice reading over your work for bias. Cultivate at least three kinds of awareness: (1) noting potential bias in the kinds of observations and characterization being made; (2) recognizing the impact of various value-laden terms; and (3) being sensitive to certain biases that are inherent in the structure of the English language.

It is a writer's job to maintain the audience's willingness to go on reading the document. Readers who are offended are likely to stop reading. Test your writing for implied or irrelevant evaluations on the basis of gender, sexual orientation, racial or ethnic group, disability, or age. Try substituting your own group for the one being discussed or imagining you are a member of the group you are discussing. If you feel excluded or offended, the material needs revision. Another suggestion is to ask people from that group to read your material and give you candid feedback.

Specify only relevant differences

Precision is a necessity in scientific writing. When you refer to a person or persons, choose words that are accurate, clear, and free from bias. For example, some writers use the generic masculine exclusively. This offends many readers, because it seems to be based on the presumption that all people are male unless proven female. Using *man* to refer to all human beings carries the same implication, and is simply less accurate than the phrase *men and women*.

Another part of writing without bias is recognizing that differences should be mentioned only when relevant. Marital status, sexual orientation, racial and ethnic identity, or the fact that a person has a disability should not be mentioned gratuitously.

Take care with group labels

Sometimes in scientific writing, participants in a study seem to lose their individuality. They are either categorized as objects (*the elderly*) or equated with their conditions (*the demented*). (Matters are not improved by changing this to *the demented group*!) Do not label people by their disabilities. Broad clinical terms such as *borderline* are loaded with innuendo unless properly explained. Calling one group *normal* may prompt the reader to make comparison to *abnormal*, stigmatizing individuals with differences (*the lesbian group* vs. *normal women*). Likewise, do not use emotionally loaded adjectives, such as "stroke *victims confined* to wheelchairs." Substitute neutral wording such as "individuals who had a stroke and use a wheelchair."

Labels such as *Group A* are not offensive, but they are not particularly descriptive either. The solution that is currently preferred places the people first, followed by a descriptive phrase (such as *people diagnosed with schizophrenia*).

Guard against the perception of bias or prejudice

Prejudice has been defined in many ways, but all include the idea of a judgment or opinion (whether positive or negative) formed beforehand or without knowledge or examination of the facts. Most of us are probably most sensitized to racism and sexism. However, many other *-isms* have been defined by groups and committees that are working to reduce perceived bias in language. Extensive discussion of this topic is beyond the scope of this book; for helpful overviews and inroads to the literature, consult the Internet and see works by groups such as the American Psychological Association (APA, 2010).

Avoiding sexist language is made more difficult by absence of a gender-neutral singular pronoun in the English language. A writer always has options, however; listed below are some of them.

- Use a gender-neutral term when speaking generically of your fellow creatures
  Instead of: man; mankind; manpower; man on the street

Use: the human race; humankind; people; workforce; personnel; average person

- Be sensitive to alternatives in titles and salutations. When a good gender-neutral term is available, use it in place of a clearly gender-oriented title.

  Instead of: spokesman; policeman; stewardess

  Use: speaker, representative; police officer; flight attendant

- Use plural constructions when you can. Often, it is possible to recast a statement in the plural, thus circumventing the need to use the third person singular pronoun. Avoid breaking the rules of English grammar, however.

  Unintentionally sexist: A doctor should advise his patients.

  Grammatically incorrect: Every doctor should advise their patients.

  Better: Doctors should advise their patients.

- Replace the third person singular possessive with articles. Often, a graceful alternative is to simply omit the possessive form in favor of more neutral wording.

  Instead of: Have the scientist send his manuscript to Dr. Blow.

  Write: Have the scientist send the manuscript to Dr. Blow.

- Address readers directly. If you can do so appropriately, substitute "you" for the third person singular pronoun. A direct instruction or command also works in many cases.

  Instead of: If the veterinary researcher cannot mail in his samples, he should ask his assistant if she can do it.

  Better: If you cannot mail in your samples, ask your assistant to do it.

  Instead of: A nurse must be sure that she uses disposable syringes.

  Better: Nurses must use disposable syringes.

**"Our goal is to establish language that is gender-neutral,
ethnic-neutral, and age-neutral, while celebrating
our spirit of diversity."**

- Use the passive voice. (Notice that this option is at the bottom of our list!)
  Instead of: Each conference participant should have received his schedule.
  Better (but only marginally): Schedules should have been received by conference participants.

Avoid awkward neologisms

In some disciplines, it is popular at the moment to alternate the use of "he" and "she" in text and oral presentations, supposedly to show sensitivity. This has the potential to be seriously distracting, however. Rather than paying attention to content, people begin playing silent games about which form will be used next. If none of the other guidelines has been helpful, one can use the slightly less awkward forms "he or she" and "him or her." Avoid s/he, he/she, and his/her. These constructions look awkward and interfere with reading.

> *Instead of:* Each technician must be sure that s/he signs his/her time card.

> *Better but awkward:* Each technician must be sure to sign his or her time card.

> *Better yet:* Each technician must be sure to sign a time card.

Some people feel strongly that a writer should avoid using words that are gender specific when the roles that they denote are not gender related. These purists have gone so far as to coin new words for any term that is gender specific, as in the substitution of *parentboard* for the computer's *motherboard*. In the words of Dupré (1998), "even if the word is awkward, it shows your reader you are sensitive."

Or does it simply make you look silly? Experimental ways of making English more neutral have not caught on very well. Many commentators vehemently argue against artificial tampering with words. So-called political correctness, an attitude that carries language sensitivity to an extreme, has come under a great deal of public ridicule. Our advice is to take the middle ground. Use gender-neutral words when they are appropriate, be aware of nuances in our changing language, and avoid awkwardly devising new words.

For practice handling language sensitively, go to Exercise 19.

Choose the right word

> The difference between the almost-right word and the right word is really a large matter – it's the difference between the lightning bug and the lightning.
>
> MARK TWAIN

The list of almost-right words is endless, and computer spellcheckers and grammar programs are little help with this problem. To rid your own writing of such mistakes, there is no easy alternative to learning what the right word is.

Some would like to believe that any widespread practice of writing or speech will become acceptable in time, and thus conclude that there is no cause for criticizing anything if it occurs regularly in the writing of educated people. If everyone confuses *affect* and *effect*, won't the dictionary eventually allow them as synonyms? And if so, can't we use them now? In a word, no. Good scientific writing is conservative.

Remember, the function of writing is to permit communication across time and space. Most of us would have trouble speaking Shakespearean English today, but we can understand written words of the King James version of the Bible, even though this edition was written centuries ago. Americans, Jamaicans, and Australians may have difficulty with each other's speech, but they have almost no problem with each other's writing.

Differentiate commonly misused and confused word pairs

Words are not always what they seem. The English language contains a great number of words that are commonly misused or mistaken for each other. Some commonly encountered "devil pairs" are given below. This list is only a beginning, and no substitute for a good dictionary.

accuracy/precision – *Accuracy* is the degree of correctness of a measurement or statement. *Precision* is the degree of refinement with which a measurement is made or stated, and implies qualities of definiteness and specificity.

acute/chronic – Reserve these terms for descriptions of symptoms, conditions, or diseases.

affect/effect – *Affect* is a verb that means to act upon. The noun *effect* means outcome. (As a verb, effect means to bring about, as in "it will effect a change," an awkward phrase worth replacing.)

aggravate/irritate – When an existing condition is made worse, it is aggravated. When tissue is caused to be inflamed or sore, it is irritated.

as/like – Rather than "like we just mentioned," say "as we just mentioned." *Like* can mean many things, but *as* is the conjunction for all but the most colloquial use.

case/patient – A *case* is a particular instance. It can be evaluated, followed, and reported. A *patient* is a person who is under medical care. (Avoid calling an animal a patient.) A sick person not receiving treatment is not a patient, so one cannot speak of untreated or normal patients.

compliment/complement – *Compliment* means praise, but *complement* means to mutually complete each other. I compliment you on finding two treatments that complement one another so very well.

continual/continuous – *Continual* means happening over and over. *Continuous* means occurring without interruption.

dose/dosage– A *dose* is the quantity to be administered at one time, or the total quantity administered. *Dosage*, the regulated administration of doses, is usually expressed in terms of a quantity per unit of time. (Give a dosage of 0.25 mg every 4 hours until the dose has been ingested.)

examine/evaluate – Patients, animals, and microscope slides are examined; conditions and diseases are evaluated.

follow/observe – A case is followed; a patient is observed. To *follow up* on either one approaches jargon, as does *follow-up study*. However, in medical writing the use of both terms is increasing.

gender/sex – *Gender* is cultural, and is the term to use when referring to men and women as social groups. *Sex* is biological; use it when the biological distinction is predominant.

imply/infer – To *imply* is to suggest, indicate, or express indirectly. To *infer* is to conclude. What you have inferred is not what I meant to imply.

infect/infest – Endoparasites such as intestinal worms *infect* to produce an infection; ectoparasites such as fleas *infest* and produce an infestation.

infectious/contagious – *Infectious* means harboring an agent that can cause infection, or having been caused by an infecting agent. *Contagious* is the adjective that means the agent in an infectious disease has a high probability of being transmitted. Under some conditions, an infectious disease is not contagious.

necessitate/require – *Necessitate* means to make necessary. *Require* means to have a need for. A patient requires treatment. The treatment may necessitate certain procedures.

negative/normal – Cultures, tests for microorganisms, tests for specific reactions, and reactions to tests may be *negative* or *positive*. Observations, results, or findings from examinations and tests are *normal* or *abnormal*.

over/more than – *Over* can be ambiguous. (The cases were followed up over two years.) Instead, say *more than*. (The cases were followed for more than two years.)

prevalence/incidence – *Prevalence* refers to the quality or state of being wide-spread or common. *Incidence* is the rate of occurrence. The prevalence of influenza makes immunizations desirable to reduce its incidence.

principal/principle – A *principal* is a leader; used as an adjective, it means highest rank. A *principle* is a fundamental truth or law. Dr. Jones was the principal investigator on a grant to study biological principles.

regime/regimen – A *regime* is a system of management of government. When a system of therapy is meant, *regimen* is the correct term.

symptoms/signs – A conservative rule states that *symptoms* apply to people, *signs* apply to animals.

toxicity/toxic –*Toxicity* is the quality, state, or degree of being poisonous. A patient does not have toxicity. *Toxic* means poisonous; a patient is not toxic.

use/utilize/employ – Generally, *use* is the intended term; *utilize* suggests the discovery of a new, profitable, or practical use for something. The word *employ* is best reserved for putting a person to work.

vaccinate/immunize – Although these words are sometimes used as synonyms, they carry different implications. To *vaccinate* means to expose a person or animal to an antigen purposively in hopes of eliciting protective antibody. To *immunize* implies that exposure successfully elicited protective antibody. Not all vaccinated organisms are immunized.

varying/various –*Varying* means changing, but *various* means of several kinds. By varying the treatment regimens, we exposed groups of animals to various medications.

while/whereas – *While* indicates time and a temporal relationship. *Whereas*, often the word the writer intended, has such meanings as "when in fact," "that being so," and "in view of the fact that."

For practice with devil pairs, go to Exercise 20.

Inspect "which" and "that"

Your manuscript is both good and original;
but the part that is good is not original,
and the part that is original is not good.

ATTRIBUTED TO SAMUEL JOHNSON

Sometimes the words "which" and "that" can be used interchangeably; more often, they cannot. A phrase or clause introduced by *that* is restrictive; as in the critique that is quoted above, it cannot be omitted without changing the meaning of the sentence. Such essential material must not be set off with commas.

A non-restrictive clause adds information but does not limit what it modifies. Because it can be omitted without changing the meaning of the main part of the sentence, a non-restrictive clause is separated from the rest of the sentence by commas. Technically, the word "which" can be either restrictive or non-restrictive. One could write "dogs which were treated recovered" or "dogs, which were treated, recovered," depending upon the sense of the sentence. However, many scientists overuse the word as a connective, perhaps in a misguided attempt to make their writing more formal. As a result, correct comma use suffers. It is much easier to rely on this simple rule: use *which* with commas with all non-restrictive clauses and use *that* without commas with all restrictive clauses.

Non-restrictive which *clause:* The researcher's decision, which did not come easily, was final.

Restrictive that *clause:* Dogs that were treated with antibiotics recovered.

Non-restrictive which *clause:* The horses, which came from six farms, were dead.

Restrictive that *clause:* The horses that died were buried.

A second reason to watch these words is that they can introduce dangling phrases. When we read the words which or that, we interpret such words to refer to whatever went immediately before them in the sentence. If either word becomes separated from its true subject, confusion results. To cure the confusion, move which or that next to the word to which it refers. Alternatively, rewrite the sentence to avoid using either word. (This is an especially desirable route if the sentence is very long and/or complex.) Consider breaking the sentence into smaller ones.

Potentially confusing: Tumors were palpable in the animals that remained. *[Which remained, the animals or the tumors?]*

Ways to clarify the meaning: In the animals that remained, tumors were palpable. OR

Tumors that remained were palpable in the animals.

For practice with which and that, go to Exercise 21.

Focus fuzzy nouns and qualifiers

Sometimes, words such as those listed below have a definite meaning:

> area, character, conditions, field, level, nature, problem, process, situation, structure, system

More often, they indicate that the thought needs to be sharpened. Think carefully about what is really meant, and substitute a more precise word.

Likewise, vague qualifiers (such as *fairly, few, minimal, much, quite, rather, several, slight, very*) usually can and should be omitted, since they add nothing. Humorist Mark Twain is said to have offered this advice: "Substitute 'damn' every time you're inclined to write 'very'; your editor will delete it and the writing will be just as it should be."

Energize the verbs

> Good writing gives energy, whatever it is about.
>
> MARILYN HACKER

Scientists are infamous for their plodding writing style. Frequently, their problem arises from poor verb use. Most of the time, they have chosen weak and overused verbs or hidden perfectly good verbs in noun form. In other cases, they have overused the passive voice, and/or lost track of subject–verb agreement.

Choose livelier verbs

Scientists often write as though only seven verbs exist: demonstrate, exhibit, present, observe, occur, report, and show. Certainly most scientific papers would be seriously crippled if these verbs were removed from the language. Consider this example:

> The mean hepatic weights observed to occur in normal and thyroidectomised rats were 154 and 27 mg, respectively. The kidney was also observed to exhibit a four-fold difference in the two groups, but as we have shown, no significant difference was demonstrated in the spleen.

These seven tired old workhorses carry another problem on their backs. To be technically accurate, they should not be coupled with nonhuman subjects. For example, a scientist may write "the results demonstrate," an action that "results" – being inanimate – cannot do. Likewise, a researcher may say,

"The tissue exhibited necrotic foci." A tissue cannot present anything for inspection, as the sentence literally implies. This misuse is so widespread that most readers have come to accept it. Nonetheless, substituting other verbs solves the problem and will usually improve the writing in other ways, too.

> *Inaccurate:* Results show dog weight increased and reduced angulation occurred.

> *Better:* Dogs weighed more and angulation decreased.

> *Inaccurate and poor word choice:* As Figure 1 indicates, disease was observed to occur in 72 of the demented group.

> *Better:* Disease developed in 72 patients with dementia (Fig. 1).

As a supplement to whatever grammar-checking program you may have or as a fairly powerful checker on its own, consider using your computer's "search" or "find" command to flag each of these weary workhorse verbs (or at least those you recognize as potential problems in your own writing). Each time that one is highlighted, examine the sentence in which it appears. You will soon become sufficiently sensitized that you no longer need mechanical help to alert you to their presence so that you can avoid or fix them.

Introduce a bit of variety. Whenever it is clear, reasonable, and possible to do so, substitute more vigorous verbs. The section headings in this book may give you some ideas. Consult a thesaurus if you need help finding more.

Unmask verbs disguised as nouns

Habitual use of nouns and pronouns is a common cause of monotonous, verbose scientific writing. Abstract nouns formed from verbs and ending in "-ion" are a particularly common offender. Such words are really verbs in disguise, richer and more concise than the lazy verbs they are capable of replacing. Consider using them directly as verbs or in their infinitive form. Experiment with their use as adjectives, adverbs, and participles, as well.

> *Overuse of abstract nouns:* Following activity termination, the patient experienced an amelioration of his condition.

> *More forceful equivalent:* After the patient stopped moving, his condition improved.

> *Buried verbal nouns:* Results showed protection by the vaccine, but degeneration of lymphocytes occurred.

> *Resurrected verb:* The vaccine protected the patients, but their lymphocytes degenerated.

Sometimes, words that are perfectly good on their own still can indicate the potential for trouble. For decades, the following "warning words" (adapted from Woodford, 1968) have remained relevant as indicators that unclear, ambiguous, or prosaic prose lurks nearby.

accomplished	achieved	attained	carried out
conducted	done	effected	experienced
facilitated	given	implemented	indicated
involved	made	obtained	required
performed	proceeded	produced	

These overused, colorless verbs occur most commonly as the past participle. They usually should be eliminated in favor of a more vital verb hidden (often in *-ion* form) in the sentence.

> *Colorless:* The provision of assistance implemented in 2007 resulted in the production of a viable method for establishment of a basis for long-term improvement.
>
> *Better:* Assistance begun in 2007 led to a method that produced long-term improvement.

For practice dealing with fuzzy words and disguised verbs, go to Exercise 22.

13 Attend to punctuation, capitalization, and other mechanics

Writing the words "a woman without her man is nothing" on the chalkboard, the professor directed the students to punctuate it correctly.

The men wrote "A woman, without her man, is nothing."

The women wrote "A woman: without her, man is nothing."

Punctuation is everything.

UNKNOWN

If effective scientific communication is like a well-designed and smoothly operating machine, then grammar – the accepted system of rules by which words are formed and put together to make sentences – forms the nuts and bolts that hold it all together. The individual fasteners of punctuation, capitalization, and such may seem simple and unexciting to look at, but they are undeniably important if the machine is to hold together and function properly.

In this chapter, we suggest ways of avoiding and correcting some common mechanical mistakes that scientific writers tend to make. For further advice, style manuals of special utility for biomedical writers include the *Publication Manual of the American Psychological Association* (2010), the *AMA Manual of Style* (2007), and the Council of Science Editors' *Scientific Style and Format* (2006). All are updated at intervals; be sure to check for the latest edition.

Punctuate for clarity

Punctuation has one purpose – to help the reader understand the structural relationship within (and thus the intention of) a sentence. For this reason, the best approach to punctuation is almost always the simplest. Punctuation should be almost automatic. If you are puzzled over how to punctuate a particular sentence, you probably have created a sentence that will puzzle readers too, no matter how you punctuate it. Rewrite the sentence in a form that requires only simple punctuation.

Prefer the period
Semicolons, colons, and dashes indicate that two statements are closely related. Their use sometimes also helps condense material. However, sentences separated in this way are usually more difficult to read, so use these

punctuation marks sparingly. The trend in scientific writing is to eliminate semicolons, substituting separate sentences with periods.

> *Older style:* A mutant strain might be designated "red"; its genetic symbol, *r*.

> *Newer style:* A mutant strain might be designated "red." Its genetic symbol would be *r*.

Semicolons are still appropriately used to separate items in a series with internal commas.

> Larval feeding habits of flies include: parasitizing beetles, moths, and other insects; mining in fern leaves, stems, and other plant tissue; burrowing in carrion, offal, and dung; and scavenging decaying vegetation.

Prevent false joining

Anytime a phrase would be nonsense without one or more commas, a dash, or parentheses, use them. This rule is the rationale behind all the more specific ones. When you have finished writing, check each sentence for reading errors associated with incorrect punctuation or lack of punctuation. If two parts might be joined erroneously, they should be separated by punctuation.

Pay particular attention to sentences that vary from the usual "subject–verb–object" word order. The possibility of erroneous joining is nearly always present when the introductory phrase contains a verb of some form, such as an infinitive or a participle. (Remember the strange linkages discussed in Chapter 11.)

> *Reading error possible:* Although additions of monensin were discontinued after 9 days the fermentors did not resume gas production.

> *Alternative interpretations clarified by punctuation:* Although additions of monensin were discontinued, after 9 days the fermentors did not resume gas production. *OR* Although additions of monensin were discontinued after 9 days, the fermentors did not resume gas production.

Insert commas for clarity and emphasis

The comma has a wide variety of uses, but its overall role is to add clarity or emphasis to a sentence. Remember this fact, and the comma's many specific applications begin to fit into a pattern.

Whenever a dependent clause or a long adverbial phrase comes before the main statement of the sentence, it needs a comma. As an example, consider the previous sentence.

To determine whether to use commas with a clause that is within a sentence, read the sentence without the clause. Proper punctuation of a clause within a sentence hinges upon whether the clause is essential (restrictive) or not. If omitting the clause does not change the meaning of the main statement of the sentence, separate the clause from the main statement with commas. If the clause is essential to the meaning, do not use commas. As noted in Chapter 12, this means commas generally are used with the word "which" but not with "that."

Punctuate the elements of series clearly

Series range from straightforward lists of like items to extremely convoluted sentences with all manner of nested phrases. For maximal clarity, they require different sorts of punctuation.

With a simple series, place a comma before *and*, *or*, and between the items. Your composition teacher may have instructed you otherwise – in literary writing, and in British scientific writing, this comma is often omitted on the grounds that it interrupts the flow of words. However, American scientific writing includes the comma, with the aim of maximizing precision. Although the comma before *and* is usually merely a nicety, sometimes it can be important to the meaning of the sentence.

Complex series need something more. When the individual elements in a series contain their own punctuation, separating the elements with commas may confuse readers. Use semicolons, numerals within the sentence, or both.

> *Confusing:* The criteria included that patients with unilateral dislocation were included but those with bilateral dislocation were not, as treatment of one hip may affect the untreated, and the child had to be less than 36 months old when treatment was begun and that no child with other anomalies such as scoliosis, arthrogryposis, or trisomy 21 was included.

> *Better:* All patients (1) exhibited unilateral, but not bilateral dislocation; (2) were younger than 36 months when treatment began; and (3) exhibited no other anomalies such as scoliosis, arthrogryposis, or trisomy 21.

Compound sentences can also be thought of as a type of series. Scientists are extraordinarily fond of coupling sentences, particularly when discussing their methodology. They also rely heavily on a single subject joined to pairs of verbs or adjectives. The words *and*, *but*, *for*, *or*, and *nor* are weak ways to join independent statements. Most critics of style shun them. Used to excess, such construction weakens the writing and creates a singsong cadence.

For stronger writing, examine each pair of sentences or compound predicates. First, consider dividing each statement into separate sentences, particularly if the statements are complex and/or long. Condense and tighten the wording. Then, if a weak connector still must be used, put a comma before it.

> *Weak writing, poorly punctuated:* Experimental subjects were kept in a climate-controlled room, and were provided with food. Artificial light was provided, and dogs were acclimated to handling. In the study described herein, the investigators found that *L. pneumophila* cannot multiply under these conditions but they do survive for they remain viable and this indicates that a great range of habitats is capable of harboring this bacterium.

> *Better:* Dogs were housed in a climate-controlled room with artificial lighting, provided with food, and handled. Under these conditions, *L. pneumophila* did not multiply, but they did survive, indicating that a range of habitats may harbor this bacterium.

Identify passages from other texts

Any time you copy another writer's or speaker's exact words directly in the text, it must be set off in a way that shows it to be a quote. How this is done is determined by such factors as the quote's length (40 words or less is a common dividing point), the nature of the material being quoted, the country in which the document is being published, and both editorial and personal preferences.

Short quotes (called run-in quotations) are usually placed directly in the text, with quotation marks at their beginning and end. American and British styles for run-in quotations differ in their punctuation (Table 13.1).

Table 13.1 Use of quotation marks in run-on quotations that appear within the text

Context	American system	British system
To set off the primary quotation	Double quotation marks at beginning and end	Single quotation marks at beginning and end
To set off a quotation within another quotation	Single quotation marks at beginning and end	Double quotation marks at beginning and end
Position of closing quotation mark in relationship to punctuation of the sentence	After a comma, period, exclamation mark, or question mark Before a semicolon or colon	"According to the sense" – before punctuation except when quotation is a complete sentence

In general, U.S. and Canadian publications follow the American style, but British and Australian publications follow the British style (Council of Science Editors, 2006).

The American style is to use single quotation marks only for a quote within a quote. The names of articles or book chapters are treated the same way. If a run-in quotation is more than a single paragraph, begin each paragraph with a quotation mark but close only the end of the last paragraph with a quotation mark.

> Matthews states that "In his 1997 book, *Digital Literacy*, Paul Gilster quotes Vannevar Bush's seminal 1945 article, 'As We May Think,' and calls it 'the first visualization of hypertext in the modern sense.'"

> According to the CDC director, recurrent polycystic kidney disease is "unparalleled in this population.

> "If the hospitalization rate for this disease continues to climb as it has done this year, we are facing a problem of enormous proportions."

Longer direct quotes (called block quotations, excerpts, or extracts) may be set off as a separate block of type by indenting each line on the left side (in the same position as a new paragraph), and single spacing without quotation marks. The right margin stays the same as for the regular text. Sometimes the excerpt is set in a smaller font size than the main text. If the text that introduces the excerpt does not make its source clear, the excerpt should end with a parenthetical indication of the source, placed after the closing punctuation mark of the excerpt.

With any direct quotation, be careful to enclose only the actual words used, not your restatement or interpretation. Follow the wording, spelling, and punctuation exactly. Whenever possible, verify the quotation from the original. To indicate an omission in quoted material, use three spaced periods (ellipses).

> Employees of the U.S. government may file a statement attesting that a typescript was prepared "as part of their official duties."

> Pauling stated that "Vitamin C . . . appears to be of value . . ."

Place other punctuation marks in proper relation to quotation marks. In American usage, the comma and period always appear inside quotation marks. The colon and semicolon are placed outside the quotation marks. Question marks and dashes go inside the closing quotation mark when they belong to the quotation, but outside when they do not.

What did the author mean by "anti-rotaviral"?

The term "pyrexia" is replacing the word "fever."

We studied "mating readiness"; the other research team studied "recalcitrance."

Know when not to use quotation marks

Quotation marks are used in two different ways – to draw attention to words or phrases, or to attribute them to some other speaker or author. Do not overuse quotation marks for emphasis. Admittedly, this is a judgment call. Slang and colloquialisms, often set off by quotation marks, are common in science publications for a general audience. However, in a scientific paper, search for more exact terms and use a more formal writing style.

In journals, quotation marks are often used around new technical terms, old terms used in an unusual way, or simply to draw attention to a word. (In books, italics are often preferred.) Used sparingly, these are acceptable when used to point out that the term is used in context for a unique or special purpose; in this way, the quotation marks substitute for the phrase *so-called*.

Indirect quotations are paraphrases of a speaker's words or ideas. They usually are introduced by the word *that*. Do not enclose indirect quotations in quotation marks.

> *Direct quotation:* Albert Einstein said, "Technological progress is like an axe in the hands of a pathological criminal."
>
> *Indirect quotation:* Jim Samuels said that he saw the sequel to the movie *Clones*, and it was the same movie!

Common nicknames, bits of humor, technical terms, and trite or well-known expressions generally can stand on their own without quotation marks. Proverbial, biblical, and well-known literary expressions do not need quotation marks. Commonly known facts available in numerous sources need neither a source citation nor quotation marks unless the material is taken word-for-word from one particular source.

Hyphenation rules are complex and changing

Hyphens have two general purposes, dividing and compounding. They function primarily as spelling devices, but also can link or separate words or replace prepositions. Their most common use is to join compound words (such as *long-term* results). They also form the compound numbers from *twenty-one* through *ninety-nine*, and fractions (such as *three-quarters*) when they are written out.

The decision whether to use hyphens with compound words – or omit them – often requires the aid of a good unabridged dictionary. The classical rules governing this set of uses are complex, covering such topics as whether

Table 13.2 Ten hyphenation rules that generally apply

Guideline	Examples
1. Use a hyphen to create compound modifiers that precede a noun	Pollen-bearing hairs; three-pronged structure
2. Use a hyphen to avoid ambiguity	The food co-op bought a chicken coop; re-cover cages so birds can recover
3. Use hyphens in compound numbers from 21 to 99	Twenty-one, ninety-nine
4. Use hyphens in fractions and ratios that function as adjectives	A four-to-one vote; three-quarters gone
5. Use a hyphen to reduce redundancy in series	The first-, second-, and third-born offspring were larger.
6. Use a hyphen with letter or number modifiers	The 5-week-old chick, H-bomb
7. Use hyphens with strings of modifiers that express a single thought when the string comes before the noun, does not have an adverb as its first word, and would not make sense if each word modified the noun without the aid of the others	Green-algae-covered ponds, scale-infested trees BUT NOT freshly collected samples, a new digital analyzer, or equipment that is out of date
8. Use a hyphen with a prefix when the root word is a proper noun	Pre-Darwinian
9. Use a hyphen when the same vowel ends the prefix and begins the root word (especially if *i* is the repeated vowel)	Anti-inflammatory; pre-existing
10. Do not use a hyphen when it isn't needed	Unless misleading or awkward letter combinations result or the rules above apply, the following prefixes may be used without hyphenation: pre, post, re, sub, super, micro, mini, multi, non

the compound word is permanent or temporary and whether the words are so closely associated that they constitute a single concept.

As a spelling device, the hyphen is supposed to make life easier, but attempts to detail all its various uses tend to only increase the hyphenation confusion that many writers feel. In addition, the rules are changing, and even the authorities do not always agree. The use of hyphens in scientific writing clearly is declining. Although some rules still seem to generally apply (Table 13.2), there is a strong tendency either to form new single-word terms or to use strings of modifiers without hyphenation. Consult your intended publication for evidence of any strong preferences, consult a standard dictionary for specific guidance, and then above all, be consistent.

Hyphens are also used to divide words at the ends of lines. Such divisions are made between syllables, but not all syllable breaks are acceptable end-of-line breaks. (Consult a dictionary.) Automatic hyphenation done by some word-processing programs can produce some unusual word divisions. In general, it is best to turn off the automatic hyphenation option on such programs.

The main context in which this hyphenation role occurs is in the production of camera-ready copy. Much typesetting today is done in "ragged-right" style, with lines left unjustified so that the right-hand margin of the type column is irregular, but occasionally you may be asked to produce text that is "justified" (aligned to both margins). If justification is done with no hyphenation, the spacing between words is adjusted, sometimes to the extent of looking very strange.

When type is set in justified lines with hyphenation, it is inevitable that some words will be broken. Such text looks attractive, but it can be difficult to read. Furthermore, if a typescript is submitted in this style, there is a good chance that at least a few line-end hyphens may be carried over mistakenly as obligatory hyphens in the typeset copy. Unless your intended journal specifies otherwise, don't justify the text. By submitting ragged-right copy, you will minimize the chances of accidental erroneous hyphenation in the typeset copy.

For practice correcting punctuation, go to Exercise 23.

Capitalize consistently

In general, most publishers are using fewer capital letters than they once did. Still, to state all the rules for employing capitals would be nearly impossible here. Usage varies, and almost every rule has exceptions and variations. This confusion is more apparent than real, however. Most capitalized words are proper nouns, major words in titles, or first words of sentences. However, a few problematic situations recur commonly enough in biomedical and biological writing to be worth special note. If you still have questions on capitalization of specific words after reviewing the guidelines below, consult a standard dictionary and follow its lead.

Remember proper and common nouns

You may not have consciously thought about this point of grammar for years, but when you were younger, language teachers almost certainly drilled you on it. A noun that designates a specific person, place, or thing is called a proper

Table 13.3 Capitalization of proper and common nouns

Type of name	Capitalization style	Examples
Proper noun	Always begins with a capital letter	Appalachian Mountains, Chemistry 605
Common noun	None (except in special situations)	the mountains, an ancient era
Common name derived from a scientific name	Like other common nouns	drosophila, canids, planarians
Common noun plus modifier derived from a proper noun	Begin modifier with capital letter; the rest of the name may or may not be capitalized	German measles; Darwinian finches. OR German Measles, Darwinian Finches.

noun. A noun that designates any and all of a class of persons, places, or things is a common noun. These two noun types differ in their capitalization requirements (Table 13.3).

Common nouns include chemicals, generic names of medicines, diseases, anatomical parts, animal breeds, and common names derived from the scientific names of plants and animals. None of these need to be capitalized, except in special situations such as titles (see the next section).

Proper nouns, on the other hand, should begin with a capital letter. Thus, one would capitalize the full names of government agencies, departments, divisions, organizations, and companies *(Department of Agriculture, Warner Communications Inc.)*.

The question becomes what to do with combinations. For example, when names include modifiers derived from proper nouns, these modifiers are usually capitalized. In the same way, one would capitalize the significant parts of the name of a manufactured product *(Pyrex glass)* and the vernacular names of plant varieties *(Yellow Dent corn)*. However, in a paper mentioning several items in a series or list, capitalizing only modifiers derived from proper nouns gives the page a very uneven appearance. Some writers and editors feel this lack of uniformity in capitalization is undesirable. They capitalize the full names of everything in the list as a matter of equality. Be sure to examine a copy of your intended journal choice for examples of their policy.

> *Uneven capitalization:* The affected animals included Virginia deer, golden hamsters, and miniature Irish wolfhounds. Their symptoms were reminiscent of depression, Prader–Willi syndrome, and Alzheimer's disease.

All entries capitalized: The second trial used French Poodles, Maine Coon Cats, and Monk Parakeets. Some of them exhibited signs of Munchausen Syndrome and Seasonal Affective Disorder.

Capitalize significant words in titles

Whether the title appears at the beginning of a work or is mentioned within running text, the role of capitalization is to help readers more readily distinguish a title from the adjacent text. There are various systems for doing this. Note that some scientific and technical publications do not follow the usual guidelines, but have their own systems.

The classic system is to capitalize the initial letters of the first and last words of a title or subtitle, as well as all major (or "significant") words. Do not capitalize articles (*a, an, the*), conjunctions (*and, but, if*) or short prepositions (*at, in, on, of*) unless they begin the title.

For the test, be sure to read the book, *How to Write and Publish a Scientific Paper*, but for now you can ignore *The 2013 Summary of Wildlife Disease Reports.*

Some systems capitalize prepositions if they contain more than four letters (*between, because, until, after*) and use lower case for shorter ones.

She suggested that the trial participants should read the new book, *Weight Loss by Dieting Without Exercise.* I prefer *Lose Ten Pounds in Ten Days.*

See Turton's 1802 classic, *System of Nature After the Three Grand Kingdoms of Animals, Vegetables, and Minerals.*

Others maintain that only a word's function, not its length, should determine whether to capitalize it. They feel that even long prepositions such as *between* nearly always are most properly put in lower case.

His career really began with the publication of his insightful book, *Behavioral Interactions of Hospitalized Patients before and since the Arrival of Viagra.*

The first word of hyphenated compounds in titles is nearly always capitalized; the second word often is not, although either of these styles is correct. Some authorities capitalize the word following the hyphen only if it is a noun or a proper adjective, or if it is equal in importance to the first word. The word after such prefixes as *anti-, ex-, re-,* and *self-* may or may not be capitalized.

Aspirin and Anti-Heartworm Therapy

The Role of Cancer-Inducing Agents

> Observations on a Hand-reared Baboon
>
> Short-term Goals and Long-term Management
>
> Self-measurements of Femoral Neck-shaft Angle

All this seeming complexity and competition between systems may change with the popularity of word processing. Most word-processing software programs include a case command with the option "sentence case" which capitalizes all words in the title automatically. Authors are certainly ready to make the switch as soon as editors are ready to embrace it.

Check journal requirements

Some journals, publishers, and graduate schools specify a capitalization style; others don't. Make every effort to mimic the style of the journal in which you intend to publish. Examine recent issues. Note the figure legends, table captions, reference lists, and typescript headings and subheadings. You will probably find a definite capitalization style, even if one has not been spelled out formally in the publication's *Instructions to Authors*.

Capitalization is particularly variable in reference citations. Sometimes, article titles have the significant words capitalized. However, many journals prefer that article or chapter titles be treated as though they were sentences.

> *Capitalized article title:* Yalow, R. S. and S. A. Bernson. 1959. Assay of Plasma Insulin in Human Subjects by Immunological Methods. *Nature* 184: 1648–1649.
>
> *Sentence-style article title:* Guhl, A. M. 1968. Social inertia and social stability in chickens. *Animal Behaviour* 16: 219–232.

For practice with capitalization, go to Exercise 24.

Treat scientific names properly

> Latin's a dead, dead language
> As dead as dead can be.
> First it killed the Romans
> And now it's killing me.
> STUDENT DOGGEREL

Few people can fail to notice that a great many scientific terms are based on foreign words. Despite what some might suspect, this is not some arbitrary plot to make students' lives difficult or a grandiloquent scheme to make science appear lofty. In earlier times, Latin and Greek were international languages that had a dominant effect upon education and culture, much as English does today.

The continuing impact of this can be seen most clearly in the worldwide system by which organisms are named and classified. The scientific names of all animals, plants, and microorganisms are based on the rules set forth in the most recent edition of one of four codes, which authors and editors are obligated to accept:

- *International Code of Nomenclature of Bacteria* (Lapage *et al.*, 1992)
- *The International Code of Virus Classification and Nomenclature* (King *et al.*, 2011)
- *International Code of Zoological Nomenclature.* 4th edn with online amendments (ICZN, 1999)
- *International Code of Nomenclature for Algae, Fungi, and Plants (Melbourne Code)* (McNeill *et al.*, 2012).

Because of differences in usage and in the nature of the organisms themselves, the four major codes differ in some aspects of terminology. For example, in botany a scientific name such as *Acer rubrum* is a "binomial" composed of a generic name and "specific epithet." In bacteriology, a name such as *Staphylococcus aureus* is a "binary combination." In zoology, *Homo sapiens* is a "binomen," and the specific epithet *sapiens* is a "specific name."

The codes also differ somewhat in practice. For example, the botanical code recognizes both subspecies and varieties. The zoological code also recognizes subspecies, but only those varieties named before 1961. The bacteriological code considers subspecies and varieties to be synonymous.

Additional useful references on bacterial nomenclature include *Approved Lists of Bacterial Names* (Skerman, 1989) and *Bergey's Manual of Determinative Bacteriology* (Holt *et al.*, 1994). Other helpful resources on biological nomenclature include Calisher and Fauquet (1992) and Jeffrey (1992).

Capitalize everything but species and variety

The basic systematic categories (*taxa*, singular *taxon*) in all biology are, in descending order: kingdom, phylum or division, class, order, family, genus, and species. ("King Phillip came over from Germany soused" is one of many easy, if irreverent, mnemonic aids.) The scientific names of all these taxa and any sub- and supra-divisions are Latin or Latinized forms. All these scientific names but the species name are considered to be proper nouns.

Do not capitalize the name of the species (except for the very rare journal that requires it). Technically, the species name is an adjective or similar modifier of the generic name, rather than a full name in its own right.

For this reason, the species name is never used alone. The same is true of varietal names. For example, you might write of the common house cat as *Felis domestica*, family Felidae, but would never refer to it as simply *domestica*. However, after first mentioning the name in full, you can shorten it to *F. domestica* if the context makes the meaning clear. Note that the shortened form should never be used to begin a sentence.

Italicize names of the genus, species, and below

Genus and species names are italicized because historically italics were always used to indicate foreign words. Because they are in Latin form like the genus and species, taxa such as subspecies or varieties are italicized as well. Names of cultivated varieties (cultivars) are not italicized when they are not Latin or Latinized, but are set off with single quotes.

> *Canis familiaris*, family Canidae
>
> *Tris tricolor* var. *hirta*
>
> *Lilium superbum* 'Calico'
>
> *Melittobia* wasps belong to the order Hymenoptera.

Do not italicize the names of higher taxa such as family or order. (This is one of the more common mistakes in popularized science writing.)

Make the first taxonomic mention a comprehensive one

Genus and species (and variety, if relevant) should be spelled out in full when an organism is first mentioned in a paper. Thereafter, a shortened form or use of the common name is acceptable.

> The pine siskin, *Carduelis pinus*, is common here. This gregarious siskin eats seeds.

The most conservative usage also adds the name of the scientist who first officially described and named the organism in print. This author citation need appear only once in the text, and usually does not appear in the title. Some publications take this concept to the extreme, and also include parts of the higher taxonomic classification of the organism.

> For an attractive ornamental plant, consider *Prunus australis* Beadle.
>
> *Spathius impus* Matthews (Hymenoptera: Braconidae) is parasitic upon bark beetles.
>
> *Musca domestica* L. is the common housefly. *[The L. is for Linnaeus, one of the scientists so widely recognized that a standard abbreviation for his name is allowed.]*

Note that the word *species* retains the *s* in both singular and plural, and that the plural of *genus* is *genera*.

> *Ixodes scapularis* is a species of tick known to transmit Lyme disease; other species of *Ixodes* may too. This genus is only one of several genera known to be involved.

When an organism has been identified only to the generic level, the abbreviation "sp." is sometimes used in place of the words "some unidentified species of." The abbreviation "spp." signifies "several species of." Neither should be underlined or italicized.

> *Zanthoxylum* spp. were abundant, but *Drypetes* sp. was apparently rare.

After its first mention, the organism may be referred to by its common (vernacular) name if you wish. Unless writing for a publication that prefers otherwise, do not capitalize this common name.

> *Solenopsis invicta* Buren ... *S. invicta* ... the red imported fire ant.
>
> The oak, *Quercus velutina* Lamarck, is found in North America. A relatively large tree, *Q. velutina* is prized for its wood. Its common name, yellow oak, alludes to the inner bark color.

Any family name can be transformed to a vernacular name by dropping the initial capitalization and the terminal *-ae*. Any generic name may be used as a vernacular name as well; this practice is common in bacteriology. Generic names are neither italicized nor capitalized when used in the vernacular sense.

The family Chironomidae includes biting chironomids.
Salmonella typhosa is a deadly species of salmonella.

For practice with scientific names, go to Exercise 25.

Be careful with other non-English words and phrases

> The chief virtue that language can have is clearness, and nothing distracts from it so much as the use of unfamiliar words.
>
> HIPPOCRATES

In addition to biological nomenclature, many other scientific terms have a Latin or Greek basis as well. Some terms have become widespread and thoroughly assimilated into English. Others have not. As a result, a number of different grammatical and punctuation conventions dealing with these words and phrases exist more or less in parallel.

Foreign words and expressions that have not been assimilated fully should generally be italicized. Examples might include *sine qua non*, *coup de grace*, and *per se*. (This rule is often bent, however. Except in the context of Greek and Latin scientific names, scientific writing is clearly moving away from the use of italicized foreign words and phrases.)

Words and phrases that have been fully assimilated into the English language do not need any sort of special treatment, although for a while they may retain their original accent marks (especially if they are of French origin).

Many scientific words that come from Latin and Greek but are no longer italicized still retain their original plurals. Words from the Greek change *-ion* to *-ia* and *-is* to *-es*. Latin words that end in *-a* are made plural by adding *-e*. Those that end in *-um* are made plural by changing the *-um* to *-a*. Those that end in *-us* change to *-i*.

For those who have not studied Latin or Greek, this admittedly can be confusing. Many scientists fail to use these words correctly.

> These data are consistent because each datum is independent of the others.
>
> Wasp larvae in general are common, but the larva of *Eumenes* is not.
>
> A microfilaria is a worm-like creature; heartworm microfilariae sometimes invade a dog's heart.
>
> An early analysis of the mitochondrion was in error, but later analyses of mitochondria from a variety of organisms rectified this.
>
> We used an agar medium but other media yielded similar results.

As foreign words become assimilated, they drop their italics, and their plural forms give way to English plurals. *Formulae* has become formulas. The plural word *sera* is becoming serums. *Indices* is becoming indexes. However, because science tends to be fairly conservative, the acceptability of the English plural forms often differs with the type of publication and its audience. Thus, one journal may pluralize calyx as *calyces*, whereas another uses calyxes.

Word order can also become confusing. In biomedical writing, certain commonly used Latin phrases most properly follow the noun they modify. These include *in vivo* (in the living body), *in vitro* (in an artificial environment), *de novo* (anew), *in vacuo* (in the absence of air or in reduced pressure), and even *in silico* (biological simulation studies done with a computer). It is incorrect to place such phrases before the noun as though they were regular adjectives. Rather than "*in vivo* tests," write and say "tests *in vivo*" if you wish to be correct and conservative. However, usage is shifting, and these Latin phrases eventually may be accepted as regular adjectives placed before nouns and without italics.

A classical education for scientists and non-scientists alike also once included learning to write in a scholarly style that included a number of Latin and Greek terms, particularly in footnotes. Despite what you may have learned in an English Composition class, avoid abbreviations such as *loc. cit.* (in the place cited), *op. cit.* (in the work cited), and *ibid.* (in the same work). For *viz.*, substitute "namely"; for *circa* use "about." These are seldom seen in literary works today, and almost never in biological or medical publications.

A prominent exception is *et al.* (*et alii*, and others), which has remained in favor for its useful role in parenthetical citations and literature reference lists. (Note that the *et* does not have a period, but the *al.* requires one, and the term may or may not be italicized.) In text narratives, more graceful alternatives are preferable.

> *Usually accepted but clumsy:* As Hirano *et al.* (2013) have shown, this result is unusual.
>
> *Less awkward:* Studies by Hirano and colleagues (2013) indicate that this result is unusual.

The use of *etc.* (and so forth), while still acceptable, is rapidly falling out of favor; it commonly is not italicized. The abbreviations below are still permissible. However, their English equivalent is acceptable or even preferred. If you must use them, confine them to parenthetical statements and punctuate them as for their English equivalent. Once again, check your intended journal's style; all these abbreviations are increasingly being used without italics and without periods.

i.e. (*id est*, that is)

cf. (*confer*, compare)

e.g. (*exempli gratia*, for example)

et al. (*et alii*, and others)

One final caution: If you are thinking you'd like to include non-scientific foreign words or phrases merely to impress your audience, think again. Seldom will it have that intended effect. Unless there are other compelling considerations, use a plainly English equivalent.

For practice with these foreign words and phrases, go to Exercise 26.

14   Address your ethical and legal responsibilities

In law a man is guilty when he violates the rights of others.
In ethics he is guilty if he only thinks of doing so.

IMMANUEL KANT

Integrity in the conduct and reporting of scientific research is a broad subject with many aspects. (Thought-provoking overviews include Buranon and Roy, 1999; Emanuel *et al.*, 2003; Lipson, 2004; Shamoo and Resnik, 2009; and Macrina, 2014.) This chapter includes some essential basic aspects, but we are not legal experts. When you have important legal questions, particularly about such things as trade names, copyrights, and patents, consult a lawyer.

Value ethical concerns

Ethics refers to the choices we make that affect others for good or ill. Obviously, this is an enormous multifaceted topic, the subject of entire religions and philosophies. Literally thousands of publications have been written on the subject of scientific ethics and both proper and improper scientific conduct.

Do they make any difference? Every month, it seems, one can find reports of scientists forging, faking, or plagiarizing their way to success. It is difficult to assess whether scientific dishonesty is on the rise, or simply being reported more widely in our shrinking world. However, it is interesting to note that as a condition of funding, the National Institutes of Health now requires all investigators to receive training in clinical research ethics.

The historical, political, and social contexts of these issues are beyond the scope of this book, but they make interesting reading. Good places to start include LaFollette (1992), Buranen and Roy (1999), and the many references included in both. For an informative examination of how various aspects of scientific integrity are defined, why and how ethical breaches occur, and how they are detected, see D'Angelo (2012).

Various ethical violations can occur in any field, of course. However, in science, two ethical errors are considered particularly unforgivable – distorting your own data and plagiarizing the work of others. Both are matters of honesty versus dishonesty, but in real life application, this distinction sometimes is not as black and white as it might seem.

Respect your data – and your readers

Scientific progress depends upon trust – trust in the personal honesty of other scientists and trust in the honesty of their data. Be careful how you approach your own research. Intentional dishonesty is easy to identify – and to avoid. Unintentional distortions can be more problematical. Was that odd result in one data set simply an anomaly? Can you ethically delete the outlier that keeps your numbers from showing statistical significance to support the result you are almost certain should occur? Should you choose to use graph intervals that downplay differences you can't readily explain?

Ask for guidance from others in your field, read the published opinions of those you respect, but realize that ultimately you may be the only one who can answer such questions. Know the conventions for data presentation in your field, and check the accuracy of all details. Try your best to walk a middle line between a meticulousness that leads to overt analysis paralysis and a casual slide down the slippery slope of dishonesty.

Write only what you know to be true

This reminder should be self-evident. It means no falsified data, no fictional notes, no creative quotations. No exceptions.

Practice humility

Be careful not to overstretch the limits when interpreting your data. There are many truths in this world, and no single set of factors can explain everything. Furthermore, whether or not we choose to consciously acknowledge it, every one of us is the product of our social and personal beliefs. As Davis (2005) notes, "Individual and cultural prejudices have troubled scientific research and reporting for centuries, and we are not without prejudices today."

Be respectful of others' opinions, even when you do not agree with them. Always remember that any single set of factors can be interpreted in a variety of ways. As a practical example, do not use the word "fact" to refer to what is actually a matter of judgment or opinion.

> *Arrogant and possibly false:* It is a fact that human exploitation has been the major cause of habitat degradation since the birth of the Roman Empire.

> *Better:* Based on our research, we suggest that human exploitation has been an important cause of habitat degradation since the birth of the Roman Empire.

"...AND TAKING THE OPPOSING VIEW, ON LEAVE FROM HIS SENTENCE AT THE STATE PRISON..."

© ScienceCartoonsPlus.com. Reprinted with permission.

Avoid ambiguities and double meanings

Unlike creative writing in the liberal arts, scientific communication does not allow readers to interpret words as they choose. Read your sentences carefully, and be sure you are not misdirecting readers through ambiguities or double meanings. Even though technical or legal experts could interpret them as accurate, the use of various abstract words, jargon, and euphemisms is unethical when they are used to mislead readers or to hide a serious or dangerous situation. Governmental groups and politicians are infamous for such cover-ups. Scientific writers should occupy ethically higher ground.

Ensure against plagiarism

> What a good thing Adam had.
> When he said a good thing, he knew nobody had said it before.
> MARK TWAIN

You've been warned about plagiarism ever since you began writing. In its simplest form, plagiarism is the act of taking words or ideas that someone else has written and presenting them as one's own. Examples encompass everything from buying term papers on the Internet to patching together a thesis introduction from unattributed sentences lifted from various publications.

Drawn from the Latin word for "kidnapping," plagiarism is viewed as a very serious offense across academia. Almost every writing book denounces it heatedly, variously describing it as illegal, unethical, immoral, or intellectually lazy (Buranen and Roy, 1999). However, perhaps nowhere is the issue of plagiarism (and the related issue of falsified data) taken as seriously as it is in science. People seemingly are willing to accept deception in politics and entertainment, and most buy into fantasy without blinking. However, almost everyone agrees that science must be held to a higher standard, because authenticity and accuracy are the foundation upon which it must stand.

Credit others fully and accurately

Scientists must use each other's ideas and inventions if progress is to be made. However, using something that belongs to someone else brings one into the realm of both ethical and legal issues. The over-arching rule is simple – be honest. If a work is not yours, find out whose it is and get permission before you use it.

Rather than moralize or editorialize any further, let us remind you once again that you have an obligation to credit others fully and accurately for their work. "Work" includes all the raw material of scholarship, be it words, ideas, drawings, or data. "Others" includes students who have helped with research, friends or informants who have provided information, and colleagues whose work you have built upon.

For a journal article, such acknowledgment is generally enough. If you are publishing a book that includes anyone else's tables, figures, or words at significant length, you will have the additional responsibility for getting written permission from each of these people and, if requested, pay a fee.

Using someone's work without giving credit may go beyond plagiarism into copyright infringement. As a responsible author, you also should understand the fundamentals of copyright law outlined later in this chapter. (In the workplace, employees often borrow and re-use material from in-house manuals, reports, and other company documents. Using such information, called boilerplate, is neither plagiarism nor a violation of copyright.)

Document paraphrased ideas

The easiest and most common way to avoid outright plagiarism is to put the essence of another writer's ideas into one's own words without distorting their meaning. The process is called paraphrasing. Quotation marks are not necessary because the paraphrase does not quote the source word for word. However, paraphrased materials still should be credited, because the ideas are taken from someone else.

A major exception to this documentation occurs when the information that is being paraphrased is common knowledge in a field. Common knowledge means that the information is widely known and readily available, as for example in handbooks, manuals, atlases, or other reference.

Watch out for redundant publication and self-plagiarism

You've worked long and hard on a study, and it seems a pity to have expended all that effort on just one publication. . . What about presenting those beautifully honed but already published words or ideas in another paper? When is it acceptable to do so? How necessary is it to cite the earlier publication? And where does the concept of "fair use" fit into all this?

Seduced by the seeming value of lengthy publication lists, many researchers repackage and republish their work in the guise of reaching different segments of their potential audience. Using essentially the same data set and blocks of nearly identical wording but changing the emphasis slightly, they submit two or three articles where one would really do. This practice is legal and common, but it is ethically questionable. Moreover, it wastes the time and energy of editors, referees, and readers alike. (See section in Chapter 1 on salami-slicing science.)

As a philosophical question, this so-called "self-plagiarism" is a matter of continuing debate (see Scanlon, 2007, and references therein). Some writers argue the term itself is an oxymoron – it is your right to re-use your own work in whatever way you please without it being plagiarism because you are not borrowing from anyone but yourself. Others argue that definitions of the word aren't the issue; it is just as fraudulent to present one's own recycled work as new as it is to present others' work as one's own. Moreover, because journals rather than individual authors usually hold legal rights to published material, recycling published words easily can run afoul of copyright laws.

However one stands on the philosophical issue, as a matter of practical ethics with legal ramifications self-plagiarism has become an area of growing concern and even alarm in many quarters, with some going as far as to call it academic fraud. Peer reviewers are being charged with the task of detecting signs of it, and some journals are running computerized pattern-matching programs such as iThenticate® to screen submitted works.

As a prudent researcher and writer, it is worth trying to avoid becoming caught in the crossfire. Situations where re-use of published words and ideas may make sense (Samuelson, 1994) include:

- When the previous work must be restated to lay the groundwork for a new contribution in the second work.
- When parts of the previous work must be repeated to deal with new evidence or arguments.

- When the audience for each work is so different that publishing the same work in different places is necessary to get the message out.
- When the author thinks they said it so well the first time that it makes no sense to say it differently a second time.

If your situation clearly fits within these criteria and you decide you must recycle some of your work, keep the recycled parts as brief as possible and cite each of them separately and fully. The American Psychological Association (2010) has summed up the issue with this useful advice:

> The general view is that the core of the new document must constitute an original contribution of knowledge, and only the amount of previously published material necessary to understand that contribution should be included, primarily in the discussion of theory and methodology. When feasible, all of the author's own words that are cited should be located in a single paragraph or a few paragraphs, with a citation at the end of each. Opening such paragraphs with a phrase like "as I have previously discussed" will also alert readers to the status of the upcoming material. *(APA, 2010, p. 16)*

Adhere to guidelines for human and animal research

Before you even began your study, if it was pertinent we trust that you checked applicable ethical, legal, and regulatory requirements for research on human subjects and for animal experimentation, both for your own institution and country and for any other institutions and country with which you may have collaborated.

Many journals request that your manuscript include a statement that you have followed these requirements. (Usually this appears in the Methods section; see Chapter 5.) Journal editors also may ask you to produce written approval of your research by an ethics committee.

For medical research involving human subjects, editors may require an explicit statement that you have adhered to the mandates outlined in the Declaration of Helsinki (WMA, 2013). Published disclosure of patient data also requires their informed consent, even when their identity is concealed so that other people are unlikely to recognize them. When anonymity is not possible, explicit written consent is required.

For animal studies, indicate that all experiments conformed to institutional, national, and international ethical guidelines, and that all efforts were made to minimize animal numbers and suffering. For more detailed discussion of both key principles and specific recommendations, see sources such as

Committee for the Update of the Guide for the Care and Use of Laboratory Animals *et al.* (2011), Bayne and Turner (2013), and Guillen (2013). The International Association of Veterinary Editors also presents guidelines and recommendations (IAVE, 2010).

Protect yourself from potential libel and slander charges

> The experiment went well because Dr. Jones was not involved.
>
> FICTITIOUS EMAIL POSTING

Scientists tend to ignore the legal problem of potential libel, believing it is something they don't have to worry about. However, in today's litigious society, this can be a naïve assumption.

Libel refers to anything untrue circulated in writing or pictures that injures someone's good reputation, particularly anything about a living person that is harmful. (The corresponding term for injury by speech is "slander.")

Libel and slander laws are complex and changing, but in general "harmful" is defined as any statement that can damage a person's status, business or profession, or social life. Groups can be the litigants and defendants as well as individuals.

> When Dr. Smithson openly charged his rival with falsifying his results, the professor sued Smithson for slander.
>
> Dr. Montgomery was quite surprised to find herself sued for libel after her hastily written editorial labeled the American Naturopathic Medical Association as "a bunch of quacks."

Even reporting about on-going investigations or decisions in fraud cases may now draw complaints. As a result, major journals like *Science* reportedly ask their attorneys to review all unflattering news reports for potential libel, because truth and accuracy are not enough to prevent a journal from being sued or bearing the cost of defending against a lawsuit (LaFollette, 1992).

If you are called upon to write about controversial events or subjects, you likewise might be wise to have a lawyer review your document.

Handle trade names responsibly

A manufactured item such as a pharmaceutical product often has as many as three different types of names. One is its scientific chemical name, which is generally complex. Another is a shorter, non-proprietary "generic" name. A third is a trade name, also called a proprietary name. This is the name a manufacturer or vendor gives to its product; usually such names are registered as trademarks.

MODERATELY CONFUSED © 2013 Jeff Stahler. Reprinted by permission of Universal Uclick for UFS. All rights reserved.

If one manufacturer's product behaves significantly differently from other similar products, readers may need to know which one you used in order to duplicate your experimental results. In such a case, the trade name should be given somewhere (often in parentheses or in a reference or footnote rather than directly in the text).

Otherwise, scientific writing generally avoids trade names. In particular, brand or trademark names should never be used in titles or summaries. One reason is that their use makes it appear as though one is advertising products. Another is that, whereas generic and scientific names generally stay the same, trade names often differ greatly from one part of the world to another. Furthermore, official trade names can be awkward to use, because many consist of a long string of words, some of which may appear in all capital

Table 14.1 Some trade names that companies are trying to keep from entering into generic use

Trade name	Generic name
Vaseline®	petroleum jelly or petrolatum
Scotch® Magic™ Tape	transparent tape
SPAM® luncheon meat	canned luncheon meat
XEROX® copier	photocopier
VELCRO® brand fasteners	hook and loop fasteners
BOTOX® Purified Neurotoxin Complex	botulinum toxin
SPACKLE®	surfacing compound

letters. (For example, the full name for those widely known sticky tapes is BAND AID® Brand Adhesive Bandages.)

Knowing whether a generally used name is proprietary is important. Considerable money has been spent, and many lawsuits have been entered into, to enforce the recognition of trade names! The problem is that when a trademarked product comes into general use, the public often loses touch with the word's commercial origins (Table 14.1). Proper names or their derivatives begin to function as common nouns, and for a period of time both styles exist side by side. Eventually, to the dismay of the company holding the trademark on the product, the product name or a variant of it may become an English word in its own right. (Aspirin, nylon, zipper, and fiberglass are examples of such lost battles.)

Don't slip into the pitfall of using trade names as though they were synonyms for generic products or processes. Usually, a quick perusal of the packaging will reveal a product's status.

Substitute generic or chemical names whenever possible

The use of generic or chemical names for products is usually preferred in the text and obligatory in titles and summaries. Generic drug names can be verified in the most recent edition of the *USP Dictionary of USAN and International Drug Names*. This useful annual guide is considered the standard source for U.S. adopted names (USAN). It includes formal chemical names of drugs, trade names, previously used generic names, and code numbers for investigational drugs, as well as an appendix that details the rules for coining new names. Many other countries have similar means for establishing non-proprietary names (see Council of Science Editors, 2006).

Chemical compounds mentioned in clinical papers can be identified either by a formal chemical name or by a shorter "trivial" (from a chemist's viewpoint) name. *The Merck Index* (O'Neill, 2013) is an authoritative source for verification of these names; check that you have the most recent edition.

Cite trade names correctly

Sometimes there are reasons why it is critical to include a trade name in the text of a paper. When this is the case, use the common name first, then the proprietary name.

Like variety names (Yellow Radiance rose), and some market terms (Choice, Prime), trade names should always be capitalized. (With two-word names such as "Sorvall centrifuge" only the first or "significant" word is capitalized.) At least the first time the product is mentioned by full trade name, one should include a suffix superscript of the symbol ® for a mark that has been officially registered with the U.S. Patent and Trademark Office or ™ for marks that have not been registered but which the manufacturer wishes to identify as its own. (However, many journals omit the symbol.) The symbol need not be repeated in subsequent uses of the trade name. For example, write "the carrier ampholyte, Ampholine®" first, then just "Ampholine" or "ampholyte."

Include the manufacturer's name and address. Often this information is treated as a footnote. (Sometimes the trade name is included in a footnote and omitted entirely from the text.)

> Diets were supplemented with a multi-vitamin tablet (Preventron®).[1] Although other tablets were tried, Preventron tablets were most easily assimilated.
>
> [1]Natural Sales Co., Pittsburgh, PA.

Understand copyright and patents

Copyright is the right of exclusive ownership by an author of the benefits resulting from the creation of his or her work. It covers the matter and form of a literary or artistic work, that is, how it is expressed. It does not cover the ideas or data themselves, nor does it cover the procedures, processes, concepts, or discoveries contained in such works. Protection of those things can sometimes be obtained through patents. (See later in this chapter.)

Copyright gives authors (or others to whom they transfer copyright ownership) control over how the work is reproduced and disseminated. Once copyrighted, a work cannot be indiscriminately reproduced unless the copyright owner gives permission, usually in exchange for royalties or other compensation.

Determine whether published material is copyrighted

The issue of copyright affects both your use of others' work and your own published writing. A work first published after March 1, 1989 receives copyright protection whether or not it bears a notice of copyright, but almost all published materials include this notice. It usually appears on the back of the title page. If a book was published after January 1, 1978, the term of the copyright is for the author's life plus 70 years. If it was published before 1978, the first copyright term covers 28 years, but it is renewable for an additional 47 years.

With the advent of the Internet, many copyrighted works formerly available solely in print are now distributed around the world in cyberspace. Copyright law applies to cyberspace works just as it does to their print counterparts. Publications that explain U.S. copyright law in detail are available from the Copyright Office, Library of Congress, Washington, DC 20559 or online at <www.copyright.gov>.

All publications created by US government agencies are in the public domain. They are not copyrighted, and may be used freely.

Realize what is (and isn't) yours

According to law, you own the copyright on any tangible expression that you create, unless it was done for an employer or commissioned as work for hire. Along with other forms, tangible expressions include written words, illustrations, printed works, electronic software, and recordings. This copyright is yours for the length of your life plus 50 years, whether or not you have formally applied for copyright protection. If you have coauthors, each of you is a co-owner of the copyright, with equal rights.

When you publish your paper in a journal, copyright is generally transferred to the publisher, who will handle such paperwork as filing the copyright application and responding to future requests to use the material. Before the Copyright Act of 1976, this transfer usually happened somewhat automatically. Now, it must be specifically written out, so most publishers ask authors to sign a copyright transfer form.

If work to which you hold copyright is to be published in electronic format, be sure to fully investigate your rights under current copyright law. Electronic publishing is a rapidly changing area. At this writing, dozens of issues await resolution.

Get help with patents

Patents do not apply to the expression of ideas, but protect the ideas as they are put into practice as machines, manufacture, processes, or composition. In general, patents cover the creations most people call "inventions." However,

© Randy Glasbergen
glasbergen.com

"I invented fire, but now everyone is using it for free. In hindsight,
maybe my first invention should have been intellectual property law."

biotechnology has added a new dimension with the decision that it is possible
to patent life forms if they have been synthesized by human efforts and do not
exist in nature without human intervention.

Copyright protection begins as soon as the expression is created but patents
must be registered to serve as protection. Copyrights protect for a long time;
U.S. patents, only for 17 years. To be patentable, an invention must be proven
to be novel, not obvious, and useful. These criteria all must be supported in
written documentation, requiring you to carefully search and read the literature on your subject. You must also keep careful records, preferably dated and
signed by witnesses, to be able to prove that you invented it first.

An important related question concerns when to publish information about
the invention. If it is described to the public before you have registered the
patent, it will be considered public information and will probably not be
patented.

(Incidentally, note that the U.S. patent literature is said to be the largest and
most comprehensive collection of technical information in the world. Certainly, disclosures on how inventions are produced and how they function can
be a storehouse of information for other scientists. When doing a literature
search, don't forget to explore your research subject in this area if it seems at
all appropriate.)

General information on U.S. patents can be obtained from the government
website <www.uspto.gov>. The laws regarding patents can be complex, and
are somewhat different in different countries. If you are thinking of patenting
an invention, get the best help you can find and afford. Scientists in academic

institutions generally have a university-supported research foundation that can advise on such matters.

Know when and how to request permissions

In the process of preparing a written paper or an oral presentation, you may find places where you want to use someone else's material. It may be a published photograph, some clip art, or a diagram downloaded off the Web. Can you legally use the material? Later you'll be preparing a classroom term paper. Can you include the material then? What about when you expand the term paper into a journal publication?

In fact, much of this material is probably copyrighted. In many cases you can use it; in other cases, you can't. A legal concept called "fair use" is involved.

Understand "fair use"

Copyright law provides a "fair use" provision that allows others such as teachers, librarians, and reviewers to reproduce a limited portion of copyrighted materials for educational and certain other purposes without compensation to the copyright owners. (The equivalent term in the U.K. is "fair use.") The provision refers to using parts of copyrighted materials for such purposes as "criticism, comment, news reporting, teaching (including multiple copies for classroom use), scholarship or research." The fair use provision does not allow you to copy complete articles and republish them without permission, even if it is not done for profit.

A small amount of material from a copyrighted source may be used in your written work without permission or payment as long as the use satisfies the fair use criteria.

The provision for "public domain" is the most straightforward of the fair use conditions. After the original copyright holders have died and their heirs have exercised their rights for 70 years, anyone can reproduce, record, perform, or otherwise use the material without the permission of the heirs or estate. Public domain can also be declared right from the start. Items such as clip art collections or certain software programs clearly announce that they are in the public domain.

A second, equally straightforward situation occurs when copyright holders give their permission for others to use their work. In addition to saying yes or no when asked, they can request money or other conditions as they grant the right to use their material.

Over the years, the courts have defined certain conditions as fair use of copyrighted material without permission. This doctrine is applied on a case-by-case basis, with decisions generally being based on four aspects: the purpose of the use, publication status, amount used, and potential for competition. Every case is unique, but, in general, classroom use has almost always been considered fair. Educational uses have been viewed more favorably than if the use is for profit. If the material has been published (for example, as a book, an article, or electronically) it generally will be viewed more favorably than if it has not been published (like a personal letter or laboratory notes). Use of only part of the work has been viewed more favorably than use of the entire work. Finally, it will be viewed more favorably if your use will not damage the potential market of the original.

It should be noted that photocopying services are sometimes still overly cautious in applying this doctrine because of lawsuits brought against them by publishers during the 1990s. During that time, many copy shops were copying material for classroom use, but also binding, packing, and selling the materials for profit. Now, once burned and twice shy, they may refuse to make copies or scan images for you. However, they usually will let you scan images and make copies yourself. Because you are simply using these materials for an educational presentation and not making a profit on them, there is no violation. (However, if you were a professional speaker, you would need to revisit the question.)

How much can be quoted or otherwise included without permission?

The *Chicago Manual of Style* (University of Chicago Press Staff, 2010) provides an often-quoted succinct guideline that a quotation of more than 500 words of prose from previously published material still in copyright requires permission from the publisher. Some editors recommend permission for as few as 300 words of prose (Germano, 2001). These 300–500 words apply to the entirety of the article or book in which they will appear. If you are using a series of brief excerpts throughout the text, it is your responsibility to tally them. (Incidentally, the rules are somewhat different for poetry and song lyrics, being limited to 4% of the original work. Play it safe and ask for permissions on these. Publishers of song lyrics, in particular, are notably stern about unauthorized use of their property.)

What are derivative works?

In academic circles, there is a widely circulated maxim that changing seven items in a published graphic makes it your own, and once you have done so, there is no longer a need to credit the original developer. This is simply untrue. There is no magic number. Instead, there is a concept called "derivative works."

A derivative work is a new, original product that includes aspects of a pre-existing, already copyrighted work. It is what most people mean when they say something is a "new version." By law, only copyright owners have the exclusive right to produce derivative works based on their original copyrighted works. Creation of a derivative work is infringement unless the copyright owner has chosen to grant permission in the form of a license or assignment (with whatever stipulations, financial or otherwise, he or she chooses to include).

The only exception is "fair use" ("fair dealing"), and legally this can be a subjective concept. You may think your use is fair, but find out that the court thinks otherwise.

If you are the copyright holder, you can create all the derivative works you want based on your original. However, if you are making changes to someone else's work, get permission or get a lawyer.

Contact publishers to secure permissions

When "fair use" provisions do not apply and you still want to reprint or adapt material that others have published, you must formally request permission from the copyright owner. Thus, the first step is to figure out whom that might be. Sometimes, copyright may be held by the author or by a third party, but in most cases the primary publisher of the material you wish to use will hold the rights. Direct your request to the publisher's permissions office.

Permission policies differ from one publisher to another, so it becomes your responsibility to learn what policies may apply. Some publishers have opted out of the requirement for express permission to use items published in their books or journals, as long as the items are cited properly. Some have joined a large consortium called the International Association of Scientific, Technical and Medical Publishers (STM), in an effort to streamline permissions procedures by establishing a common framework. Permission may be granted globally or only for specific uses (such as print-only publication or in only the current edition of a book). Often, there is a fee involved.

Many publishers have fillable online forms on their websites, which theoretically should speed up the process. However, it is best to allow ample time for securing permissions. Most publishers will not allow your paper to enter production before you have secured these permissions and sent copies to them.

Always remember to give credit

Remember the issue of avoiding plagiarism. Although the information you include may not be an infringement of copyright, you still are using someone else's material. It is both appropriate and ethical to give the original creator

Table 14.2 Ethical and legal compliance questions to ask oneself before submitting any manuscript in the biological and medical sciences

Aspect	Questions
Human research subjects	Does the manuscript violate anyone's rights?
	Have I been careful to protect the confidentiality of everyone who was a source for information I have presented?
	Has my work passed institutional review, including informed consent and debriefing procedures?
Animal subjects	Has my work passed institutional review, including humane care and responsible use of animals?
The manuscript	Is my document honest and truthful?
	Is it ethically consistent?
	Have I properly credited others' work?
	Have I respected trade names?
	If parts of this study have been published before, have I made this clear?
Coauthors	Have all authors reviewed the final manuscript?
	Have all authors agreed on responsibility for its content?
	Have all authors agreed to order of authorship?
Permissions	Have I obtained permission to use any unpublished procedures, data, or other materials that others might consider theirs?
	Have I obtained permission for any copyrighted material I have used?
Potential bias	Have I treated any possible conflicts of interest with caution?
	Have I disclosed them fully and openly?
Audience	If I were the intended audience, would my paper's message be acceptable and respectful?
	Am I willing to take responsibility, both publicly and privately, for what my document says?

credit for his or her work. Before you copy it, add a citation indicating the author and copyright holder.

The format for credit citations may be specified by your publisher or by the copyright holder. Otherwise, however, you can generally follow the examples below.

If you obtained written permission to use an illustration, you might write:

©2007 Robert W. Matthews. Used with permission.

For material that did not require permission because it was taken from the public domain, you could write:

From the public domain via <www.freemaps.org> 28 Feb. 2007

From Freeman, F.N. and Johnson, E.M. (1929, p. 279). "Are you starved for sunlight?" Child-story Readers. Chicago: Lyons and Carnahan.

Verify that you have addressed all potential concerns

Much of this book addresses customary writing style, a subject that differs from one field of endeavor to another and generally involves as many opinions as fixed decrees. However, basic ethical and legal matters involve goals and principles that are fundamental, stretching across the entire landscape of research and publication.

Clearly, ethical concerns deserve attention at every step along the path of scientific enterprise. However, as you approach publication, it is particularly important to check explicitly whether (and how) you have addressed them (Table 14.2). Someone – be it a professor, graduate committee, editor, or member of the public – is almost certain to bring the matter up at some point. Don't let this be the first time you've thought about your answers!

Note also that journals differ in the degree to which they explicitly speak to ethical and legal concerns, making it is advisable to check requirements about these matters before submitting your work for publication. Many journals require quite specific statements of conformity to various policies and mandates.

For practice concerning ethical and legal concerns, go to Exercise 27.

15 Oral presentations: adapt the text and visuals

Since the days of the cave man carving stuff on the cave walls, people have wanted stories, and storytellers have wanted an audience.

That is still the case. The changes are really a matter of format.

SUSAN WIGGS

At some point in time, and perhaps sooner than you realize, you almost certainly will be called upon to make an oral presentation to colleagues, administrators, or a general audience whose background lies outside your specialized area of expertise. The opportunity may appear in the guise of a dissertation defense, a job interview, or as a speaker to a community group.

Nearly every such presentation has two basic components – text and illustrations. Although both elements have long received attention in the context of the primary research article, scientific writing instruction has tended to treat these other communication channels as a relatively minor afterthought. The implicit assumption has been that oral presentations involve only minor repackaging of a written document.

In recent years, however, this assumption has been challenged by new developments that have increased the status of visual communication and given it a surprisingly powerful role to play in modern scientific exchanges. Visual materials have become easy and inexpensive to produce, and in response, people are tending to use them more. Presentation software makes it relatively straightforward to generate materials that once took hours or days to create. As a consequence, visual communication has become a basic part of almost all effective scientific presentations.

In some ways, written and spoken communications are quite similar. In other ways, they differ markedly. However, for both, the content of your message must be king and graphics must be but court attendants.

Choose your design tools

To design is to communicate clearly by whatever means you can control or master.

MILTON GLASER

Launched in 1990, Microsoft PowerPoint® is the elephant in the arena of oral presentation design and delivery. It holds an estimated 90–95% market share and is installed on over a billion computers. It is difficult to overstate the impact that this software has had upon presentations in academia, business, and professional societies. In fact, the name "powerpoint" is rapidly becoming a generic synonym for bulleted lists and presentations.

At the same time, as a result of this popularity, outline-style electronics-based presentations have become so predictable, commonplace, and generic that, for the audience, they all begin to look and feel the same. Speakers compound the problem by trying to use a single set of slides not only as speaker's notes and slides the audience will see, but also as handouts to be studied after the talk and as a substitute for a written paper. Almost never can this all be done simultaneously and well.

Rather than automatically turning to PowerPoint when asked to address a group, begin by learning what is expected and customary for this particular type of presentation. Consider your audience and purpose. Perhaps you will even find that presentation software would be overkill. If so, choose one of the other presentation formats. A presentation doesn't have to be PowerPoint to be professional.

Simple choices still work well

The simplest of visual aids for a spoken talk is a chalkboard, whiteboard, or large paper pad (flipchart). From the presenter's point of view, the downside of these simple aids is that they can be difficult to prepare in advance. However, from the audience perspective, this is an advantage because a live performance is always more interesting to observe than a pre-packaged one.

The most effective way to use these aids is selectively. Intersperse face-to-face commentary with written items. By underlining, circling important points, or writing words in the margins, you can give your presentation extra life. If this is done in response to audience input, listeners will be drawn closely into your talk and feel a stronger connection with you than you would ever attain with a canned approach. (There are ways for the manually dexterous user to do all this with PowerPoint, too, but not as simply or intuitively.)

The old-fashioned "slide show" is still popular, though photographs now generally are imported into a computerized presentation as digital copy. Audiences tend to enjoy the movie-like atmosphere. However, avoid showing a single long series of pictures with your voice droning away in the darkness. Many people will get drowsy, and will disconnect from you and your message. Instead, dim the room lights only enough so that slides can be seen while some light is still focused on you. Show slides in batches, with

Podiatry 101

© Mark Anderson. Reprinted with permission.

breaks between where you turn away from the projector and connect directly with your audience.

As we urged in the context of written works, regardless of the presentation style you choose, it's important to know when enough is enough. Don't overdo the technical features or use too much glitziness. Audiences welcome a simple layout, with well-planned color and graphics that emphasize your message rather than competing with it.

Investigate electronic alternatives

If you decide to stay with a computer-driven approach, you have choices. Several excellent alternatives exist (Table 15.1). One of these may be just the tool you're looking for. Don't be afraid this will put you out on a limb by yourself. If you decide to use an alternative application, most of these allow you to "save as" to other formats, including PowerPoint. This handy feature makes it relatively easy to share your presentation with others who may be using other systems.

Teleconferencing (also known as interactive television or ITV) connects presenters and an audience in another location. Popular both as a way to save travel costs and as a way to provide distance education to students in different physical locations, it shares similarities with face-to-face oral presentations.

Table 15.1 Some slideshow creation choices to investigate

Application	Brief description	Helpful aspects	Possible drawbacks
PowerPoint	Well-known branded program from Microsoft.	Most powerful choice with the most features. Used widely. Is "expected."	Overuse or inappropriate use. Oversimplification of complicated messages. Audience boredom.
Keynote	Part of Apple iWork suite.	Elegant, simple. Attractive themes, animations, and formatting options. Handles embedded media and graphics well.	Apple only.
Prezi	Cloud-based app. Groups topics.	Presenter can flow easily in and out of topics, showing context.	Non-linear format takes adjustment and practice.
Google Presentations	Part of Google Docs suite. Cloud-based.	Basic, flexible. Easiest to use for collaboration because teams can make edits live at the same time.	Less powerful than some other choices. Some users have reported problems inputting images from other sources.
Sliderocket	Cloud-based, richly featured app.	Wide access to one's presentation, incl. via smart phone. Plug-ins can display content from websites such as Flickr, Twitter, and YouTube.	To use many of its nicest features, one must upgrade to paid subscription.
OpenOffice Impress	Part of free, cross-platform, open-source suite.	Available for years, very stable. Works like PowerPoint.	May have fewer fancy elements than latest version of other apps.
Ezvid	Free. Quickly uploads to YouTube.	Useful for creating how-to tutorials or demos.	Available only for Windows.

However, a good teleconference is more than simply a camera aimed at a presenter. Ask for advice from professionals, and take it.

Close cousins to teleconferencing include multimedia modules, massive online open courses (MOOCs), and computer-based training (CBT), but these relatives are not live presentations, and thus they lack the real-life interactions that occur between a presenter and an audience. They are more akin to conventional writing, spiffed up with heavy use of graphic aids and specialized computer capabilities.

Present text effectively

It is important to remember that although PowerPoint and its kin have eased the mechanics of preparing slides, they are just tools. In actuality the process of preparing an effective oral presentation hasn't changed all that much. The first step is to design a presentation according to sound communication principles and techniques. The second is to create slides that outline an introduction, main points, and a conclusion. The third is to insert transitions, graphics, and other aids to understanding. Then, before the fateful moment when you stand in front of your primary audience, practice the talk not only in private but also before a small group of interested individuals who (one hopes!) will give appropriate input to help identify and polish any rough edges the presentation might still have. Then practice some more.

Decide upon your content

Talks come in various lengths and have different target audiences, and this simple recognition will have a major influence on content you choose to present. It may seem counterintuitive, but shorter talks are often more difficult to prepare and present than longer ones are, largely because time limitations usually necessitate extremely selective decisions and severe self-editing. In a 10-minute conference talk, there is simply no way to present the details that could be included in a full-hour seminar.

Generally, any scientific talk will follow the overall format of introduction, results, and discussion. (Methods are usually omitted or given only very briefly, unless they are the actual point of the presentation.) One's intended audience should guide the relative proportion of time spent upon these sections. The further removed that listeners are from your specialized area, the more time should be spent providing the background and orientation necessary to understand your work and its implications. A surprisingly large number of speakers fail in this regard, and lose much of their audience's attention within the first few sentences that are spoken.

New presenters sometimes approach this task backwards, asking how many slides they should use. The best answer is: As many as it will take to effectively present your story to your audience in a clear, concise, understandable way within the constraints of your time limit. That many – no fewer and no more. The number of slides is less important than how well they are used. Sometimes you'll hear someone say, "Don't worry about having so many slides. If you run out of time, you can just skip the last few." Never take this advice. Listeners will recognize this sure sign of a careless, poorly organized presentation.

If you must have an absolute number as a guide, the well-known venture capitalist Guy Kawasaki, who regularly listens to hundreds of PowerPoint presentations, offers his 10/20/30 Rule of PowerPoint: his ideal presentation has ten slides, lasts no more than twenty minutes, and contains no font smaller than thirty points (Kawasaki, 2005). He suggests that if you have an hour time slot, give your pitch in 20 minutes and have 40 minutes left for discussion. Taking this advice probably takes a lot of gumption and self-confidence, but it would be a refreshing change from the usual long-winded talks so prevalent not only in the biomedical sciences but wherever presentations occur.

Adjust your written material for the spoken word

All the technical expertise in the world will not be enough if a talk is poorly organized. If you want an audience to follow along, you must provide a road map. This is as true for spoken exchanges as it is for written ones. To the degree that you are planning to use computer-based text-heavy graphics, it is doubly true.

A spoken presentation needs more than an IMRAD rehash of your written paper. Talks generally are organized on a deductive or inductive pattern. With deductive organization, you present your bottom line (conclusion, solution) at the onset. Then, you provide the background and information that led you to this conclusion. Inductive organization is more or less the opposite of deductive. First, you give a general sense of the main topic, then present specific instances or examples as evidence, leading to the conclusion that you state at the end.

Deductive organization is probably the more common approach to scientific presentation, with good reason. This scheme helps audiences understand and follow a speaker, because they can see clearly how supporting material fits into a bigger picture. In contrast, even a well-done inductively organized presentation can be difficult to follow. For this reason, we recommend avoiding this approach unless you are sure it is the only possible alternative. For example, inductive presentations are sometimes useful if you know the audience might not readily agree with your conclusion unless they are led through the train of thought leading up to it.

Craft visual elements of the text with the audience in mind

The user-friendly nature of slide presentation software has made the specific "how" of slide production less important than the "what." The mechanics are fairly straightforward and most graphic software does a good job of guiding you through the steps involved. As with any other area of art and design, experts often disagree on specific recommendations and generally have their own personal preferences, but in general, simplicity is key. Present one main idea per slide and emphasize this message when speaking. Follow the suggestions in Table 15.2, and it will be difficult to go wrong.

Table 15.2 Creating an effective electronic presentation (based on material from University of Georgia Center for Teaching and Learning)

Area of concern	Guidelines
Content	Include only one idea, point, or comparison per slide.
	Present concisely worded material in outline form.
	Include some interactive elements (e.g. questions, polls) to keep audience engaged.
Format	Limit slide titles to 2–5 words.
	Use horizontal orientation rather than vertical.
	Left-justify text and left-align bullet points.
	Use color with caution.
Graphic aids	Use charts or graphics rather than data tables.
	Place graphics off-center to the left (leaves more room for text and leads eye to text).
	Simplify graphics.
Things to avoid	Complex drawings lifted directly from paper publications.
	Extraneous or excessive information.
	Lengthy data tables.
	Gratuitous sound effects and slide transitions.
	Slides read directly to the audience.
Back-up plan	Know at least two ways to advance the slides, in case one method doesn't work.
	Know how to black out the screen to draw audience attention back to you.
	Know how to get directly to any slide in the presentation.
	If technology fails, spend no more than 5 minutes maximum trying to fix it.
	Be prepared to speak directly to the audience without any aids.

If a slide will contain only text, make sure it contrasts well with the background color. Avoid either white text on yellow fills or dark text on dark backgrounds or fills.

Despite the many instances of white text on blue you may have seen in other presentations, know that audiences generally prefer dark text on a light background rather than the reverse However, when projected, the brightness of a stark white background sometimes gives people headaches. A pale pastel with black or dark blue text works well.

Learn the terminology

Mainstream type fonts are of two basic kinds, serif and sans serif. A serif is a "foot," one of the crosslines at the bottom or top of a letter such as I. Serif fonts have these crossbars; sans serif fonts do not. Helvetica and Arial are two common sans serif typefaces; the block strokes that form their letters are straight up and down.

Type also comes in two kinds of dimensional spacing: monospace and variable width (proportional). With monospace fonts such as Courier, every letter occupies the same amount of space, just as they did on an old typewriter. Proportional typefaces have letters of varying widths, more akin to traditional printing styles.

Most conventionally published journals use a proportional serif font style such as New York or Times for their basic text. (Electronic journals often use only sans serif fonts.) Serif fonts are often considered the most readable, because the serifs help guide the eye from letter to letter. Serif typefaces include the oldest type styles, and thus are the most familiar. They are also considered more formal.

Type size is based on points, an old system of measuring type that has carried over into the digital age. For most typefaces, the size in points approximates the distance between the tops of the tallest letters (which may be either the capitals or the lowercase letters with ascenders, like b and h) and the bottoms of the letters with descenders, like p and q. For this reason, a given point size may change in measurement when a different font is selected.

Choose visually effective typefaces and fonts

Historically, with conventional printing, fonts were expensive. Each font was an actual physical device that the typographer purchased. For any given typeface, most typographers had four basic fonts (regular, bold, italic, bold italic). Today, with computerized printing, the choices are endless, and fonts and typefaces can be easily changed with a simple click. But such easy choices bring with them the temptation to mix and match so much that you end up with a mishmash that distracts the audience.

Unless specified otherwise by the group sponsoring your presentation, the following conventions are generally accepted. (The same guidelines should follow for handouts, the printed materials you may wish to distribute as part of your message.)

Stay within one family of typefaces, or use one family for the body copy and another for the headings. For example, consider using Helvetica bold for headings, Times New Roman for body copy, and plain Helvetica for captions and labels on charts and graphs.

Use primarily plain text fonts. Avoid ALL CAPS and use italic and bold sparingly.

How big should slide text be?

The most effective type size for a screen presentation is generally larger than you first think is right. Remember the 30-point type in Kawasaki's 10/20/30 rule? Never plan to include tiny material with the falsely apologetic comment, "I know you can't read this, but ..."

An exact size can't really be mandated, of course, because viewing distance matters and within a given point size, the choice of font will change the actual size of the letters. However, experts generally suggest boldface sans serif type that is approximately 30 points for large rooms; even for a small conference room, they urge using more than 14 points. More mathematical than most, Swinford (2006) suggests basing text size on the "8H rule"– the maximum viewing distance should be no more than eight times the height (H) of the screen. If you then keep your font size at least 1/50th the height of the screen, your text will be legible at the maximum viewing distance. In PowerPoint, this once again translates to an absolute minimum font size of roughly 14 points in a font such as Arial or Helvetica. If the text seems too small, it should be increased to roughly 28 points.

Whatever size you use for the body text, make all headings at least 2 points larger. Slightly more is even better.

Adapt and simplify the supporting graphics

> We are visual creatures. Visual things stay put, whereas sounds fade.
>
> STEVEN PINKER

Slides composed solely of text, accompanied by an oral commentary, can be the most boring talks imaginable. Well-chosen drawings, diagrams, photographs, and other illustrations capture audience interest and attention, and can help explain complex ideas. Adding them to your text message can enliven a

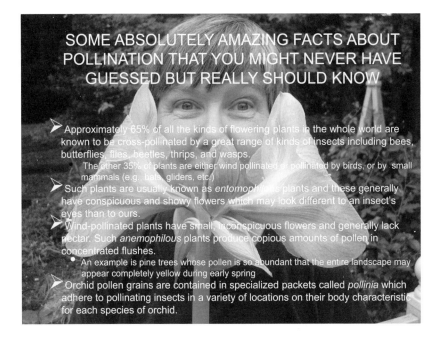

Fig. 15.1 This visual is overdone in many ways, with too much information, extreme verbosity, fancy fonts, and distracting background. Never overwhelm your audience with glitz and chartjunk.

presentation and make information more understandable. On the other hand, poorly thought-out slides can be so horrible they are funny (Fig. 15.1).

When people look at a visual pattern, they process it differently than text (Gurak, 2000). Humans read each word of text and decipher it, but they quickly and efficiently perceive visual information as a unit. (How many times have you tried to assemble something and after puzzling over the written instructions, found yourself turning to the diagram?) However, indiscriminate importing of unaltered tables and figures from your written paper will not suffice if you want to produce a successful or even memorable talk. For best results, the illustrations you prepared for publication need some alteration before being included in an oral presentation.

As you revise and adapt your visual aids, pay attention to proportion and scale. In general, graphics should be greater in width than in height unless the nature of the data suggests otherwise. Tufte (2001) suggests that graphics be about 50% wider than tall. He uses the horizon as an analogy; our eye is naturally practiced in detecting deviations from the horizon, he says, and graphic design should take advantage of this fact. Furthermore, horizontal graphics accept labels more gracefully. It is easier to write and read words that stretch horizontally from left to right, rather than vertically.

Present data details in handouts, not on slides

A table is a good visual device to show choices between categories of information, but spreadsheets or tables containing too much information have the potential to become the worst type of visual aid possible. Audiences simply cannot assimilate all those columns and rows. Furthermore, overloaded tables can be difficult to read on a screen. When you feel you absolutely must share complex information in table format, make a simpler version of the table to put on the slide for the talk. Then bring along handouts of more complex or detailed tables for your audience to review later if they wish.

Bar charts, line graphs, and pie charts need similar visual simplification. Take care not to use too many different types of shading and screening to separate their components. Again, save complex details for handouts, and make certain that simplification has not unintentionally distorted your data (see Chapter 8).

Divorce your handouts from your slides. They serve different purposes. If you have prepared your talk and graphic aids to complement – not duplicate – one another, the seeming shortcut of printing out the screen shots as a handout makes little sense.

Develop appropriate and interesting illustrations

Illustrations drawn from material prepared for print publication often include too much detail for effective use in an oral presentation. Everything on your slide should be visible to the back row. Simplify whenever possible. If the larger picture is necessary, briefly orient the audience to it. Then isolate the relevant portion, enlarge it, and present just that part.

Some experts (Alley, 2013) recommend that you include only those visuals that provide evidence to directly support the text assertion that appears on a given slide. Others note that images relevant to one's message can provide a kind of pictorial label that enlivens and underscores it, even when used only as a background (Kosslyn, 2006).

When an image is being used as background, extend it all the way to the edges of the slide rather than confining it to a box. Make sure it has sufficient resolution to avoid graininess, but be willing to lighten or fade it if necessary to keep it from competing with the text. Pay attention to placement, cropping, and overlaps to be sure you haven't produced an unintended amusing result.

Use color wisely

Like fonts, charts, and other visual communication, color was once a scarce commodity. Color printing was expensive, and color overheads required hand-applied overlays. New technologies have simplified the technical aspects, but wise color use is still a complex issue. Judge each situation on its own merits; just because you can use color doesn't mean you necessarily need to, and more is not always better.

If you will be speaking to an international audience, be aware that certain colors take on different meanings in different cultures. Red means prosperity in China but implies death in many African countries. An Internet search almost certainly will yield the background you need, but do your homework.

If you will be speaking to an organization, company, or industry group, you may be required to use a specified color palette and/or format template. Check in advance.

Instead of relying solely on color to make your points evident, build in some redundancy. Remember that an estimated one of every 10–12 men has some type of color perception problem. (Blue–green and red–green combinations are particularly problematical.) If you are presenting a line graph, for example, define the lines both with color and with line thickness or pattern.

Give your graphics a test run

Before you spend a lot of time refining a particular visual aid, make sure it reproduces well in your visual medium. Sometimes a chart or table doesn't look the same when it is copied into presentation software, or a graphic that looked passable on a small computer screen appears too detailed when projected. Remember, if you present too much information, people won't understand any of it.

Pay attention to details. Is your graphic large enough for the room in which you'll be presenting? Are all the axes and parts labeled? Does the graphic itself have a short, clear informative title? If some of the material is not wholly your own, have you included a reference stating where you obtained this information? (A simple author and source citation will usually suffice. Use a slightly smaller font size than other text.)

Ideally, also test your visuals on a sample audience. What looks clear to you may be confusing to others. Don't expect the audience to know what to look for. Point out the important features by using appropriate indicators such as type of a different color, bold type, highlighting, or arrows.

Employ an effective slide presentation style

Few scientists have escaped becoming familiar with the generic PowerPoint slide: a phrase headline hovering above a bulleted list (Fig. 15.2). This graphic is easy to make, but can turn intellectually noxious as a presentation tool. Detractors speak of PowerPoint Hell, Death by PowerPoint, and PowerPoint Poisoning. Use of this default slide design has been blamed for everything from the Space Shuttle

---

HONEY FACTS

- Honey is significantly sweeter than table sugar and has attractive chemical properties for baking.

- Liquid honey does not spoil. Because of its high sugar concentration, it kills bacteria by osmotic lysis.

- Natural airborne yeasts cannot become active in it because its moisture content is too low.

- Natural, raw honey varies from 14% to 18% moisture content. As long as the moisture content remains under 18%, virtually no organism can successfully multiply to significant amounts in honey.

Fig. 15.2 What not to do – full sentence points on a presentation slide. The only way to make it worse would be to subsequently read them verbatim to the audience.

Columbia disaster (Tufte, 2003) to economic losses in the business community (Simons, 2004). Editorials have asked, "Is PowerPoint the devil?" (Keller, 2004) and "Does PowerPoint make you stupid?" (Simons, 2004). Why are critics so acerbic? And if a bulleted list is not the answer, then what is?

Be aware of the PowerPoint controversy

As outlined by a host of critics, PowerPoint's short phrase headings and bulleted lists limit the amount of detail that can reasonably be presented. They create many layers of hierarchy, and these ultimately obscure logical connections (or the lack of them) between the facts used to make an argument. Their use oversimplifies and fragments the subject matter. Other criticisms include the fact that bullet points may leave critical assumptions unstated, and that the format gives an illusion of preparation, whether or not it is justified (Bell, 2004).

Supporters who defend PowerPoint generally agree as to the validity of the criticisms. However, they endorse the program itself as an extremely efficient timesaving, enabling tool that can be used poorly or well. An intelligent approach, these advocates say, is to avoid simply slipping mindlessly into what everyone else is doing. Among the most vocal advocates of "intelligent use" is Atkinson (2005). He views PowerPoint not as a presentation method, but as a medium – an entirely new category of mass communication in which, almost like a second language, it takes a significant effort to become fluent.

These advocates urge presenters to learn how to override the program's defaults and start developing slides in styles that better address the needs of the audience and the specific nature of the material being presented (Kosslyn, 2011).

(This task may or may not become easier as newer, more sophisticated versions of presentation software arrive on the scene.) They also urge that a presentation be understood as a total experience of which slides are just one part, paying thoughtful attention to non-slide aspects of design, structure, and delivery.

Consider the assertion–evidence approach

Alley (2013) and various colleagues have been leaders in the search for a more effective slide format to substitute for PowerPoint's topic–subtopic approach. As part of this search, Alley and Neeley (2005) undertook a 4-year study that involved interactive critique sessions of more than 400 technical presentations. The results included the guidelines given in Table 15.3.

Table 15.3 Guidelines for assertion–evidence, an alternative approach to electronic slide design (based on Alley and Neeley, 2005; Atkinson, 2005; Alley, 2013)

Area of concern	Guidelines
Style	State each slide's main assertion in a sentence headline. (If you can't phrase an assertion, omit the slide.)
	On every slide, include supporting evidence presented in a visual way (image, graph, table).
	Avoid bullet lists and merely decorative images, including PowerPoint background art.
	Include visually oriented "mapping slides" to keep audience oriented.
Layout	Limit blocks of text, including headlines, to one or two lines.
	Left-justify the headline in the slide's upper left corner.
	Limit lists to two, three, or (rarely) four items.
	Instead of bullets and sub-bullets, use vertical white space and indention to indicate separations and subordinate points.
	List items in parallel grammatical construction.
	Avoid sub-lists, if possible.
	Be generous with white space.
Typography	Use the bold version of a sans serif typeface such as Arial, Helvetica, or Comic Sans MS.
	Choose an appropriate type size for the room, generally 32–44 points for slide title, 28–32 points for slide headlines, 18–28 points for body text, and 14 points for reference listings.
	Avoid presenting any text in all capital letters.
Timing	Limit number of slides so that at least 1 minute can be spent on each.
	In a longer presentation (such as a 1-hour seminar) spend even more time per slide.

The two most striking differences between traditional PowerPoint slides and their alternative are the use of a full sentence headline and the inclusion of supporting graphics in every slide. The use of a sentence headline (rather than the traditional phrase) better directs an audience toward the slide's main point, they say, both during the presentation and later when the slides are used as a set of notes. Furthermore, presenting details in a visual graphic (rather than with a bullet list) makes them more memorable. Although it sounds counterintuitive, research shows that audiences actually pay more attention when less written information appears on a slide (Atkinson, 2005; Mayer, 2001). Furthermore, other research (Sweller, 2005) indicates that when too many written and spoken words are being presented concurrently, listeners' comprehension rate drops even below their rate for having no slides at all!

The contrast between the two slide presentation styles is striking when slides of both types are compared (Fig. 15.3, a and b). Note also the difference between both of these slides and the same subject matter in Figure 15.2.

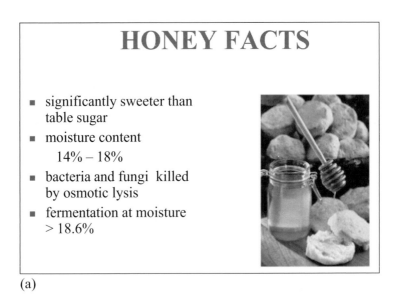

(a)

Fig. 15.3 The information from Figure 15.2 presented in two more effective ways:
(a) as a traditional text-heavy presentation slide, but with illustrative graphics;
(b) in assertion–evidence format, with a full topic sentence headline and a supporting graph.

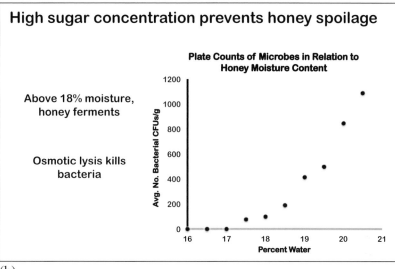

(b)

Fig. 15.3 (cont.)

Whether or not you choose to embrace the other guidelines of assertion–evidence design, consider including more graphics to support your words. In Alley and Neeley's (2005) long-term studies, respondents found this recommendation sufficiently useful that 3 months later, 45% of them were still using visual aids for most of their slides and 37% reported using them on all their slides.

Base choices on personal effectiveness rather than convention

It is said that there are three kinds of people in the world – those who make things happen, those who watch things happen, and those who ask, "What happened?" A challenge is always implicit in the invitation to do something that is unusual. Even when a new idea has observable merit, its acceptance is enhanced by a critical mass of supporters who make the others feel willing and perhaps even slightly pressured to try the new idea.

PowerPoint's bulleted presentations are clearly the mainstream approach, and a safe choice if you fear the possibility of skepticism or criticism should you challenge the status quo. However, we encourage you to read more about this alternative approach, try it and judge its effectiveness for yourself.

Although it is probably not the ultimate best answer for presentations, it may be a significant step forward. Compared to the default bullet-point presentation, the assertion–evidence approach better follows established principles of effective presentation, is more original, and when well done, generally appears to be more responsive to an audience's needs.

For practice with slide presentation format, go to Exercise 28.

16 Share your story in public: presenting talks and posters

> The human brain is a wonderful organ.
> It starts to work as soon as you are born
> and doesn't stop until you get up to deliver a speech.
>
> GEORGE JESSEL

Every oral presentation has three major facets: content, design, and delivery. The quality of each of these aspects affects both the overall quality of the presentation and the extent to which the other aspects can be realized. For example, a confident delivery is much easier when you have good content and good organization. On the other hand, if the design of the talk is poor, even if the delivery is polished, it will be difficult for the audience to understand the content. We've presented guidelines for content and design. In this chapter, attention turns to delivery – the human elements in the way a spoken presentation actually occurs.

The human factor

It is often said that people rank speaking before a group as one of their biggest fears, and this may well be true. Most of us have relatively little experience of it and the potential for embarrassment seems high because speaking occurs in real time, so mistakes can't be sucked back in for correction. The physical symptoms of nervousness – butterflies in one's stomach, pounding heart, squeaky voice – are familiar to most of us as well. They are a result of adrenaline released by the body to escape an uncomfortable or threatening situation. (If it helps, think of nervousness as nature's way of keeping you on your toes!) First let's consider ways to get this under control. Then we can turn our attention to other aspects of delivery.

Keep your composure
Thankfully, nervous reactions can be controlled or minimized in two powerful ways. The first is to change one's state of mind. The other is to prepare, organize, and deliver the presentation in ways that reduce anxiety.

Although it may not feel like it, state of mind is a choice. You can dwell on personal shortcomings, or you can take an optimistic, enthusiastic view about the excitement of talking about something you enjoy to an audience that is on your side and wants you to succeed. Your audience can't tell whether you are nervous inside, but only whether you show it outside.

A speaker actually should feel some tension in order to be alert and enthusiastic. This is far better than sounding tired and bored with the entire presentation! Don't let these feelings frighten you. Confidence will soon take over if you are well prepared.

Take concrete action to be well prepared

The decisions you make about content and design will help convert your high adrenaline level to enthusiasm. Whenever you have a choice, select a subject that you know well. Be extremely well prepared. Develop interesting, organized visual aids so that people's eyes will be on them, not just on you. (But don't plan on hiding behind them!)

Put together a particularly interesting introduction and conclusion. Rehearse them to the point of near or complete memorization. A well-mastered introduction will provide your talk with a solid framework to get you beyond your initial nervousness; most people find that after the first few moments of speaking, their anxiety lowers significantly. Rehearse the conclusion just as thoroughly. A well-mastered conclusion will leave your audience with a good impression even if you should stumble somewhere in the body of the presentation.

Don't memorize everything word for word, however. For one thing, it can sound stuffy, singsong, and insincere. For another, if you forget one word or phrase, you will lose your place – and probably your composure. Instead, memorize the outline's key points, along with key words you want to use. You will sound polished and professional, yet natural.

Develop notes to cue your talk

We've all had that bad experience – the speaker who bores us to death while facing the screen to read verbatim what seems like a hundred words in illegible 10-point type on countless slides that appear and disappear with magical whooshing sounds.

Don't be that speaker! As soon as your audience realizes that you are reading the text, they will begin to read ahead of you. They can read faster than you can speak. If you and the screen are presenting the same information, one of you is unnecessary.

Writing every word of the presentation in the side-notes section of the program and simply reading them from there is not the right answer, either. This is a bad idea for at least two reasons. First, instead of making eye contact or engaging people's attention, you may find yourself imitating a chicken, bobbing your head back and forth between notes on the laptop's screen and words on the big screen. Second, with so many words in those little boxes, if you glance up momentarily, you may lose your place entirely.

What about reading the entire speech from a paper copy? This is not a good option unless you are forced into it by legal requirements. It will negate any image of spontaneity you might otherwise achieve, and will have your audience shifting restlessly in their seats, wishing for your talk to be over.

So what should a nervous or inexperienced presenter do? The same thing nearly every good speaker does. Develop a set of notes. Make them easily readable, using extra-large print if necessary. Most of these notes should be in brief, telegraphic, outline style. An important exception is that any time you want to quote someone directly, write this out in full.

If you are using presentation software, you can transfer your notes into the Notes section where you will be able to display them using the presenter's view during your presentation, but to really cover your bases and connect with your audience, consider also putting these brief notes on numbered 3 × 5 index cards. These are small enough to fit in your pocket and to be unobtrusive in your hand. If the microphone is portable, index cards will allow you to relax your death-grip on the lectern and come around to where the audience can actually see you. Furthermore, even if worse came to worst and the entire computer system died, with written cards you would still be able to give a smooth presentation.

Pay attention to transitions and the conclusion

Bridging words and phrases (Table 16.1) play a particularly important role in a well-done oral presentation, where they provide an overview for listeners and ease the shift from one topic to the next. These sorts of fillers are less necessary in published research articles, but once again, oral presentations are different from written communication. When people read information, they can always turn back a few pages if they forget something. As a speaker, you have to remind your audience where you are headed as you advance through the presentation.

Bridges and overview phrases traditionally have been called transitions, but the term has also been co-opted by presentation software to mean the zooming, blinking or otherwise distracting animation-like effects that can be made to occur when you move from one slide to the next during

Table 16.1 Bridging words and phrases help listeners follow the logical flow of a presentation

Type of bridge	Sample wording
Repeated theme or idea	This same phenomenon occurs when... We wondered if this same explanation would be sufficient in those cases in which...
Soft transitions	For instance, ... Once again, ... Just as an aside, ... Please consider ...
Overview words and phrases	What I'm going to talk about today is ... To start, I'd like to discuss... Now I'd like to move on to... On the next slide, ...
Rhetorical questions	Would this same idea apply when...? Does this finding negate our hypothesis?

an on-screen presentation. Use traditional transitions generously; use electronic ones stingily.

Write these bridges and overview words explicitly in your notes so that you'll remember to include them. However, don't use them on the slide your audience sees. You want them to pay attention to you, not jump ahead conceptually by reading the screen. Furthermore, your spoken transitions will strengthen the perception that you are so well prepared you know what is coming next and where every part of your story fits.

Conclusions are just as important in oral presentations as in paper copy, because they are the part of the talk that people remember best. To create a solid organization, construct the conclusion at the same time as you create the introduction. Even though your manuscript's Discussion may include suggestions for further research, avoid introducing new ideas or new topics in the conclusion of an oral presentation. (You can always mention them afterwards if an audience member raises an appropriate question.) Instead, close your presentation by succinctly reminding your audience about the points you have made and why you consider them to be important. When appropriate, restate an appeal for action, and/or provide resources for further information.

In a gracious way, make it clear that you have finished. Don't just say, "Well, that's all I have for you today." Instead, use a traditional bridging phrase to lead to your conclusion, just as you bridged the rest of the talk.

It can be simply the time-honored phrase, "In conclusion." Other possibilities include "Let me close with a few final ideas" or "Where does this leave us?"

Murphy was an optimist

> Anything that can go wrong will, and at the worst possible moment.
> If nothing can go wrong, it will anyway.
>
> FOLK WISDOM ATTRIBUTED TO U.S. AIR FORCE CAPT. E. A. MURPHY
> AND OTHERS

Mix-ups, snafus, and such are a part of life. The best way to handle them is by being well prepared for the possibility of their occurrence. Don't worry that careful preparation might make you look paranoid. As the old saying goes, "You're only paranoid if you're actually wrong."

Preview and rehearse

Before your talk is scheduled to start, familiarize yourself with the room and the equipment. (If talks are back to back, perhaps you can get into the room over the lunch hour, during a break, or on the previous day.) Pay attention to such aspects as room size, how the lights are controlled, and where you will be expected to stand relative to the audience.

Practice with the equipment – it may differ from what you've been using to date. Determine how to focus and zoom to fit screen size. Try out the pointer, the remote control, and the microphone. Figure out the volume control so you won't need the famous "testing-testing-one-two-three" drill once the audience is seated and ready to begin.

Make ancillary plans

Have a contingency plan for any technology you plan to use. No matter what tool you choose to use, it can fail you at some time in some way. Even the simple chalkboard can turn out to be missing its chalk. Decide what you will do if the computer fails to work. Slip extra batteries for the projector's remote control into your pocket. Put your speaking notes on index cards and number them. Accidents happen; things get dropped. You know the rest.

Finally, as your ultimate backup plan, be prepared to give your presentation on your own, with no technology or visual aids. Knowing you are able to do so brings a measure of confidence and security that is hard to match.

Deliver a successful speech or presentation

> When at a loss how to go on, cough.
>
> GREEK PROVERB

At this point, you have organized your material carefully, constructed slides you are proud of, psyched yourself into a positive frame of mind, and practiced your talk before a small but helpful audience. Now it's time to consider the mechanics of actually giving the presentation.

Several general tips can improve presentations with any visual medium (Table 16.2). For starters, look at the audience. Don't talk to the projector, the screen, or the board on the wall. Casually move around the room, if possible. Don't pace, but don't stand in the same location for the entire talk. Remember, your primary role is not to be a robot imparting information, but to be a human being making a connection with the audience.

Use your visual aids effectively. Whenever possible, reveal information sequentially. With PowerPoint, design slides so that bulleted points appear as you talk about them. If you must put material on a chalkboard or white-board in advance, see if there is a pull-down projection screen mounted above it. If so, consider writing the points in reverse order; by raising the screen gradually, you can reveal points as needed.

If you are using a remote and suddenly it won't move the slides forward, first check to be sure you're pointing it at the remote receiver, not at the screen! Then try moving forward; you may be too far away from the receiver for the remote to pick up the signal. If this fails and you're using a computer, note that keyboard keys (usually the right and up arrow keys and several others) can be used to advance the slides.

During the talk, if your mind momentarily goes blank, don't panic. As Swinford (2006) reminds us, silence is golden – it is all right to look at your slides and collect your thoughts. Don't keep talking when you're doing it. Although the silent moment will seem long and awkward to you, the audience will find it to be natural.

Plan to start strong

As you craft your presentation, think about how you will open it. Your audience has assembled expectantly, hoping for a lot from you; do your best to give them something noteworthy, right from the start. (On a practical note, too, if you start off in a strong, interesting way, the audience will be on your side from the beginning. Then, should you stumble somewhere in the middle, they will probably be sympathetic or may not even notice.)

There are many ways to do this. Simply thanking the audience is a common one. Everyone likes to be appreciated. Be sure to sound genuine rather than perfunctory. If asked sincerely, a question also can be effective at breaking the ice, engaging your audience, and telling you a bit more about them. Ask something relevant to your talk, rather than just making small talk. Attendees

Table 16.2 Speaking in public: some body language presentation guidelines to appear relaxed, confident, and in control

Do this:	Not that:
Walk calmly to the podium, arrange your notes, make eye contact with the audience, and thank the moderator and the attendees.	Hurry toward the podium and begin speaking when only partway there. "Ping" on the microphone or ask, "Can you hear me in the back?"
Speak from your notes using a spoken English style, but more slowly than during normal conversation and in shorter sentences.	Read anything (except quotes) word for word. Use stilted academic language. Speed up under stress.
Take a deep breath, pull the microphone toward your chest, and pitch your voice as low, deep, and full as you can.	Mumble or speak so softly you can't be heard. Blast your speech into the microphone so loudly and closely that it squeals.
Keep the laser pointer steady (prop your arm if necessary). Turn it off when you are talking.	Absentmindedly swing the laser pointer around wildly or point it shakily.
Turn your body toward the audience even when your head turns toward the screen. Relax arms and hands at your sides and place both feet on the floor.	Turn your back on the audience. Pace, fiddle with objects, play with your hair, scratch your nose, put hands in your pockets or arms across your chest, sit on the table, or cross and uncross your legs.
Respond to glitches, mishaps, and slips of the tongue calmly. Prefer relaxed pauses to frantic space-fillers.	Let the audience see you sweat or panic! (They want to be on your side.)
Finish just slightly ahead of your allotted time. Be unfailingly polite.	Encourage audience to interrupt during the talk. Go past your allotted time. Argue with the moderator, other presenters, or questioners from the audience. Utter profanity, coarse words, or sexist or racist statements.
Appear immaculately presentable, with appropriate clothing and well-groomed hair.	Appear to have treated the occasion more casually than your audience does.

will just be annoyed at listening to the same trite or trivial question they've probably heard at every session at this meeting. (No more "So what do you think of this weather, huh?")

A more comprehensive but very effective technique is not only to begin with a question but continue on to engage a few people in the audience in a real but short conversation that ties into your topic, and then make a point that leads into the presentation. This process will help relax your jittery nerves while it gives the impression that you are relaxed and in command.

A personal story can be powerful and memorable if it relates closely to your topic or ties your presentation together. Keep it short and to the point. A joke is a slightly different sort of story; use caution with this. Unless you know your audience well and are good at telling stories, even the best of jokes can backfire, either being met with dead silence or actively offending someone. If you must poke fun at foibles, it's safer to make them be your own. In any case, avoid any hint of profanity or sexual innuendos, and steer clear of politics and religion.

A strong affirmation that surprises or shocks the audience is a common technique in business presentations. This approach is unusual in biomedical talks, but in some situations it could be used to good advantage. Suppose you heard a speaker start a talk by saying, "According to statistics, three people in this room will die of bacterial infections in the next 2 years. Our study may help you avoid being one of them." Wouldn't he or she have your attention? Then, of course, having raised expectations the speaker must be careful to meet them.

Watch the clock

Know how long your presentation will take. Most of us either speed up or slow down our speech when we are under stress. If you have rehearsed your talk in front of a small trial audience rather than just practicing in front of a mirror, your estimate will be more accurate.

Staying within your allotted time is common courtesy, both to your audience and to the speakers who will follow you. The moderator may have a system in place to alert you when you are approaching your limit. If not, consider having a compatriot give you a signal from the audience. Your listeners will not be impressed if you ramble on until forced to stop, then try to cover your transgression with the pseudo-apologetic boast, "I could talk about this subject all day!"

Maintain eye contact with the audience most of the time, and remember their needs. If you see shuffling about, or people cupping hands to their ears, pay attention.

Set aside an appropriate time for questions

Sometimes, a presenter will say to the audience, "Feel free to break in with questions at any time." Don't take this approach. It can annoy listeners, and it usually signals a certain lack of preparation on the speaker's part. If an audience

© 2002 Ted Goff

"Did you skip over the interesting
parts of your talk on purpose? "

member interrupts your presentation with a question, politely respond to the
effect that the questioner may find the answer as your talk progresses and if not,
you'll be happy to address their concerns at the end of the presentation. (For
help on ways to do this, see the last section of this chapter.)

Always plan to end your formal presentation with some time left for
questions. Sometimes, there truly may be no questions. That's all right. It's
not a sign you failed somewhere. Thank the audience and the moderator, and
sit down. More often, there will be questions but they may take a moment or
two to begin. Be patient; the silence will seem longer to you than it really is. It
is all right to fill the awkward-feeling pause by saying in a relaxed manner
something like, "While you are collecting your thoughts, I'd like to just
elaborate on one of the points I made earlier." (However, if you do this, be
extremely brief!)

Make a conscious effort to take questions from various parts of the room.
When you respond, look around the entire room, not just at the individual
who has asked a question. Although one person is asking, you should be
answering to them all. If one person seems to want to monopolize the floor,
suggest that you meet to discuss the matter further after the session.

To the very end, remain professional and self-assured. Many speakers tend
to shed their professional image at the conclusion of their formal presentation.

Don't loosen a tie, lean on the podium, or relax your diction. As Davis (2005) notes, "Yeah" is not a good way to begin the answer to a question.

If questions continue as your time limit approaches, and the moderator doesn't end them, do so yourself. Make an ultimate summarizing statement if possible, and thank the audience one more time. You're finished, and you survived!

Present a poster, the happy hybrid

> A drug is a substance that
> when injected into a white rat
> produces a scientific poster.
>
> UNKNOWN

Poster presentations were almost unknown before being introduced into scientific meetings in the United States in the mid-1970s. Since then, however, they have rapidly become a major format for scientific communication at conferences and other scientific meetings worldwide. In general, a given poster will be displayed, as one of a dozen to hundreds, during a given time frame; for at least part of this time, the author will be on hand to discuss the subject with a relatively small number of interested viewers who stop wandering among the poster displays long enough to listen and converse.

Conference organizers tend to love poster sessions, because posters offer advantages both for meeting arrangements and for communication efficiency. Compared to oral presentations, more posters can be scheduled in less space, and more research can be presented in the same amount of time. In addition, posters do not require numerous meeting rooms and visual projection equipment.

Presenters find posters appealing, too. They are generally less stressful than a standard scientific presentation. Instead of imparting information to a room full of strangers, one generally converses more informally with a small group of truly interested people. Both the presenter and the audience derive mutual benefit from the discussion, and following up on ideas is easier because contact information can easily be exchanged.

Perhaps more than any other form of scientific communication, a successful poster combines visual, oral, and written elements. Because poster sessions have evolved so rapidly, their format is still more flexible than better-established forms of scientific communication. Despite this leeway, poster design still require paying attention to elements of text, type size and style, color and texture, shape and arrangement, and the ways in which data are presented and illustrated. If you feel you need guidance beyond the points briefly mentioned here, good information is available from Woolsey (1989), Briscoe (1996), Davis (2005), and Hofmann (2010).

Learn of any requirements and restraints

Before you begin to develop or lay out your poster, check carefully for any information that conference organizers may have provided about poster size, shape, or arrangement. At different meetings, poster display boards may be as small as 3 ft × 3 ft (1 m × 1 m) or as large or larger than 4 ft × 8 ft (1.3 m × 2.6 m). Sometimes they must be mounted horizontally on a stand or table, whereas others must stand vertically on the floor. If possible, find out the exact dimensions that will be allowed for the display board.

Choose a construction and printing method

Section the poster into modules based on the organization of the material. Then construct the poster in such a way that sizes and shapes are roughly balanced, with no more than four or five blocks or columns on the board.

Increasingly, posters are being printed as a single large page after developing them with PowerPoint templates. It can seem strange at first to think of using a slide format for such a large item, but many people find it works well.

By combining slide size and printing size options, you can produce various poster sizes. Posters are often 60 × 48 inches (152 × 122 cm); set the slide size to 30 × 24 inches (76 × 61 cm), and print the slide at 200%. If you do not have ready access to a large format printer, check availability through commercial businesses that provide office support, photocopy services, or architectural blueprints.

It is best to set the slide size before you begin. Changing the proportions of your slide after it has been created may distort the graphics and text. If you find you need to change the proportions of a poster after your slide is already finished, you will probably find it easiest to start a new slide with the revised proportions. Then select, copy, and paste the text and graphics from your original slide into the new presentation.

Before these options came along, the favored approach for poster construction was to print logical sections of the text separately, frame each on a stiff colored backing, and assemble them together on a larger background. The resultant posters were time-consuming to prepare, but when carefully done they were very attractive. This look can also be achieved now by printing each of a series of PowerPoint slides individually, then mounting them on foam core or similar material using spray adhesive.

A poster is a synopsis, not a paper

A scientific poster should follow the same organizational conventions used for other scientific writing, with an Introduction, Objectives, Materials and Methods, and Results. The Discussion should be limited, and generally can be included under the single heading of Results and Discussion. If literature is cited, a References section must be included; however, it can be in smaller type and in a less prominent position than other sections. Include Acknowledgments to recognize contributions to the research or poster construction.

Despite following the same general organization, however, a poster differs in many ways from a paper written for publication. Poster format demands concise presentation of information. In comparison to a written paper, add more photographs, graphics, and color. Omit the separate abstract unless the sponsoring society requires it.

Many people find it helpful to view the poster-writing process not as trying to condense a paper but rather as expanding and enriching its abstract. The most common problem with poster presentations is the attempt to present too much text and too many data.

Make sure the text of the poster can stand on its own merits. Viewers will pause to look at your poster even when you are not present to answer questions. Most will not read the poster in order from beginning to end. Most commonly, they will begin by scanning the data in tables and figures, then read the conclusions or objectives. Try reading these independently yourself, and see if they carry your central point of emphasis.

Pay attention to legibility and readability

Easy reading – which includes both legibility and readability – is of primary importance with a poster. The title needs to be legible from a distance of 5–10 m if it is to catch people's attention. Viewers generally stand 1–2 m away as they read a poster, so body of the text itself must be clearly legible at that distance.

Readability is affected by the size and style of type. Common typefaces generally recommended for titles include Helvetica, Tahoma, and similar block sans serif styles. A mix of capital letters and lowercase is easier to read than all capitals. These same typefaces may be used for text, or choose a conservative serif type such as Times New Roman, Bookman Old Style, or Palatino Linotype. Use italics only where scientifically required.

Text readability also depends on line length. (With current software and a wide sheet of paper, you could actually produce a one-page poster containing a single line of type 2 m long – imagine the nightmare of trying to read it!) Use short expanses of text and short paragraphs. Good limits would be fewer

"I don't know, it's a little formulaic."

than 65 characters and spaces per line and no more than 20 lines of text in a section. Whenever possible, present material in lists rather than sentences. Sections such as Objectives, Methods, and Conclusions especially benefit from this.

To be viewed to best advantage, graphics also must be large and may need to be simplified. For photographs to show at their best, they should be at least 5 inches by 8 inches (12 × 20 cm), and larger is better. Table entries should be limited to 20 items or fewer. Graphs should include no more than 3–4 lines or 6–8 bars.

Blank space is important, too. It gives the eye a place to rest. Some design experts suggest that as much as 50% of the area of the poster page should be blank, including space used to separate parts of the poster.

Tips for talking about your poster

Despite the relative informality of the poster situation, it is still your responsibility to maintain a professional attitude. Be at your poster when you are scheduled to be; some people will make a point of being there to talk with you. If friends stop by for unrelated small talk, be sure any poster audience takes precedence over the social one.

Resist the temptation to do competitive head-counts. Your success does not depend on the number of people who stop by your poster versus someone else's display. As you stand by your poster watching people pass in the aisles, it can feel disheartening. Most will walk on by. If they stop, they will generally look at only your main points, usually for less than 90 seconds.

Remind yourself that your audience is not all these people, but a small subgroup of people who are already interested in your general subject, but are not familiar with your data. If you design your poster in such a way that you attract and keep their interest, and as a result have the opportunity for clear communication conveyed with knowledge and sincerity, the experience will be worth their time and yours.

Handle questions with respect and assurance

> The answers I remember longest are the ones that answer questions that I didn't think of asking.
>
> JONATHAN KOZOL

It is little wonder that some presenters approach the idea of answering questions with a great deal of trepidation, because whether the context is a poster session, a class report, a dissertation defense, a job interview, or a presentation at a scientific meeting, the stakes can feel high. What if someone asks a question that you can't answer? Or one that seems to negate the whole study? Or is openly hostile?

There are ways to handle all these situations (Table 16.3). Be prepared, and then relax. Stay cool. It's important to realize that whatever happens, you are still in charge.

First, be sure you understand the question. Listen closely. Make sure the questioner is asking what you think he or she is. Don't interrupt before the question is complete, even if you think you know what is being asked. Ask for clarification if necessary. As a courtesy to your audience, if necessary repeat, rephrase, or recast the question. Then pause to think for two or three seconds before answering. Your answer will probably be better for having done so.

Answer briefly and directly. Never laugh at a question or dismiss a question without a response. Any question is important even if it sounds trivial. If one listener has missed a basic detail, others may have also. However, don't belabor any point either. This is not the time or place to start a new speech.

Don't bluff. When you don't know an answer, honestly say so. Don't just guess. Suggest ways that an answer might be found. If you are confident that someone else in the audience might have an answer, it is acceptable to redirect

Table 16.3 Some suggested ways to handle difficult questions

Situation	Possible responses
You don't know the answer.	Say simply that your research has not supplied an answer to that question. Suggest how you would investigate the question. Offer an educated speculation on the topic. Offer information on a closely related area. Ask the questioner his or her thoughts.
Question is too complicated.	Acknowledge that it is a difficult question. Give the beginning part of an answer, and suggest more discussion afterwards.
Questioner seems hostile.	Stay cool. Accept the question with a smile, followed by a serious, professional reply that is related to the subject.
Questioner asks repeated questions or wants extended discussion.	Make a positive comment about the complexity of the subject, and suggest you meet to discuss the matter further after the session.
Questioner interrupts during your talk.	Respond courteously, answer as briefly as you can, and return to the prepared speech. Politely suggest that "we" hold the question until the end of the talk, because points "we" are about to cover may help answer it.

the question to them in a polite manner that avoids putting them in an awkward situation. Alternatively, remember the old dictum attributed to politicians: "The question they ask doesn't have to be the question you answer." It also is perfectly acceptable to steer your answers in directions you'd like to discuss as long as you don't appear devious or deceitful while doing so.

Never answer sarcastically or with anger. If you feel someone is asking a "loaded" question only for purposes of impressing others, remain courteous and patient. Even if you feel that a question or comment was not asked with respect, you can dignify it by supplying a serious, professional reply.

For practice answering difficult questions, go to Exercise 29.

17   Publication: the rest of the story

And now you know ... the *r-r-rest* of the story!

PAUL HARVEY

Each week from the 1950s through the 1990s, as many as 24 million people listened to an American newscaster named Paul Harvey broadcast a radio segment called *The Rest of the Story*. It always began as a quaint, apparently historical tale about someone that seemed very average until the very end, when Harvey dramatically exposed a missing element that revealed the deeper significance hidden within.

Even before publication you have become a writer, but now you stand poised at the threshold of dramatic reveal, ready to share the significance of your scientific message with the world. Only relatively minor details stand between you and scientific publication. Go forward with confidence. Soon you will be celebrating, and soon afterward, planning your next project.

Get it all together – then send it off!

Modern technology has greatly simplified the mechanics of manuscript submission. Whereas in the past, authors had to worry about the safe arrival of (sometimes multiple) copies of paper-based text and figures sent through the postal system, today most journals welcome or require electronic copy from the beginning. Clearly, this saves time, money, and hassle for everyone involved. Editors can edit the typescript on the computer screen, and, if necessary, reformat it to their specific printing requirements. Reviewers can receive it as an email attachment. After annotating their suggested changes as they read through it, they can email this to the editor, who in turn can add his or her own comments and send it back to the author. All these advances hold the potential to make the entire review process more efficient and (theoretically at least) shorten the time involved.

Nonetheless, the details may have changed but the basic process remains the same. To ensure that your manuscript and its associated documents, including your cover letter to the editor, are treated well, you must make a final careful inspection to ensure that all these documents are present, accurate, well written and complete. Your job at this stage is to make the editor's life easier by paying attention to details.

Inspect your document one last time

You've just finished going through your document for what seems like the hundredth time. Take a break, and get some sleep, then come back to the document one last time. Nine basic questions provide a good framework for a final review of the text of nearly any scientific paper. If any of them cause you problems, refer to the material in earlier chapters.

- *Is the Title accurate, succinct, and effective?*
  Titles are more effective when they begin with a keyword. Check *ITA* for any limits on length. Assure that the title is grammatically correct; pay attention to the placement of modifiers.
- *Does the Abstract represent all the content but stay within the allowed length?*
  An abstract of a research report should include the study design, experimental subjects, methods, results, and interpretations. An abstract of a case report should briefly characterize the patient as well as the unusual features of the case. A review article abstract usually tells what the review is about, rather than representing its content in highly condensed form.
- *Does the Introduction set the stage adequately but concisely?*
  It should orient the reader, disclose the gap to be filled, and present the question you propose to answer. At its end, it should clearly spell out the focus of your research.
- *Is the rest of the text in the right sequence?*
  Most full-length research papers have an IMRAD format, but the position of the Abstract, Acknowledgments, and footnoted material may vary. Case reports, review articles, editorials, and book reviews appear in many different formats, and are more likely to show deviations in sequence.
- *Is all the text really needed?*
  Sometimes papers are overwritten. Your document will be judged by content, not its length.
- *Is any needed content missing?*
  Sometimes – especially if a writer is interrupted while working – important material gets left out.
- *Do data in the text agree with data in the tables?*
  If you wrote the text with the tables sitting beside you, there should be no problems. Check anyway. Surprising things sometimes happen.

- *Should any of the tables or illustrations be omitted, restructured, or combined?* The more time you have invested in tables and illustrations already, the more psychologically difficult this question can be, but ask it anyway. If some graphics seem now to be of only tangential importance, delete them. Then remember to renumber those that remain.
- *Do the citations and references agree with one another?* Check both for missing references and for unnecessary references. Use only enough citations to support key statements. (Theses and dissertations sometimes require extensive review and referencing to showcase a graduate student's mastery of the literature; for research papers that arise from this work, delete all but the most directly relevant.) Then make sure that the text citations and the full references match.

When the typescript finally seems done, read it once more. Have coauthors or a colleague read it as well. It still undoubtedly will harbor a few surprises. Finding them now is a bit embarrassing, but less so than facing them on the journal reviewer's edited copy or the published page!

Double-check references and attributions
Several studies of the accuracy of citations and presentations of others' assertions in the biomedical literature have revealed surprisingly high rates of error. An analysis of 300 randomly selected references in six frequently cited veterinary journals found major errors in 30% of them (Hinchcliff *et al.*, 1993). Misquotation rates of 12% in medical journals (de Lacey *et al.*, 1985) and 27% in surgical journals (Evans *et al.*, 1990) have been reported.

Spelling problems were the most common error, a particularly important concern because misspellings have the potential to impede computerized retrieval systems or to obscure author identity. Another common error was a failure to cite the original source of information, a disturbing finding because it suggests that authors frequently do not read the original reference. Misquotations of findings in studies by others also were common, carrying the risk that through repeated secondary citation, a major inaccuracy may become established as accepted fact.

Take the time to check every nitty-gritty detail, including spelling of authors' names, publication dates, exact titles of articles, and the journal name, volume, and page numbers.

Verify submission format
Long before now you have, of course, chosen a journal. Now it is time for one last check to be certain that you have tailored your submission to its requirements. Check the journal's website for the latest version of the *Instructions to*

Authors; print versions of the *ITA* also often can be found in the January issue for the journal's current year of publication. Journal *ITAs* vary widely in their comprehensiveness, however. You may also wish to refer to recent issues for examples of accepted format.

Most probably, you will be submitting your document as electronic copy, though a few journals still require paper and some want both. Standard practice dictates that printed copy should appear in Pica or Elite type, and the spirit of this requirement has carried forward into electronic manuscript preparation. Although computer-generated fonts differ from one another in size, typewritten Pica and Elite type are roughly equivalent to 12-point and 10-point computer-generated type, respectively. Unless specified otherwise, double space everything that is typed, including tables, figure legends, and footnotes. Use wide margins (a full inch at sides, and at least an inch at top and bottom).

Check that you have all the required entries on the first page. Many journals request that author names and affiliations be placed on a separate page from the title in order to facilitate blind reviews. The Abstract or Summary usually appears by itself on the second or third page, sometimes followed by keywords.

Begin the Introduction on the third page. Either run the text matter continuously or start each subsequent major section on a separate page. Many journals require the latter approach.

Footnotes to text material, if used, are grouped on a separate page, as are figure legends. Each table, with its title, should be on a separate page. Rather than interspersing these non-textual materials throughout the text, assemble all of them in numerical order at the back of the manuscript. Some journals may also require notations within the text margins to indicate approximate locations for tables and figures.

Number all pages

When documents were all typewritten by hand, omitting page numbers was a tempting shortcut, because it allowed material to be inserted or changed later without retyping the entire document. Use of word processing removes this excuse. However, if paper copy is required, starting major sections on separate pages still can help to minimize reprinting.

Always number all pages, including (generally in this order) the Title page, Abstract, the text itself, and such materials as Acknowledgments, References, Tables, Figure legends, and footnote lists. Editors and reviewers must be able to refer to pages by number in their written comments. (Some journals also require that lines be numbered along the left margin for easy reference during editing.)

Check that you've addressed all additional requirements

Often, a journal may require special statements or permissions for legal reasons. Check the *Instructions to Authors* and recent issues. Failure to include these will significantly delay your paper's review. Commonly, these requirements may include:

- A statement that all authors have contributed significantly to the paper, understand and endorse it, and have read and approved the version being submitted for publication. This may include explicit attributions for each author's responsibility or role. Some journals require such a statement to be signed by all the coauthors.
- A signed permission statement from anyone you've mentioned in the acknowledgments and anyone cited under "personal communication" for use of their name and/or data.
- A statement certifying that no part has been submitted, accepted for publication, or published elsewhere.
- A statement that the article is original work of the authors except for material in the public domain or excerpts from others' works for which written permission of the copyright owners has been obtained.
- A conflict of interest disclosure.

Assemble these, and include them with your submission as directed in the *ITA*.

If the paper depends critically on another unpublished paper or one that is "in press" in another journal, mention this fact. Though it may or may not be a requirement, it is common courtesy to include electronic or paper copies of the related paper for the reviewers.

Write a brief but effective cover letter

Write and edit this letter carefully – it forms an editor's first impression of you and your work. Be certain to spell the editor's name correctly. Ensure that this information is current and correct. Sending a submission to the wrong person can delay it considerably.

In the letter, name the journal and say something nice (but not effusive) about why it is the appropriate place to publish this particular paper. State the title of your document. Identify yourself as corresponding author, and include your full current postal and email addresses and your phone number. Mention any additional information that may facilitate editorial processing, such as the type of article (short communication, research article, case study).

It is quite appropriate to offer suggestions for potential non-local reviewers. Naming people who should not review it can be a trickier matter.

Thrust your manuscript into the world

It's time to let your baby grow up. Take a deep breath, and send everything off to your intended journal, but recognize that none of us live in a perfectly error-free world. Assume that packages will become lost in the mail, that electronic files will crash or be corrupted or lost, that photographs will become separated from text, and that figures will be misplaced. Never send off your only copy of anything! If submission is electronic, maintain a backup copy of the final file in a separate location – not just on your hard drive! An easy way to accomplish this is to send a copy to your own email.

The relatively few journals still asking for paper documents usually require at least two copies of the typescript, including any supporting materials such as photographs. (Again, check the *Instructions to Authors*.) Save an additional paper copy for yourself. Be especially careful to fully label any illustrations. For prints, this is usually done with a sticker label on the reverse side. Indicate the top edge of the illustration.

For electronic copy, use a descriptor that explicitly identifies the content, even when the file name appears in abbreviated form. Illustrations are processed differently than text at the publishers, and if they are not fully identified, proper association of figures and text in the final assembly of the journal can be a headache or worse.

Having done your best, don't waste time worrying. Find something else to do for a while. (If you have not already done so, this can be a good time to work on developing an oral presentation or a poster!) The journal office may notify you (often via form letter) that they have received your submission, but it probably will be weeks before you hear more than that.

Understand the process of editorial review

> Writing is an adventure. To begin with, it is a toy and an amusement.
> Then it becomes a mistress, then it becomes a master, then it becomes
> a tyrant.
> The last phase is that just as you are about to be reconciled to your
> servitude, you kill the monster and fling him to the public.
>
> WINSTON CHURCHILL

Receipt by the editor marks the beginning of a whole series of steps that conclude with publication in printed or electronic media or both. Only two of these steps require direct action from the corresponding author: dealing with reviewers' comments and correcting proofs. However, understanding what happens once the editor receives your typescript can help to alleviate those natural feelings of worry and wondering that can gnaw at you while you await a response.

What happens at the editor's office: Round one

When it arrives at the editorial office, your typescript is logged in, dated, and assigned a typescript number that allows the editor to track its progress through the subsequent steps. The typescript is also given a cursory review at this stage to ensure that all the illustrations are included and that it meets the journal's criteria for submission for publication. The editor then identifies two or three external referees qualified to review your typescript, and sends a copy of your typescript to each.

Referees usually are requested to return their reviews within 3 weeks. In an ideal world, all referees would return their reviews promptly, because reviewers usually are researchers who submit their own work to the same journal and generally they are impatient if they do not receive their own reviews in a timely manner. However, because these reviewers volunteer their time, some are less conscientious than others about meeting return deadlines.

Once the editor has all the external reviews in hand, he or she decides if the paper should be accepted in its current form, accepted with the provision that certain changes or objections can be handled in a satisfactory manner, or rejected outright. The paper then is returned to the corresponding author, along with copies of the referees' comments and the editor's decision and recommendations.

Acceptance is nearly always contingent on some revision. Be prepared for this possibility (see the following section). If a submission is rejected outright, you have the option of appealing the decision to the editor or editorial board. Alternatively, you can choose to reformat the article, incorporate whatever of the reviewers' and editor's recommendations seem warranted, and submit the typescript to another journal, thereby beginning the publication process anew.

PEANUTS   by Charles Schulz

Deal respectfully with reviewers' comments

The system of peer review – wherein anonymous reviewers funnel comments about your typescript back to you through the editor, who usually appends his or her own comments – is rarely a wholly pleasant one, no matter how common it is (Arthur and Weintraub, 2010). Even if you have carefully followed all the suggestions in this book, be prepared for the possibility of negative comments and misunderstandings. Sometimes these may not be even diplomatically worded. Nonetheless, treat the entire process with respect. As noted by Dizon and Rosenberg (1990), "The peer review process is not a perfect system – just a necessary one."

The worst thing that you can do, should critical reviews appear, is to treat them as an affront to your professional image. Instead, calmly and carefully evaluate each comment, point by point. Make the suggested changes that seem to have value. Review those that seem wrong. If a reviewer misunderstood you, try to determine why. The misunderstanding may reveal a weakness in your argument or analysis, or a spot where the writing is weak.

Return the revised typescript to the editor. In your letter of reply to the editor, respond to each reviewer comment in turn. Indicate acceptance of those suggestions that seem to have merit. If you chose not to accept a reviewer's comment, indicate why not. Diplomatically and briefly explain your reasoning concerning suggested changes that you feel are unjustified.

Avoid anger and any tendency to sarcasm in your responses. Editors sometimes pass your comments back to the reviewer, to whom you may not be anonymous. The world is really a very small place.

What happens at the editor's office: Round two

If an author's revisions have been extensive or have substantially changed the paper, an editor may elect to repeat the review process, essentially returning to round one. If he or she is satisfied, however, the paper is officially accepted. The editor or an assistant marks the copy for the typesetter to conform to the particular details of journal design and format. Then the editor forwards it to the publisher.

Other paperwork may also appear at this time. Generally the publisher includes an order form for the author to order reprints of the article. If page charges are journal policy, the author receives a bill or invoice for the number of printed pages with the galley proof. Open-access journals may send their invoices as well. Many journals require authors to execute a copyright release form, and such forms are often also enclosed with the galley. In addition to your signature as corresponding author, these forms may need to be signed by all coauthors.

Correct galley and page proofs conscientiously

When the publisher has typeset the paper, both your typescript and the publisher's "galley proof" will be returned to you (sometimes by way of the journal's editor, who may also check the proof). Galley proof originally was the name for a typeset copy of a document used to permit correction of errors before the type was made up in pages; its name comes from the galley, a tray for holding composed type. With computerized typesetting, the term is also used as a synonym for a "page proof" that shows how the made-up pages will appear.

Checking galley proof is an important step in the publication process. Take it seriously, and give the proof the attention and care it deserves. With the increase in electronic submissions, the typesetting process generally introduces fewer errors, but proofs totally without errors are exceedingly rare.

Read the proof carefully. Errors at this stage can be difficult to catch when working alone. If possible, enlist a friend's aid, so that one person can slowly read the original typescript aloud while the other checks the proof. If you must work alone, examine individual sentences slowly, word by word and line by line. To detect spelling errors, try reading lines backward to view each word separately. Compare the typeset material with the original typescript to ensure that no material has been omitted or repeated. Examine numbers carefully, especially in tables. Check that the figures and their legends are properly associated with one another, and that figure placement in the text is correct.

Documents slated for paper copy pass through many hands between the author's submission and their final appearance as printed pages. Common sense suggests that a standard method of marking corrections will reduce the chances of misunderstandings. Proofreaders' marks form an internationally recognized convention, although British and American systems differ slightly. When sending you the proofs, editors often include a list of preferred marks, with examples of their use.

Errors and omissions should be marked twice – once as corrections in the margin, and a second time by way of proofreaders' marks in the body of the text where the errors occur. Never write the full correction itself above the lines of type within the printed matter, where it would be almost impossible to read clearly.

Checking over a galley or page proof, the printer will look for marginal notations, and makes only the alterations noted there. He or she will not, and cannot be expected to, make sweeping corrections on the basis of a single command such as "change this word to italics throughout the document." Mark

A proofreader's nightmare

Can you read this? Olny srmat poelpe can.

I cdnuolt blveiee that I cluod aulaclty uesdnatnrd waht I was rdanieg.

Bceuase of the pheonmneal pweor of the hmuan mnid, aoccdrnig to a rseearch at Cmabrigde Uinervtisy, it deosn't mttaer in waht oredr the ltteers in a wrod are. The olny iprmoatnt tihng is taht the frist and lsat ltteer be in the rghit pclae. The rset can be a taotl mses and you can sitll raed it wouthit a porbelm. Tihs is bcuseae the huamn mnid deos not raed ervey lteter by istlef, but the wrod as a wlohe.

Amzanig, huh? Yaeh, and I awlyas tghuhot slpeling was ipmorantt!

UNKNOWN

each change on the proof where it occurs. When more than one correction must be written in the margin next to a single line of type, arrange the corrections in sequence from left to right, and separate them by slashes (slant lines).

The time for revision or adding new information has passed. Changes in the typescript at this point should only be to correct errors. Resist any impulse to further polish style. In fact, such changes are usually expressly forbidden, and any changes made that are not the fault of the typesetter may be charged to the author as "penalty copy" at considerable expense. (Rarely, a journal will allow a brief appendix to be added that includes late-breaking new information that supports work in the paper.)

Finally, read and correct the proof promptly, and return it immediately to the editor. Proofs are extremely time-sensitive from the publisher's standpoint. Delays at this point are costly to everyone.

Celebrate – You have published!

As the final step in the publication process, the editor organizes and makes up an issue from proofed papers, and sends the entire issue to the publisher. The publisher then prints and mails the issue to journal subscribers. Reprints, if ordered, are usually mailed to authors within a week or two of publication.

FOR BETTER OR FOR WORSE © 2000 Lynn Johnston Productions. Distributed by Universal Uclick. Reprinted with permission. All rights reserved.

Also, the editor generally provides the author with a copy of the final print version.

Now you can at last rejoice! With pride, add this title credit to your growing resume and begin your next publication.

Tips for international publication

> To think justly we must understand what others mean; to know the value of our thoughts, we must try their effect on other minds.
>
> WILLIAM HAZLITT

Scientific writing today has taken on a distinctly international nature, but when the writer and readers do not share the same first language, clear communication takes an extra degree of effort.

Translation is often touted as the answer. However, there is a shortage of qualified translators, and the expense can be prohibitive. Translation also delays the publication of scientific research. Furthermore, some languages have not developed the vocabulary required for science, so that in effect, translation requires the artificial development of terminology. Various software and online services also promise translation, but as of this writing, they have yet to be refined to the point where they can be recommended for scientific documents.

In this section, we offer some pointers for both the native English speaker writing for a reader with a different first language, and for the writer seeking to publish in English although it is not his or her primary language. A comprehensive introduction to the extensive literature on this topic can be found in Leki, Cumming and Silva (2008) and references therein. For additional practical help, Glasman-Deal (2009) and the appendices in Markel (1994) offer good places to begin.

As a native English speaker, remember second-language learners

This advice is addressed to those who, like us, grew up speaking and writing in English. Sometime in your writing career, you almost certainly will be called upon to write a document addressed to readers for whom English is a secondary language. Their task will be greatly eased if you pay careful attention to yours.

What MacNeil (1995) calls "the glorious messiness of English" has resulted in an estimated vocabulary of over one million words. (Other major languages have far fewer; French, for example, has only about 75,000.) This massive vocabulary poses formidable obstacles to those attempting to master what has become, to a very real extent, the first truly global language.

There are ways in which you can ease this problem. One is to use a simplified version of English. Just after World War II, this idea gained great popularity as a possible tool for better international understanding and hopefully, world peace. Over the years, various experts have proposed special assemblages of restricted vocabularies and simplified grammar. For example, Basic English was designed around an 850-word lexicon; its creator (Ogden, 1930) claimed it would take someone seven years to learn English but only seven weeks for Basic English!

A form called Special English has a core vocabulary of 1500 words. Like Basic English, it uses the active voice and short, simple sentences that contain only one idea. This system has been used in *Voice of America* broadcasts since 1959; tune in online if you'd like to hear how it sounds.

Another variant is Simplified English, a limited and standardized subset of Standard English intended for science or technical communication. Its most extensive use, in a version called Simplified Technical English, is for instruction and maintenance manuals (Gingras, 1987; Sanderlin, 1988), particularly in the aerospace industry. It has been shown not only to reduce ambiguity and improve comprehension, but also to facilitate automated translation and thus make translation cheaper and easier.

Simplified English is both a vocabulary and a technique. It starts with a basic lexicon of less than 300 nontechnical words, grouped by function (with definitions) in a thesaurus. To this, one can add one's own limited list of terms required by the specific document, and include their definitions in a glossary with example sentences. Words must have only one meaning and they can only be used in certain ways. Use of jargon, vernacular phrases, and abbreviations is discouraged.

Because Simplified English is designed with science in mind, using its reduced vocabulary plus target terms works surprisingly well for most purposes. Often, clarity is actually improved by the change.

Instead of: Unless one implements the modifications, there is a potential for damage.
Write: Make the modifications, or damage can occur.

Although they were developed primarily for non-native English speakers, the constraints imposed by such systems also improve the readability of text for native speakers. For example, Simplified Technical English requires writers to:

- Use the active voice
- Use articles wherever possible
- Use simple verb tenses
- Use language and terminology consistently
- Avoid lengthy compound words
- Use relatively short sentences

Additional guidelines are designed to keep sentence structure as simple as possible. Sentences are to be kept below 20 words in length, and no more than one sentence in ten on a page should exceed 16 words in length. The less skill and training in English the intended audience has, the shorter the sentences should be.

When you are called upon to write a document addressed to non-native English speakers, remember the general principles set forth in these systems. For further guidance, including the Simplified English lexicon and numerous examples of basic usage, see *Science and Technical Writing* (Rubens, 2002) or various online sites.

When writing English as a second language, decide what approach to take

Among multilingual writers whose first language is not English but who choose that language of publication, three writing methods are common. You could:

- Draft the paper in English from the start, doing the best you can. This is the most desirable way, because it usually results in the most readable text in the least time.
- Write the first draft in your own language, then translate it into English yourself. This takes longer, and is more apt to lead to grammatical difficulties and stylistic awkwardness.
- Write the paper entirely in your own language, and then employ a professional translator who is familiar with the terminology of your branch of science. This can be expensive. Learn whether you can include the translation fee if you apply for a research grant.

FOXTROT © 1996 Bill Amend.

Whichever method you choose, your primary task remains the same as for any other scientific writer – that is, to ensure that your material is well organized, complete, and clear. Pay attention to the level and type of details that appear in papers published in your chosen journal, and try to emulate them. Referees and editors will probably not mind correcting minor grammatical mistakes, but they will reject a paper if they cannot even decipher the text's basic meaning.

Seek editorial advice from a colleague fluent in scientific English

As you begin writing in English, find a willing native English speaker to serve as your first editor. Such people can be your most important resource – treat them well! Do not overwhelm them with a lengthy manuscript or ask for help with every small grammatical matter in the text. Instead, show them early sections of your paper and use their initial comments about your grammar, style, and organization to improve your writing skills as you progress.

Watch to avoid some specific pitfalls

Most of the usage and grammar questions that confront scientific writers are the same whether or not one's native language is English. If this were not true, there would be little place for books like this one! However, a few areas seem to cause special problems for those for whom English is a secondary language. Writers feeling the need for more help may wish to consult a highly regarded older book, *Grammar Troublespots: An Editing Guide for ESL Students* (Raimes, 1988). Widely available in the online used book market, it is an excellent investment. A useful, comprehensive dictionary that includes extensive grammatical guidance is the *Longman Dictionary of American English* (Pearson Education, 2008).

Recognize, too, that cultures differ in their attitudes toward material taken directly from other people's writing. In some countries where English is not the first language, cultural norms may include a tolerant view of plagiarism. Maintain a strict policy here.

Read in order to write

Finally, a bit of advice directed to everyone called upon to write in a language they did not learn at their mother's knee... Learning to write well takes effort and practice, and writing well in a second language takes even more. Although consulting books such as this one can help your effort, ultimately no book can actually teach you how to write, any more than a rule book could teach you how to play soccer or a music theory book teach you to play a symphony. Just as with sport or music skills, writing skills can be developed only by actual practice over time.

Even for native English speakers, the scientific English in your chosen field of study could be considered to be a dialect (Montgomery, 2003), and learning to write this dialect proceeds much like learning to speak any other foreign language. Although one can attempt to memorize words and rules, the fastest learning occurs by imitation and observation. Success comes from studying examples of proper use and trying to emulate them.

A major way that both native and acquired English speakers learn to speak like scientists is through constant reading of literature until they develop a sense of what "sounds right" and what doesn't. For many people, this can be a haphazard process, but it doesn't need to be. A more effective approach is to seek out especially well-written recent articles in your field, reread them at frequent intervals, and imitate their writing style as part of your overall language training. If this idea appeals to you, consult Montgomery (2003) for detailed guidance.

Thirty exercises to improve anyone's scientific writing skills

1. Publication readiness: message, format, and audience

How would you answer these questions? More than one answer is possible; justify your decision.

1. A 75-year-old woman brought to your clinic has contracted a rare form of viral infection previously known to be associated primarily with children. A quick library search shows that the oldest affected person in the published literature was 62 years old. Should you publish your new information? Why or why not?

2. Your supervisor suggests that you both review the records of the last 50 cases of canine heartworm disease referred to your clinic and coauthor a paper on the findings. You ask what question the paper is going to answer. "We are not trying to answer a question," he says irritably. He just wants to report a summary of these data because colleagues elsewhere will be interested. Does the paper have a purpose? Does it have a message? What format would be most appropriate?

3. The two of you proceed to analyse those 50 cases of heartworm disease. Your analysis doesn't yield any new important findings, but does lend additional support to some previously published views. Is it still publishable? If so, in what form?

4. You've written a concise, clearly worded summary of the genetics of horn development in jackalopes. A series of examples from the literature, combined with your own laboratory analyses and a field-based population study, all point to the conclusion that a single gene controls this trait. You reason that geneticists, veterinary pathologists, and wildlife biologists all should know this important new information. How many papers could justifiably arise from your study? Explain your reasoning.

5. You've gone back through psychiatric clinic records for the past 18 years, and made a startling discovery. Nearly 80% of all the children hospitalized for manic depression had been previously identified in school tests as being highly creative. Who might be the potential audience for your message?

2. Search strategy and Boolean logic

This is an exercise in thinking logically, not in finding answers on the Web. Here are ten publication titles. Use them to answer the questions below.

a. Trap-Nesting Wasps And Bees: Life Histories, Nests, And Associates
b. Behavior Of Three Florida Solitary Wasps
c. Winged Warriors: Insects In The Garden
d. A Cluster Of Bees
e. The Wasps Of The Genus *Pisonopsis* Fox
f. Beeswax, Twine, and Time: The Art of Candlemaking
g. Cowfly Tigers: An Account Of The Bembicine Wasps Of British Guyana
h. Honeybees Attacked At Their Hive Entrance By *Philanthus* Wasps
i. A Life History of Stinging Insects
j. A Comparative Study Of The Nesting Habits Of Solitary Bees And Wasps

Write the number(s) corresponding to the title(s) that would be retrieved for each of the following Boolean statements.

1. Wasps AND Bees
2. Wasps NOT Bees
3. Bees NOT Wasps
4. Wasps OR Bees
5. When using terms in a subject directory, you will usually get only relevant titles. When using terms in a search engine, you should expect a mixture of relevant and irrelevant titles. If you were searching for Wasps OR Bees using a search engine, which of the above titles would probably be retrieved but have little to do with them?
6. When you search one of the better subject directories, you search not only titles but annotations written by a staff person. Which of the above titles would be missed by a search engine using the keywords Wasps OR Bees, but might contain relevant information that would be retrieved by a good subject directory?

3. Organizing ideas

Reorganize the following outline of ideas, using a concept map or an issue tree.

ABUNDANCE OF SAND FLIES

A. Determining population dynamics
   1. Aspirating flies from resting sites
      a. 6-ft high tree holes (most were here)
      b. Ground level

    2. Light traps at different levels
B. Determining offspring age
    1. Laboratory studies
        a. Maximum age, 5 weeks
        b. 50% mortality by 2 weeks
    2. Field studies
        a. Most were 2–3 weeks old
        b. Youngest found, 1 week old

4. Spellchecker programs

Find the errors that the spellchecker missed.

1. The young of the hoatzin, curious foul native to South America, are remarkable in having clawed fingers on their wings, by moans of which they are able to climb about trees like quadruplets.
2. These imported trees are so profligate they are crowding out the more fragile naïve species.
3. The client has a congenial hip disease.
4. His prostrate gland problem had persisted for many years.
5. The animals that normally inhabit the pond were dyeing because it had too much green allergy.
6. The experimental group included three Great Dames and eight puppies from a German Shepherd and an Alaskan Hussy.
7. She had a seizure, fell, and went unconscious. She was in a comma, and she never woke up.
8. The pistol of a flower is it's only protection against insects.
9. The doctor advised the patent to rest until the stitches were out and that there would be a permanent scare.
10. Our Spellwriter Program has the power to check wards within a document in as many as eight different languages, and this is only the tap of the iceberg.

5. Grammar programs

Enjoy these examples inspired by *Anguished English* (Lederer, 1987). Then rewrite the sentences to correct the errors a grammar checker would miss.

1. Migraines strike twice as many women as do men.
2. Wanted: Worker to take care of cow that does not smoke or drink.

3. As a baboon who grew up wild in the jungle, I realized that Wiki had special nutritional needs.
4. The patient was referred to a psychiatrist with a severe emotional problem.
5. In the photograph, veterinarian Joe Mobbs hoists a cow injured while giving birth to its feet.
6. About two years ago, a wart appeared on his left hand, which he wanted removed.
7. People who use birth control methods that smoke are in danger of having mentally disabled children.
8. The woman wants to have the dog's tail operated on again, and if it doesn't heal this time, she'll have to be euthanized.

6. Title choices

How could the following manuscript titles be improved? Explain the reasons for your choices.

1. Plantar Wart Removal: Report of a Case of Recurrence of Verruca after Curative Excision
2. Characteristics of Columbine Flowers are Correlated with Their Pollinators
3. Panda Mating Fails: Veterinarian Takes Over
4. Gleanings On The Bionomics And Behavior Of The East Asiatic Nonsocial Wasps. III. The Subfamily Crabroninae With A Key To The Species Of The Tribe Crabronini Occurring In Formosa And The Ryukyus, Contributions To The Knowledge Of The Behavior Of Crabronine Fauna, And Changes In The Taxonomic Position Of Three Species Of Crabronini Occurring In Japan
5. Report of New Health Data Results from the 1999 National ASAPFYI-ERGO Health Study: Lung Cancer in Women Mushrooms

7. Table and figure choices

The choice of a format in which to present data is a judgment call. What would you use for the examples below? Your choices need not match ours if you feel you have sound justification for them.

1. You've gathered a series of data concerning serum electrolyte values and acid–base variables for patients with Rocky Mountain spotted fever. How should you present this information?
2. You've examined mortality rates for male and female cats with thyroid disease in individual states of the United States. Should you use a table, graph, or figure?

3. You've measured maximum systolic blood pressure after giving white rats various doses of epinephrine, and have measured changes in their blood pressure throughout a 2-week period. You also have a really nice photograph of one of your control rats. What should you publish, and in what form?

4. In a case series study, you have collected data from a physical examination of animals at admittance, from observations during the course of the illness, and from final autopsies. You've decided to present the data in a table; how should they be arranged?

5. You have written a paper about a new species of a bacterial pathogen implicated in a case of pneumonia. You have a chest roentgenogram showing typical findings of pneumonia, and an electron micrograph of newly discovered structural details of the bacterium's flagellum. Should you include either or both in your paper?

6. You have identified a genetic syndrome that appears in members of a canine lineage as a Mendelian autosomal dominant trait. Should you present your evidence as a table, a graph, or text?

7. You have researched deaths from mycoplasmal diseases in turkeys and ducks, and found a significant difference in mortality rates. How should you show this difference?

8. Number use and interpretation

Treat these sentences conservatively, spelling out numbers or changing them to Arabic numerals as appropriate.

1. A full 3/4 (75 percent) of the experimental animals died with 15 hours, but 17 horses (10%) were still alive forty-five days later.

2. The chemicals for the experiment weighed less than 1/5 of a milligram.

3. Approximately 20 500 cells were calculated to be affected.

4. The control group recovered more quickly but a chi-square test of P equals 11 showed the difference was insignificant. We felt this was significant, however, because it showed the drug's effect.

5. The test plot contained ten species of grasses, two species of legumes, six species of trees, and 15 species of cruciferous plants.

9. Person and point of view

Change the use of third and first person in the following sentences. Many variations are possible.

1. The laboratory technician will find that the new procedure is an improvement; you will not need to sterilize the skin.

2. Kristen Preston and colleagues showed that some bacteria do not give off molecular oxygen but the authors herein contend that they still photosynthesize.
3. The authors wish to gratefully acknowledge and thank Dr. C. F. Snow for technical assistance and expertise.
4. It was found that the disease is contagious and that you should avoid contamination (van der Veen, 1850); the author concurs that cleanliness is essential.
5. It is postulated by the author, working alone and writing herein, that we have discovered a new species of *Australopithecus*.

10. Readability

Improve the readability of these sample paragraphs by changing the sentence lengths, word order, or other aspects as needed.

1. The Haversian system consists of a canal in the center containing blood vessels and a nerve surrounded by concentric rings of bony matrix and between them scattered tiny spaces called lacunae filled with bone cells connected by canaliculi to one another and the central canal. Through this canal the cells are nourished and kept alive.
2. The kidney is a very important organ. It has the ability to secrete substances selectively. This makes it able to maintain proper composition of the blood and other body fluids. The various end products of metabolism are injurious if allowed to accumulate.
3. Sex-linked genes explain red–green color blindness in man, and if a woman heterozygous for color blindness marries a normal-visioned man, all of the daughters of this combination will have normal vision, but half of the sons will be color blind; however, half of the daughters will be heterozygous for the defect but the normal sons will show no trace of the anomaly and will never transmit it to their children; while the heterozygous daughters can have color blind sons, the homozygous daughters will never pass the trait on to their sons or daughters.
4. Fertilized medaka embryos exposed to different concentrations of alcohol affect the embryogenesis by delay in initiating the vessel circulation, forming thrombus in many regions of the body including the brain, microcephaly (small head size), malformed neurocranial and trabecular cartilages and alteration in oxidative stress enzymes.
5. AMDRO fed to weanling castrated Holstein calves for 7 weeks experienced leucopenia by 2 weeks into the regimen that included significant reductions of eosinophils and lymphocytes.

11. Clarity and brevity

A. Rewrite each of these at least twice to express different meanings clearly.
   1. mature muscle iron
   2. chronic depression symptoms
   3. renal lithium excretion
   4. The three cases all had histologically confirmed metastatic malignant intraabdominal tumors.
   5. The present study examines various immunospecific drug sample combinations and their inhibition producing effects upon human peripheral blood leukocytes.
B. Reduce the following examples to a single hedge word apiece. Your interpretation may influence which hedge word to keep.
   1. These observations serve to suggest the probable existence of a possible female sex pheromone.
   2. It seems that it might possibly be very wise to follow the outlined procedure.
   3. Our belief is that the study may show an apparent link between cigarette smoking and lung cancer.
   4. A possible cause-and-effect relationship is not unlikely.
   5. The results appear to indicate that the mixture may have been more or less saturated with oil.
C. Identify and remove redundancy.
   1. It is interesting to note that the new organism is green in color, round in shape, 5 × 10 mm in size, and active with respect to motility.
   2. The authors envision that approximately 20–30 steps that are collectively referred to as electrophoresis will be necessary in the majority of cases.
   3. In the event that we hold a meeting at this point in time with reference to the data, consensus should not be difficult to attain.
   4. It is not irrelevant to mention here that the caseload included 15 young juveniles and 10 mature adults.
   5. Fig. 1. This figure shows the lateral white cells as they appear in a living abdominal ganglion of a cockroach. The ventral view has the anterior at top. The scale bar is 0.1 mm.
   6. The total absence of visible color was absolutely unique.
   7. To determine the mobility activity of the organism, new state-of the-art equipment was used.
   8. For a full and complete understanding of the impacts and ramifications of the hot temperature upon the organism, it is our personal opinion that future plans should include a chilling procedure.

12. When short may be too short

The following abbreviations are used incorrectly. Why?

1. *A title:* Assay for TCGF Activity in SPAFAS Chickens in the U.S.
2. *An abstract:* The present study provides first evidence for the presence of TCGF in supernatants of Con A stimulated chicken spleen cells incubated for several hrs.
3. *A text sentence:* Con A stimulated BALB/C spleen cells were used to prepare TCGF preparations by the MF I and MF II methods.
4. *A table title:* Distribution of ATPase in El treated membranes expressed as μ/mg of protein and total U.
5. *A footnote:* Pheasants were obtained from hatcheries in Ala., TN, and S. Carolina.

13. Tense use

Indicate preferred tense use in the sentences below. If you feel that a sentence is correct as it stands, simply note the fact.

1. Work by Matthews (2007) showed that *Vespula* nests readily in the laboratory.
2. Bird size shows an increase in our study with width of wooded habitat, as Figure 2 indicates.
3. Beal (1960) also observed that size increased with meadow width.
4. In our study we find that there are significantly fewer antibody-producing cells in copper-deficient mice than in copper-supplemented mice (see Fig. 3).
5. In a study by Sengelaub and Finlay (1981), the average costal width for normal animals was 0.81 mm.
6. Conover and Kynard (1981) reported that sex determination in the Atlantic silverside fish was under the control of both genotype and temperature.
7. Recently published work by Fruchter *et al.* (1) characterizes the ash from the Mount St. Helens eruption of 18 May 1980.
8. Many researchers have confirmed that the balance of hydrostatic and osmotic pressures in the capillaries is a very delicate one.
9. ABSTRACT: The cell-to-cell channels in the insect salivary gland are probed with fluorescent molecules. From the molecular dimensions, a permeation-limiting channel diameter of 16–20 angstroms is obtained.

10. SUMMARY: Germinal and somatic functions in *Tetrahymena* are found to be performed separately by the micro- and macronuclei, respectively. Cells with haploid micronuclei are mated with diploids to yield monosomic progeny.

14. Active and passive voice

Rewrite these passive sentences in the active voice. Condense and clarify the wording if you can.

1. It might be expected that this treatment would be effective.
2. No feed was available to the pathologist to analyse.
3. Inoculation was performed on 25 chickens by Jones and colleagues.
4. A collecting trip was made by this writer to Georgia for the purpose of collecting Lepidoptera.
5. Passages A and B should be marked for revision.
6. If certain words are discovered to be missing from this medical dictionary, it must be remembered that no equivalents for modern technical words were to be had by ancient speakers of Greek and Latin.
7. Three incineration systems are being studied for the university president by administrative personnel at the Biology Building.

15. Subject–verb agreement

Correct the following sentences if needed. Explain your reasoning.

1. The remaining fluid was drawn off and the kidneys washed.
2. Due to the small number of test animals used, that data was not significant.
3. Karyorrhexis, karyolysis, and cellular degeneration of hepatocytes was evident within the centrilobular regions.
4. None of the animals was harmed in the course of this study.
5. A sample was assessed by radiocarbon dating and sections analysed by potassium–argon methods.
6. Neither the rats nor the chimpanzee were kept in the laboratory.

16. Collective nouns, comparisons, and lists

A. Recast these sentences so that the collective noun or quantity is no longer the subject.

1. Ten to 50 parts per million of chloramphenicol is an appropriate dose.
2. A committee of 30 scientists was convened by the university president.
3. A total of 12 liters of serum were infused into the elephant by the veterinarian.

B. Rewrite the following sentences to correct their comparisons and lists.
   1. The authors' mild pulmonary hypertensive stage was similar to our present study.
   2. In comparison to Group B, Group A was more unique.
   3. The cat had a recovery that was better than the other cats.
   4. The emergency medical kit contained a bandage, applicator, towel, brush, and a rubber sponge.
   5. The fox was heavier than all the other animals in the study group.
   6. Of the two alternatives, this is the most interesting.

17. Dangling participles and other misplaced modifiers

Untangle the sentences below. Transform the sentences into the active voice when you can.

1. Progressing toward the anterior chamber a lamination was evident.
2. No bacteria were observed using dimethyl sulfoxide.
3. Following experimentation, bacteria multiplied.
4. Using this method the result demonstrated a correlation between the variables.
5. Intestinal sections can be examined for metazoan parasites using an inverted ocular.
6. Two stopwatches belonging to researchers that had been left leaning against cabinets were badly damaged.
7. For sale: Laboratory table suitable for researcher with thick legs and large drawers.
8. Two microscopes were reported stolen by the campus police last night.
9. Commercials have been prepared by the French government encouraging the use of condoms that are thought to be blunt enough to shock even liberal Americans.

18. Jargon and wordiness

A. Find a substitute for the following pretentious words and phrases.
   1. a sufficient number of
   2. has the capability of

3. produced an inhibitory effect
4. on a theoretical level
5. on a regular basis

B. What do the following sentences literally mean? What did the author intend?
1. The etiology of this disease is puzzling.
2. Histopathology stages were based on 10 dogs.
3. The necrology confirmed the intestinal occlusions.

C. Reword these sentences to remove jargon and extra words.
1. The bovine was postoperatively traumatized by a defective electrified fencing enclosure, necessitating euthanatization.
2. Positionize the slide carefully to visualize the quite unique spatial configurations with a high degree of accuracy.
3. It is the author's opinion that it is not an unjustifiable assumption that this chemotherapeutic agent has the capability of significantly ameliorating and attenuating the symptomology of the disease process.

19. Handling language sensitively

Improve the word choice in these examples.

1. A researcher must be sure that he double-checks all his references.
2. The sample consisted of 200 Orientals.
3. The depressives and the epileptics reacted differently to the drug.
4. The chairman confronted the female for plagiarizing.
5. The ten ladies in the study included one who was afflicted with cerebral palsy.
6. Breast cancer is one of the oldest diseases known to man.
7. A scientific writer's point of view must be clearly stated by him at the beginning.
8. We need 14 females willing to man the project.

20. Devil pairs

Place each member of the devil pair in the proper place in the sentences below.

1. The results of our study were (like/as) those of McGowen (1967). A significant number of study animals staggered (like/as) drunks do.
2. Young dogs are very susceptible to distemper, (while/whereas) older dogs are often immune. Cattle often develop respiratory disease (while/whereas) being shipped to market.

3. Clients often have ponds, which may be of (varying/various) sizes. Each group received (varying/various) combinations of antibiotics over the study period.

4. Although we gave penicillin and terramycin, the drugs had little (affect/effect). The (affect/effect) of the treatment was minimal.

5. Trypsin-catalyzed digestion has the (affect/effect) of converting the substrate to short-chained peptides. Giving erythromycin (affected/effected) a change in the nuclear shape. In double-blind experiments, researcher bias does not (affect/effect) experimental results.

6. He resigned as a matter of (principal/principle). The (principal/principle) effect of centrifugation was to separate cell types. The (principal/principle) of independent segregation is fundamental to genetics.

7. To determine the appropriate value, one must find the (complement/compliment) of the angle. The authors would like to (complement/compliment) Ms. Jones on her diligent effort. In the replication process, DNA and RNA (complement/compliment) each other.

21. Which and that

Improve the following sentences in whatever ways seem sensible and correct, paying particular attention to "which" and "that."

1. It is relevant to mention here that novel paleontological findings have uncovered the strong probability that the genus *Cantius*, an early genus of primates of a primitive nature, had a large pedal digit that could grasp and which possibly may have figured in the evolutionary scenario of all of today's more modern primates.

2. It should be noted that the use of low molecular weight dextrans should be avoided in these patients which appear to pass through the damaged endothelium of pulmonary vessels.

3. Occasionally a parasite will be noted by the client on a fish which is more worrisome to the owner than to the fish.

4. According to this interpretation it is then concluded by the authors of this present study that ten thousand five hundred tons of lead, that are in addition to the ninety thousand tons which are presently being emitted, will be emitted into the atmospheric envelope during the course of the next calendar year.

5. Our efforts did not result in the location of the proposal which was missing.

22. Fuzzy words and disguised verbs

A. Improve the following sentences in whatever ways seem correct and appropriate. Be alert for lazy verbs.
  1. By early adulthood, more of the males than females were observed to exhibit severe symptoms characteristic of the occurrence of copper deficiency.
  2. Under standard conditions, diazepam was chosen for inhibition of the initial rate of protein phosphorylation, as Figure 1 demonstrates.
  3. The site of action of soap is observed to be at the cell surface.
  4. Stanozolol caused prolongation of appetite, as the results demonstrate.
  5. Isolation of *A. hydrophila* occurred.

B. Use infinitives to replace verbal nouns, and improve the wording of the following sentences.
  1. The physicists' hope is for the solution of the question of whether science can harness alternative energy sources.
  2. Transformation of the data was necessary for the statistical analyses relevant to resolution of the hypotheses.

23. Punctuation

Correct the punctuation in these sentences.

1. Indicate optimum instrument settings for temperature humidity rainfall and performance.
2. When examined closely, the skeleton bears many bumpy spines, that project from the surface of the animal
3. Class Echinoidea which includes sea urchins sand dollars and heart urchins is not closely related to class "Ascomyceteae."
4. The adults are radially symmetrical but the larvae are bilateral and it is generally held that this phylum evolved from bilateral ancestors and that radial symmetry arose as an adaptation to a sessile way of life.
5. The clinician asked, How did the patient die?; the answer was not obvious.
6. The essay, The Future of Veterinary Medicine, appeared in the early 1960's.

24. Capitalization

Indicate accepted capitalization in the following sentences and titles.

1. The afghan hound ate plaster of paris.

2. The Study Sample included 15 greyhounds, 14 malamutes, and 10 spanish terriers.

3. adenine and guanine are nucleotides called purines.

4. A person can live normally without the Adrenal Medullae, but not without the Cortices.

5. these bacteria inhabit all Biomes of the northern hemisphere.

6. *A book title:* what's so funny about science? by sidney harris

7. *The title of a scientific research paper capitalized by the "significant word" system:* assessment of the role of alcohol in the human stress response

8. *A research paper title capitalized by the sentence system:* A Synopsis Of The Taxonomy Of North American And West Indian Birds

25. Scientific names

Indicate how the following scientific names should be handled.

1. the parasitic wasp, m. atrata

2. the dandelion, taraxacum officionale, family compositae, class dicotyledonae

3. the honeybee, apis mellifera var. ligustica

4. the human malarial parasite, plasmodium falciparum Bignami

5. the starfish (asterias) belongs to class asteroidea, phylum echinodermata, in the section deuterostomia.

26. Foreign words and phrases

Indicate correct type use (italics or Roman) and format in the following sentences. Follow the most conservative route.

1. When acceptable, use the formulas already given in the book, Official Methods in Microbiology.

2. For information on the in vivo action of green plant pigments, i.e. chlorophyll, see Arnon's article in Scientific American and Calvin and Bassham's book, The Photosynthesis of Carbon Compounds.

3. Our experiments cannot identify the underlying biophysical alterations, viz., effects within the membrane itself.

4. Reduced oxygen tension provides the best environment for in vitro parasite development, as shown by Udeinya *et al* (2005).

27. Ethical and legal issues

A. Indicate how you might handle the following situations. Explain your answer.

   1. You have redrawn an illustration from an 1890 book to use in a research article. Do you need to credit the original work?

   2. You are publishing a book about DNA, and it includes several excerpts from Watson and Crick's original 1953 letter to *Nature*. In all, you estimate they number about 600 words, and you feel that the context makes it fairly clear who wrote them. Are you free to use the excerpts without explicit citation? What do you need to consider?

   3. Your research on genetic factors underlying the development of juvenile diabetes has been accepted in *PLoS Medicine*. With a grin, you mention this to a colleague. She suggests you contact *Parents Magazine* to do a popular article on your research. What is your reaction? Does this constitute duplicate publication?

   4. You listen in astonishment at a faculty meeting as your department head says that although he can't prove it, he suspects that the dean of one of the other colleges has been bribing the provost. The next day you learn that the dean has brought legal charges against the department head. Would the charges be libel? Slander? Why or why not?

   5. You made a pioneering discovery and wrote it up for publication, but the manuscript disappeared from your desk before you could send it to *Science*. Now a team of rivals has published the essence of it. You have the computer files, but you never copyrighted the manuscript. Might you pursue legal action? On what grounds?

   6. You are writing a research article about chicken diseases, and would like to include some tables from a 2011 USDA publication. Do you need permission? Does the source need to be cited?

   7. While trying to develop a new reagent, you accidentally spill the chemical on the lab bench and realize that you have invented an incredibly effective new cleaning compound. Your assistant excitedly suggests that you contact the campus newspaper and get a bit of publicity. Should you? Why or why not?

   8. Preparing to give a guest lecture, you have found some wonderful articles on the Internet. How much can you copy into your PowerPoint presentation without having to cite them? How much before you must formally ask permission?

B. Many former trade names have become generic, but other trademarked names are still defended in court. Which of these were once trademarked but are now considered to be generic, and which are still protected?

Clorox, Lanolin, Freon, Sharpie, Tarmac, Teflon, Xerox, Q-tip, Heroin, Zipper

28. Slide presentation format

A. Organize this text in traditional slide format with a short-phrase title and bulleted sentence fragments:

> "Carbon dioxide dissolves readily in water and forms small quantities of carbonic acid. The salts of carbonic acid and simple carbonates usually account for the largest part of the electrolytes in aquarium water. This means the absorption of carbon dioxide by plants is closely linked to the complex system of aqueous carbonic acid and carbonates."

B. Organize this text in assertion–evidence format, and suggest a graphic aid that would be helpful:

> "Twenty-one species in the order Crocodylia are known around the world. Of these, only the American Alligator and the American Crocodile are native to the United States. However, a third species, the Spectacled Caiman, has been introduced in extreme southern Florida."

C. Match the numbered and lettered items to identify optimal visual elements for an effective computer-generated slide.

1. Good font for body text
2. Preferred typeface for headings
3. Minimum type size for body text
4. Good type size for projection in large room
5. Worst kind of slide graphic
6. Preferred graphic orientation
7. Preferred color combination for text-only slides
8. Preferred design for assertion–evidence title
9. Best kind of slide graphic
10. Worst style for headings

a. All capital letters
b. Complex spreadsheet
c. 14 point type
d. Sans serif font such as Arial or Helvetica
e. Vertical
f. Serif font such as Times New Roman
g. White letters on blue background
h. Decorative image with sound effects
i. 28–30 point type
j. 24 point type
k. Visually based support for the title's claim
l. Horizontal
m. Dark letters on a light but not white background
n. Complete sentence

29. Answering questions

Determine how you would handle these imaginary scenarios. More than one correct answer is, of course, possible.

1. You've just finished a talk in which you presented evidence that bacteria can break down a commonly used flame retardant into more toxic forms. An industry representative in the audience challenges your findings on the basis that no one has found massive amounts of the breakdown products in the environment. How might you respond?
2. The same industry representative gains the floor again, and launches into a long speech on the lives saved by these chemicals. How might you respond?
3. You've presented research showing that children with bipolar disorder are more likely than other children to read hostility in bland facial expressions. A teacher in the audience interrupts during your talk to note that she sees classroom evidence that these children miss facial cues altogether. She wonders if your work could be developed into a test to help therapists better diagnose and treat bipolar disorder. How do you handle this interruption?
4. Scrub jays will steal food from one another. You've done some clever experiments to show that these birds get sneakier about hiding food if they know another jay is watching them. A questioner in the audience asks whether parrots might show the same behavior. You don't know. How might you respond?
5. In a stunning presentation, you've revealed the isolation of a protein from white blood cells that could offer a new way to repair damaged nerve cells. A graduate student excitedly asks how long it will be until you can completely regenerate injured nerves and restore full function to paraplegics. How do you handle his question?

30. Practicing mixed corrections

Find the errors, comment on them, and write a corrected version of the sentences. Your interpretation of certain sentences may differ from ours, but responses should aim in the same direction – toward increased accuracy, precision, and clarity.

1. The authors conclude that there is evidence that the limiting diameter lies between sixteen and twenty angstroms in these cells taken from mammals.
2. The inhibitory activity of the various combinations was studied and isobolograms plotted.

3. The site of action of EDTA is at the cell surface by increasing cell wall permeability.

4. Measurements were made of the pronounced lesions that were in the heart.

5. Numerous strains of T. cruzi are reported to cause chronic *chagas disease*.

6. In the present study, treatment is terminated when fish appear irritated.

7. The wasp S. maculata is a progressive provisioner and transports the flies held ventrally by the middle legs.

8. Figure 24 is a cichlid fish from a Florida pond where metacercariae (at arrow) were found in the gill cavity.

9. You should mix 1500 grams of dye with 7,000 ml of water.

10. Fruits in the diet of Artibeus included an orange, pear, apple and peach.

11. Ichthyophthirius is one of the few parasites of fish with cilia.

12. The authors encountered amorphous material of varying density.

13. The animals were equally divided into 5 groups of 22 each.

14. Cotton swabs were obtained from tracheas.

15. Many of their published results indicated that perhaps MG organisms may be poorly transmitted at times.

16. The results were obtained from HPLC a useful technique for the analysis of aflatoxins in feeds with excellent resolution.

17. There is a possible cause which must be faced up to. It is in regard to whether aflatoxin enters into the blood stream.

18. An excessive amount of solar radiation received at a rapid rate has been shown by a large body of data to have the capability of inflicting epidermal damage.

19. When the horse was circled to the left and right, lameness was evidenced which was not cyclic but continual.

20. None of these dogs, that were housed in runs and were not challenged by exercise, developed any clinical signs of heartworm disease

SUGGESTED RESPONSES TO EXERCISES

1. Publication readiness: message, format, and audience

1. Probably not. Simple novelty or extension of a previous record usually is not enough to warrant publication. A case study must change, improve, or enlarge how people think.
2. The paper your colleague has proposed would have a purpose – to report the case findings – but as a research paper it would not have a message. However, a critical review of case records, coupled with a careful and critical assessment of the literature, might result in a valuable document. A case-series analysis or review article would help busy clinicians get information without laboriously sifting through the primary literature. It would tell investigators where things stand on particular aspects of the disease. And, if well written, it could suggest directions new research should take.
3. Yes, with proper choice of format. Written as a "me-too" series of case histories, the paper will probably be rejected. However, a case-series analysis that would include these data could be a useful contribution.
4. Only one primary research publication is justifiable, because all the results bear upon your single message. However, this could be supplemented with general articles written for the popular press to reach other target audiences.
5. Psychological researchers, clinicians, psychologists, teachers, school administrators, parents.

2. Search strategy and Boolean logic

1. a, h, j.   2. b, e, g.   3. d, f.   4. a, b, d, e, f, g, h, j.   5. f.   6. c, i.

3. Organizing ideas.

Answers will vary.

4. Spellchecker programs

1. fowl, means, quadrupeds
2. prolific, native
3. congenital
4. prostate

5. dying, algae
6. Danes, Husky
7. coma
8. pistil, its
9. patient, scar
10. words, tip

5. Grammar programs

1. Twice as many women as men experience migraines.
2. Wanted: Nonsmoking, nondrinking worker to care for cow.
3. I realized that because she was a baboon that grew up wild in the jungle, Wiki had special nutritional needs.
4. The patient with a severe emotional problem was referred to a psychiatrist.
5. Veterinarian Joe Mobbs hoists to its feet a cow injured while giving birth.
6. He wanted a wart removed that had appeared on his left hand about two years ago.
7. Birth control users who smoke are in danger of having mentally disabled children.
8. The woman wants us to operate on the dog's tail again. If it doesn't heal this time, the dog must be humanely killed.

6. Title choices

1. *Comments:* Overuse of prepositions and trivial phrases takes title over the 10–12 word limit. Two-part title is not accepted by some journals. *Revision:* Verruca [*or* Plantar Wart] Recurrence after Curative Excision
2. *Comments:* Some (but not all) editors ban titles that make claims about the findings in the paper. *Revision:* Correlation of Columbine Flower Characteristics and Pollinators
3. *Comments:* Unintended humor arises from careless word choice. *Revision:* Veterinarian Offers Medical Assistance After Panda Mating Fails
4. *Comments:* A century ago, long titles like this one were common. Today they are no longer accepted. *Revision:* Bionomics, Behavior, and Taxonomy of Some East Asiatic Crabronine Wasps
5. *Comments:* Another overly wordy two-part title, with unintended humor. Titles should not be thinly disguised abstracts. *Revision:* National Health Study on Lung Cancer in Women

7. Table and figure choices

1. Present the data in a table; some readers might be interested in carrying out their own calculations of relationships among the data.
2. Present these data in a table (if exact values are of interest) or by ranges on a map (to show geographical patterns).
3. Present your data in tables or graphs; the relationships are as important as the actual values. Omit the rat photo; it adds no new information.
4. Reading from left to right, the table columns might correspond to the temporal order in which the data were collected, like this: Age; Sex; Complaint; Physical Findings; Laboratory Data; Autopsy Findings
5. Use the electronmicrograph; it presents new evidence of the bacterial structure. Omit the roentgenogram; no new evidence is provided by a typical example of previously published information.
6. You could present it in a table, a graph, or in the text, but readers will see the point more quickly in a genealogical chart, which is a type of graph.
7. A bar graph would emphasize the difference in mortality, but the same point could be made with equal efficiency in the text. In a lecture or talk, a bar graph might be perfect for added visual emphasis, but readers can scan the text of a paper again if they have missed a point.

8. Number use and interpretation

1. Three-quarters (75%) of the experimental animals died within 15 hours, but 17 horses (10%) were still alive 45 days later.
2. The chemicals for the experiment weighed less than 0.2 mg.
3. We calculated that 20 500 cells were affected.
4. The control group recovered more quickly, but the difference was not statistically significant (chi-square test, $P = 11$).
5. The test plot contained 10 species of grasses, 2 species of legumes, 6 species of trees, and 15 species of cruciferous plants.

9. Person and point of view

1. As a laboratory technician, you will find that the new procedure is an improvement; you will not need to sterilize the skin. *OR* Laboratory technicians will find the new procedure an improvement because they will not need to sterilize the skin.

2. Change "the authors herein" to "we."
3. Change "the authors wish to gratefully acknowledge and thank" to "we thank."
4. The disease is contagious and contamination should be avoided (van der Veen, 1850); cleanliness is essential. *OR* Van der Veen (1850) found that the disease is contagious and contamination should be avoided. I agree that cleanliness is essential.
5. I believe that I have discovered a new species of *Australopithecus*.

10. Readability

1. The Haversian system consists of a central canal containing blood vessels and a nerve, surrounded by concentric rings of bony matrix. Between them, scattered tiny spaces called lacunae are filled with bone cells and connected by canaliculi to one another and the central canal. Through these canals the cells are nourished and kept alive.
2. The kidney, a very important organ, has the ability to secrete substances selectively. This enables it to maintain proper composition of the blood and other body fluids. Some metabolic end products are injurious if allowed to accumulate.
3. Sex-linked genes explain red–green color blindness in humans. If a woman heterozygous for color blindness marries a normal-visioned man, half her sons will be color blind. Her normal sons will show no trace of anomaly and will never transmit it to their children. All her daughters will have normal vision. However, half of these will be heterozygous for the defect and can have color-blind sons. The homozygous daughters will never pass the trait on to either sons or daughters.
4. Alcohol-induced teratogenic effects in fertilized medaka embryos include: (1) delayed initiation of vessel circulation, (2) formation of thrombi in many regions of the body including the brain, (3) microcephaly (small head size), (4) malformed neurocranial and trabecular cartilages, and (5) alterations in oxidative stress enzymes.
5. Weanling castrated Holstein calves fed AMDRO for 7 weeks experienced leucopenia by 2 weeks into the regimen. The leucopenia was characterized by significant reductions in eosinophils and lymphocytes.

11. Clarity and brevity

A. 1. mature iron from muscle; iron that is from mature muscle
   2. chronic symptoms of depression; symptoms of chronic depression
   3. excretion of renal lithium; renal excretion of lithium

    4. In their abdomens, the three patients all had tumors that were confirmed to be metastatic and malignant. (Avoid saying "cases" had tumors.)
The three patients had intraabdominal tumors confirmed to be metastatic and malignant.

    5. We examined various combinations of immunospecific drugs to see whether any inhibited leukocytes in the peripheral blood of humans. (Avoid saying a study "examines" something.)
Various combinations of immunospecific drugs were examined to determine whether they inhibited human peripheral blood leukocytes.

B. 1. These observations suggest a female sex pheromone. (Still marginally incorrect, for an "observation" can't suggest anything, but the meaning would be clear to readers.)

    2. Following the outlined procedure might be wise.

    3. The study shows an apparent link between cigarette smoking and lung cancer. (Longer but more technically correct: Based on this study, cigarette smoking and lung cancer may be linked.)

    4. A cause-and-effect relationship appears likely.

    5. The results indicate that the mixture was somewhat saturated with oil. *OR* On the basis of these results, the mixture was somewhat saturated with oil.

C. 1. The new organism is green, round, 5 × 10 mm, and active *OR* motile.

    2. Twenty to thirty electrophoretic steps usually will be needed.

    3. If we meet now about the data, consensus should be easy to attain.

    4. The case load included 15 juveniles and 10 adults. (By definition, juveniles are young and adults are mature; here, "case load" is not jargon, but specialized vocabulary of the field.)

    5. Figure 1. Lateral white cells in abdominal ganglion of live cockroach. Ventral view, anterior at top. (Scale bar, 0.1 mm.)

    6. The absence of color was unique.

    7. To determine the organism's mobility, state-of-the-art equipment was used.

    8. To understand the effects of temperature on the organism, we plan to refrigerate it.

12. When short may be too short

1. Do not use abbreviations (TCGF, SPAFAS) in titles. Do not abbreviate U.S. except as an adjective.
2. Do not include undefined abbreviations in abstracts. Do not abbreviate units of measurement (hrs.) when they are used without numerals.

3. This alphabet soup sentence is annoyingly cryptic.
4. Do not abbreviate units of measurement used without numerals.
5. Abbreviation of state names is inconsistent and that of South Carolina follows neither approved system.

13. Tense use

1. Work by Matthews (2007) shows that *Vespula* nests readily in the laboratory. *[Sentence is also correct as it stands, though slightly less smooth.]*
2. In our study, bird size increased with width of wooded habitat, as Figure 2 indicates.
3. Beal (1960) also observed [or observes] that size increases with meadow width.
4. In our study we found that there were significantly fewer antibody-producing cells in copper-deficient mice than in copper-supplemented mice (see Figure 3).
5. Correct as it stands; these results cannot be generalized.
6. Conover and Kynard (1981) reported that sex determination in the Atlantic silverside fish is under the control of both genotype and temperature.
7. Correct as it stands.
8. Correct as it stands.
9. ABSTRACT: The cell-to-cell channels in the insect salivary gland were probed with fluorescent molecules. From the molecular dimensions, a permeation-limiting channel diameter of 16–20 angstroms was obtained.
10. SUMMARY: Germinal and somatic functions in *Tetrahymena* were found to be performed separately by the micro- and macronuclei, respectively. Cells with haploid micronuclei were mated with diploids to yield monosomic progeny.

14. Active and passive voice

1. One might expect this treatment to be effective. *OR* We expect this treatment to be effective.
2. The pathologist had no feed to analyse.
3. Jones and her colleagues inoculated 25 chickens.
4. I travelled to Georgia to collect Lepidoptera.
5. Mark passages A and B for revision.

6. This dictionary does not include modern technical words that had no equivalent in ancient spoken Greek and Latin.
7. At the request of the university president, administrative personnel at the Biology Building are studying three incineration systems.

15. Subject–verb agreement

1. The remaining fluid was drawn off, and the kidneys were washed.
2. Due to the small number of test animals used, the data were not statistically significant *OR* (if no statistical tests were involved) Due to the small number of test animals used, the data were not meaningful.
3. Karyorrhexis, karyolysis, and hepatocyte degeneration were evident within the centrilobular regions. ("Cellular" is redundant, for hepatocytes couldn't degenerate any other way.)
4. Not one of the animals was harmed in the course of this study. *OR* None of the animals were harmed in the course of this study.
5. After a sample was assessed by radiocarbon dating, sections were subjected to potassium–argon analysis.
6. Neither the rats nor the chimpanzee was kept in the laboratory. *OR* Neither the chimpanzee nor the rats were kept in the laboratory.

16. Collective nouns, comparisons, and lists

A. 1. An appropriate dose is 10–50 parts per million of chloramphenicol.
    2. The university president convened a committee of 30 scientists.
    3. We infused 12 liters of serum into the elephant.
B. 1. The authors' mild pulmonary hypertensive stage was similar to this stage in our study.
    2. Group A was more unusual than Group B.
    3. The cat recovered better than any of the other cats did.
    4. The emergency medical kit contained a bandage, an applicator, a towel, a brush, and a rubber sponge.
    5. The fox was heavier than any of the other animals in the study group.
    6. Of the two alternatives, this one is the more interesting.

17. Dangling participles and other misplaced modifiers

1. Toward the anterior chamber, a lamination was evident.
2. Using dimethyl sulfoxide, we observed no bacteria.

3. After experimentation, bacteria multiplied.
4. A correlation between the variables was evident with this method.
5. With an inverted ocular, one can examine intestinal sections for metazoan parasites.
6. Two of the researchers' stopwatches that had been left leaning against cabinets were badly damaged.
7. For sale: Laboratory table with thick legs and large drawers; suitable for researcher.
8. Last night, the campus police reported that two microscopes were stolen.
9. To encourage condom use, the French government has prepared commercials blunt enough to shock even liberal Americans.

18. Jargon and wordiness

A. 1. enough.
   2. can.
   3. inhibited.
   4. in theory.
   5. regularly.
B. 1. The "etiology of this disease" means the "study of the cause of this disease." The author intended to say "the cause of this disease."
   2. Literally, "histopathology stages" would be stages in the study of the pathology of tissues. The author probably intended to say "histopathological."
   3. A "necrology" is a list of persons who have died within a certain time. The author probably meant "necropsy." Avoid saying that the necropsy could "confirm" something; necropsy is the tool that the scientist uses to confirm it.
C. 1. After the operation, the cow ran into a defective electric fence and had to be humanely killed.
   2. Position the slide carefully to see the unique shape clearly.
   3. I think the drug can relieve and curtail disease symptoms.

19. Handling language sensitively

1. A researcher must be sure to double-check all references.
2. There were 200 Asian participants.
3. Depressed individuals and those with epilepsy reacted to the drug in different ways.

4. The chairperson confronted the person for plagiarizing.
5. The ten women in the study included one with cerebral palsy.
6. Breast cancer is one of the oldest diseases known.
7. As a scientific writer, you should state your point clearly at the beginning.
8. We need 14 women who are willing to staff the project.

20. Devil pairs

1. like; as
2. whereas; while
3. various; varying
4. effect; effect
5. effect; effected (awkward usage); affect
6. principle; principal; principle
7. complement; compliment; complement

21. Which and that

1. New fossil evidence indicates that *Cantius*, a primitive primate, had a grasping big toe, which may have figured in the evolution of all modern primates.
2. The use of low molecular weight dextrans should be avoided in these patients. These drugs appear to pass through the damaged endothelium of pulmonary vessels.
3. Occasionally a client will notice a parasite on a fish. The situation is more worrisome to the owner than to the fish.
4. We conclude that during the next year, 10.5 thousand (*OR* 10 500) tons of lead will be emitted into the air in addition to the 90 thousand (*OR* 90 000) tons that are being emitted now.
5. We could not find the proposal that was missing.

22. Fuzzy words and disguised verbs

A. 1. By early adulthood, more males than females expressed severe symptoms of copper deficiency.
   2. Under standard conditions, diazepam inhibited the initial rate of protein phosphorylation (Fig. 1).
   3. Soap acts at the cell surface.
   4. Stanozolol prolonged appetite.
   5. We isolated *A. hydrophila*.

B. 1. Physicists hope to solve the question of whether science can harness alternative energy sources.
   2. Data were transformed to perform relevant statistical analyses.

23. Punctuation

1. Indicate optimum instrument settings for temperature, humidity, rainfall, and performance.
2. When examined closely, the skeleton bears many bumpy spines that project from the surface of the animal.
3. Class Echinoidea, which includes sea urchins, sand dollars, and heart urchins, is not closely related to class Ascomyceteae.
4. The adults are radially symmetrical, but the larvae are bilateral. It is generally held that this phylum evolved from bilateral ancestors and that radial symmetry arose as an adaptation to a sessile way of life.
5. The clinician asked, "How did the patient die?" The answer was not obvious.
6. The essay, "The Future of Veterinary Medicine," appeared in the early 1960s.

24. Capitalization

1. The Afghan hound ate plaster of Paris.
2. The study sample included 15 Greyhounds, 14 Malamutes, and 10 Spanish Terriers. OR The study sample included 15 greyhounds, 14 malamutes, and 10 Spanish terriers.
3. Adenine and guanine are nucleotides called purines.
4. A person can live normally without the adrenal medullae, but not without the cortices.
5. These bacteria inhabit all biomes in the Northern Hemisphere.
6. *What's So Funny about Science?* by Sidney Harris
7. Assessment of the Role of Alcohol in the Human Stress Response
8. A synopsis of the taxonomy of North American and West Indian birds

25. Scientific names

1. the parasitic wasp, *M. atrata*
2. the dandelion, *Taraxacum officionale*, family Compositae, class Dicotyledonae
3. the honeybee, *Apis mellifera* var. *ligustica*

4. the human malarial parasite, *Plasmodium falciparum* Bignami
5. The starfish *(Asterias)* belongs to the class Asteroidea, phylum Echinodermata, in the section Deuterostomia.

26. Foreign words and phrases

1. When acceptable, use the formulas already given in the book, *Official Methods in Microbiology.*
2. For information on the action of green plant pigments, *i.e.*, chlorophyll, *in vivo* see Arnon's article in *Scientific American* and Bassham's book, *The Photosynthesis of Carbon Compounds.*
3. Our experiments cannot identify the underlying biophysical alterations, namely, effects within the membrane itself.
4. Reduced oxygen tension provides the best environment for parasite development *in vitro*, as shown by Udeinya *et al.* (2005).

27. Ethical and legal issues

A. 1. Yes. With a publication that old, copyright would no longer be an issue. However, to clearly avoid plagiarism, the credits should state "based on..." the original citation.
   2. No. You have exceeded the 500-word limit and a book is considered to be for profit rather than "fair use." Whether the authors or the journal hold the copyright, it almost certainly is still active.
   3. You should consider doing so. It would not constitute duplicate publication because both your audience and the nature of your manuscript would be quite different. However, it would be best to publish the scholarly version first.
   4. The charges would probably be slander because spoken words were involved and the comments fit the definition of harmful.
   5. You could, particularly since you have your computer files and perhaps also earlier printed drafts. If sections of your manuscript appear verbatim in the rivals' paper, possible charges could include both plagiarism and copyright infringement. Copyright is in effect as soon as a work is created, even without formal registration.
   6. Government publications are in the public domain, so you do not need formal permission. However, any time you include something that is not your own, it should be cited.

7. First, you should contact your institution's legal affairs office. They would probably advise that the publicity could adversely affect potential patent application.
8. Always cite your sources. Internet regulations are in flux, but many sites indicate whether or not their materials require permission.

B. All the listed terms were once trademarked. Products still defended as trade names in the United States include Clorox, Freon, Sharpie, Teflon, Xerox, and Q-tip.

28. Slide presentation format

A. Several answers possible.
B. Several answers possible.
C. 1 – f, 2 – d, 3 – c, 4 – i, 5 – b, 6 – l, 7 – m, 8 – n, 9 – k, 10 – a.

29. Answering questions

More than one answer is possible. Judge by suitability.

30. Mixed corrections

1. *Comments:* Wordy; change numbers to Arabic; use first person. *Revision:* We conclude that these mammalian cells have a limiting diameter of 16–20 Å.
2. *Comments:* Subject–verb disagreement; use of passive could be changed. *Revision:* We studied the inhibitory activity of the various combinations and plotted isobolograms.
3. *Comments:* Wordy, awkward; "at ... by" construction sounds like location; "increasing" may be interpreted two ways. *Revision:* At the cell surface, EDTA increases cell wall permeability. (Remember not to start a sentence with an abbreviation.)
4. *Comments:* Wordy. *Revision:* The pronounced heart lesions were measured.
5. *Comments:* Two meanings possible for "numerous" – many strains, or strains that have many individuals; incorrect use of italics and capitalization. An exception to the usual rule regarding diseases, Chagas is capitalized because it is derived from a proper noun, the name of its describer. *Revision:* Many strains of *T. cruzi* cause Chagas disease.

6. *Comments:* A report of one's current research requires past tense; "irritated" gives sentence an amusing double meaning. (Author probably meant it in the sense of "inflamed," not "annoyed.") *Revision:* Treatment stopped when fish showed signs of physical irritation.

7. *Comments:* Dangling phrase – whose middle legs, those of the wasp or those of the fly? Which does "ventrally" refer to? Scientific name needs italics. Progressive provisioner is an acceptable technical term. *Revision:* A progressive provisioner, *S. maculata* carries flies beneath its body with its middle legs.

8. *Comments:* How can a figure be a fish? Does a pond have metacercariae or a gill cavity? *Revision:* Metacercariae (arrow, Figure 24) were evident in the gill cavity of a cichlid fish found in a Florida pond.

9. *Comments:* Unnecessary words; measurements could be simplified. *Revision:* Mix 1.5 kg dye with 7 L water.

10. *Comments:* Generic names should be underlined or italicized. A list in which some items begin with a vowel and some do not requires an article with each; a series requires a comma before "and." Pluralizing (if statement is still accurate) would make the sentence read more smoothly. *Revision:* Fruits in the *Artibeus* diet included an orange, a pear, an apple, and a peach. *OR* Fruits in the *Artibeus* diet included oranges, pears, apples, and peaches.

11. *Comments:* Misplaced modifier sounds like fish have cilia. Generic names should be underlined or italicized. *Revision: Ichthyophthirius* is one of the few ciliated parasites infesting fish.

12. *Comments:* "Varying" means changing; authors probably meant "various." Use of "the authors" is unclear; if it means authors of this sentence substitute "we." *Revision:* We found amorphous material of various densities.

13. *Comments:* "Equally" and "each" are redundant; "divided" has two meanings. *Revision:* The animals were placed in 5 groups of 22.

14. *Comments:* Sounds like a magician, pulling swabs out of tracheas. *Revision:* With cotton swabs, we obtained tracheal samples.

15. *Comments:* Too much hedging; use present tense for published findings that can be generalized. The qualifiers "many" and "sometimes" (or "at times") both are needed to avoid changing the meaning. *Revision:* Many of their published results indicate that MG organisms sometimes are transmitted poorly.

16. *Comments:* Misplaced phrase – feeds with resolution? Punctuation needed; active tense improves sentence. *Revision:* We used HPLC, a technique with excellent resolution, to analyse aflatoxins in feeds.

17. *Comments:* Hiccups; redundancy; wordiness. *Revision:* A possible cause is aflatoxin entering the bloodstream.

18. *Comments:* Wordy and pretentious. *Revision:* Too much sunlight can burn skin.

19. *Comments:* For a restrictive clause, "that" is preferable; passive, colorless verb; "continual" is used improperly; some redundancy. *Revision:* When it circled, the horse was continuously lame.

20. *Comments:* A restrictive clause should not be set off by commas; rewording would make sentence read more smoothly. *Revision:* The unexercised dogs housed in runs developed no clinical signs of heartworm disease.

Selected resources

Aad, G., Abat, E. Abdallah, J., *et al.* (2008). The ATLAS experiment at the CERN Large Hadron Collider. *Journal of Instrumentation*, **3**(8), SO80003.

Alley, M. (1996). *The Craft of Scientific Writing.* 3rd edn. New York: Springer.

Alley, M. (2013). *The Craft of Scientific Presentations: Critical Steps to Succeed and Critical Errors to Avoid.* 2nd edn. New York: Springer.

Alley, M. and Neeley, K. A. (2005). Rethinking the design of presentation slides: A case for sentence headlines and visual evidence. *Technical Communication*, **52**, 417–426.

Altman, D. G., Schul, K. F., Moher, D., *et al.* (2001). The CONSORT statement: revised recommendations for improving the quality of parallel-group randomized trials. *Lancet*, **357**, 1191–1194.

American Medical Association (AMA). (2007). *AMA Manual of Style: A Guide for Authors and Editors.* 10th edn. Oxford, UK: Oxford University Press.

American Psychological Association (APA). (2010). *The Publication Manual of the American Psychological Association.* 6th edn. Washington DC: American Psychological Association.

Arthur, F. H. and Weintraub, P. G. (2010). Publications and the peer review system. *American Entomologist*, **56**(3), 138–139.

Aslett, D. (1996). *How to Have a 48-Hour Day.* Cincinnati, OH: F & W Publications, Inc.

Aslett, D. (2008). *The Office Clutter Cure: Get Organized, Get Results.* 2nd edn. New York: Adams Media.

Atkinson, C. (2005). *Beyond Bullet Points.* Buffalo, NY: Microsoft Press.

Bakker, M. and Wicherts, J. M. (2011). The (mis) reporting of statistical results in psychology journals. *Behavioral Research Methods*, **43**(3), 666–678.

Baron, D. N. (1994). *Units, Symbols, and Abbreviations: A Guide for Biological and Medical Editors.* 5th edn. London: Royal Society of Medicine.

Bayne, K. and Turner, P.V. (2013). *Laboratory Animal Welfare: American College of Laboratory Animal Medicine.* Waltham, MA: Academic Press.

Bell, S. J. (2004). End PowerPoint dependency now! *American Libraries*, **35**(6), 56–59.

Benson, B. W. and Boege, S. (2002). *Handbook of Good Laboratory Practices.* Bristol, PA: Hemisphere Publishing.

Bjelland, H. (1990). *Writing Better Technical Articles*. Blue Ridge Summit, PA: TAB Books.

Bohannon, J. (2013). Who's afraid of peer review? *Science*, **342**(6154), 60–65.

Boice, R. (1990). *Professors as Writers: A Self-help Guide to Productive Writing*. Stillwater, OK: New Forums Press.

Boice, R. (2000). *Advice for New Faculty Members: Nihil Nimus*. Needham Heights, MA: Allyn & Bacon.

Bolker, J. (1998). *Writing Your Dissertation in Fifteen Minutes a Day*. New York: Henry Holt.

Briscoe, M. H. (1996). *Preparing Scientific Illustrations: A Guide to Better Posters, Presentations, and Publications*. 2nd edn. New York: Springer-Verlag.

Broad, W. J. (1981). The publishing game: getting more for less. *Science*, **211**(4487), 1137–1139.

Buranen, L. and Roy, A. M. (eds) (1999). *Perspectives on Plagiarism and Intellectual Property in a Postmodern World*. Albany, NY: State University of New York Press.

Calisher, C. H. and Fauquet, C. M. (1992). *Stedman's ICTV Virus Words*. Baltimore, MD: Lippincott, Williams & Wilkins.

Cargill, M. and O'Connor, P. (2009). *Writing Scientific Research Articles: Strategy and Steps*. New York: Wiley-Blackwell.

Cleveland, W. S. (1994). *The Elements of Graphing Data*. 2nd edn. Summit, NJ: Wadsworth Hobart Press.

Collins, R., Gray, R., Godwin, J., *et al.* (1987). Avoidance of large biases and large random errors in the assessment of moderate treatment effects: the need for systematic overviews. *Statistics in Medicine*, **6**(3), 245–250.

Committee for the Update of the Guide for the Care and Use of Laboratory Animals, Institute for Laboratory Animal Research, Division on Earth and Life Studies, and National Research Council. (2011). *Guide for the Care and Use of Laboratory Animals*. 8th edn. Washington DC: National Academies Press.

Cooper, H. (1998). *Synthesizing Research*. 3rd edn. Thousand Oaks, CA: Sage.

Council of Science Editors (CSE). (2006). *Scientific Style and Format: The CSE Style Manual for Authors, Editors, and Publishers*. 7th edn. New York: Cambridge University Press.

D'Angelo, J. (2012). *Ethics in Science: Ethical Misconduct in Scientific Research*. New York: CRC Press.

Darwin, F. (ed.) (1897). *The Life and Letters of Charles Darwin, Including an Autobiographical Chapter*. New York: D. Appleton and Company.

Davis, M. (2005). *Scientific Papers and Presentations.* 2nd edn. Burlington, MA: Academic Press (Elsevier).

Day, R. A. and Gastel, B. (2011). *How to Write and Publish a Scientific Paper.* 7th edn. Westport, CT: Greenwood Press.

de Lacey, G., Record, C., and Wade, J. (1985). How accurate are quotations and references in medical journals? *British Medical Journal,* **291**, 884–886.

Dizon, A. E., and Rosenberg, J. E. (1990). We don't care, Professor Einstein, the Instructions to the Authors specifically said double-spaced. In *Writing for Fishery Journals,* ed. J. Hunter. Bethesda, MD: American Fisheries Society. pp. 65–74.

Dorland's Illustrated Medical Dictionary. (2011). 32nd edn. Philadelphia, PA: W. B. Saunders Co.

Dupré, L. (1998). *BUGS in Writing: A Guide to Debugging your Prose.* Revised edn. Reading, MA: Addison Wesley Longman, Inc.

Emanuel, E. J., Crouch, R. A., Arras, J. D., *et al.* (eds) (2003). *Ethics and Regulatory Aspects of Clinical Research: Readings and Commentary.* Baltimore, MD: Johns Hopkins University Press.

Evans, J.T., Nadjari, H. I., and Burchell, S. A. (1990). Quotational and reference accuracy in surgical journals: A continuing peer review problem. *Journal of the American Medical Association,* **263**, 1353–1354.

Flower, L. (2000). *Problem Solving Strategies for Writing.* 5th edn. San Diego, CA: Harcourt Brace Jovanovich.

Friedland, A. J. and Folt, C. L. (2009). *Writing Successful Science Proposals.* New Haven, CN: Yale University Press.

Germano, W. (2001). *Getting It Published.* Chicago, IL: University of Chicago Press.

Gilbert, N. (2009). Editor will quit over hoax paper. *Nature.com/news.* DOI: 10.1038/news.2009.571.

Gillan, D. J., Wickens, C. D., Hollands, J. G., *et al.* (1998). Guidelines for presenting quantitative data in HFES publications. *Human Factors: The Journal of the Human Factors and Ergonomics Society* **40**, 28–41.

Gingras, B. (1987). Simplified English in maintenance manuals. *Technical Communications,* **34**(1), 24–28.

Glasman-Deal, H. (2009). *Science Research Writing for Non-native Speakers of English.* London: Imperial College Press.

Gopen, G. D. and Swan, J. A. (1990). The science of scientific writing. *American Scientist,* **78**(6), 550–558.

Graham, S. and Sandmel, K. (2011). The Process Writing Approach: a meta-analysis. *Journal of Educational Research,* **104**(6), 396–407.

Guillen, J. (2013). *Laboratory Animals: Regulations and Recommendations for Global Collaborative Research*. Burlington, MA: Academic Press.

Gurak, L. J. (2000). *Oral Presentations for Technical Communication*. Needham Heights, MA: Allyn & Bacon.

Gustavii, B. (2008). *How to Write and Illustrate a Scientific Paper*. 2nd edn. Cambridge, UK: Cambridge University Press.

Hailman, J. P., and Strier, K. B. (1997). *Planning, Proposing, and Presenting Science Effectively*. Cambridge, UK: Cambridge University Press.

Healy, R. (2013). *Speed Writing for Nonfiction Writers: How to Double or Triple Your Daily Word Count*. Kindle edn. Seattle, WA: Amazon Digital Services, Inc.

Hinchcliff, K. W., Bruce, M. J., Powers, J. D., *et al.* (1993). Accuracy of references and quotations in veterinary journals. *Journal of the American Veterinary Medical Association*, **202**(3), 397–400.

Hofmann, A. H. (2010). *Scientific Writing and Communication: Papers, Proposals, and Presentations*. Oxford, UK: Oxford University Press.

Holt, J. G. (1994). *Bergey's Manual of Determinative Bacteriology*. 9th edn. Baltimore, MD: Lippincott, Williams & Wilkins.

Hoogendam, A., Stalenhoef, F. H., de Vries Robbé, P. F., *et al.* (2008). Analysis of queries sent to PubMed at the point of care: Observation of search behaviour in a medical teaching hospital. *BMC Medical Informatics and Decision Making* **8**, 42.

Huff, D. (1993). *How to Lie with Statistics*. New York: W. W. Norton and Company.

International Association of Veterinary Editors (IAVE). (2010). International Association of Veterinary Editors' Consensus Author Guidelines on Animal Ethics and Welfare. www.veteditors.org/ethicsconsensusguidelines.html (23 July 2010).

International Commission on Zoological Nomenclature (ICZN). (1999). *International Code of Zoological Nomenclature*. International Trust for Zoological Nomenclature History Museum. Code that incorporates subsequent amendments can be obtained online at www.nhm.ac.uk/hosted-sites/iczn/code/.

International Committee of Medical Journal Editors (ICMJE). (2013). Recommendations for the Conduct, Reporting, Editing, and Publication of Scholarly Work in Medical Journals. *www.ICJME.org*.

International Union of Microbiological Societies. (1992). *International Code of Nomenclature of Bacteria*. 1990 revision, ed. P. H. A. Sneath, E. F. Lessel, V. B. D. Skerman, H. P. R. Seeliger, and W. A. Clark. Washington DC: American Society for Microbiology.

Jablonski, S. (ed.). (2008). *Jablonski's Dictionary of Medical Acronyms and Abbreviations.* 6th edn. Philadelphia, PA: W. B. Saunders Co.

Jeffrey, C. (ed.). (1992). *Biological Nomenclature.* 3rd edn. New York: Cambridge University Press.

Jensen, L. J., Saric, J., and Bork, P. (2006). Literature mining for the biologist: from information retrieval to biological discovery. *Nature Reviews/Genetics*, 7, 119–129.

Jones, G.E. (2006) *How to Lie with Charts.* 2nd edn. Charleston, SC: Book-Surge Publishing.

Kawasaki, G. (2005). How to change the world: the 10/20/30 rule of Power-Point. Available online at http://blog.guykawasaki.com/2005/12/the_102030_rule.html.

Keller, J. (2004). Is PowerPoint the devil? *Chicago Tribune*, 23 January.

King, A. M. Q., Adams, M. J., Carstens, E. B., *et al.* (2011). *Virus Taxonomy. Ninth Report of the International Committee on Taxonomy of Viruses.* London: Elsevier Academic Press.

Körner, A. M. (2008). *Guide to Publishing a Scientific Paper.* New York: Routledge.

Kosslyn, S. M. (2006). *Graph Design for the Eye and Mind.* Oxford, UK: Oxford University Press.

Kosslyn, S. M. (2011). *Better PowerPoint: Quick Fixes Based on How Your Audience Thinks.* Oxford, UK: Oxford University Press.

LaFollette, M. C. (1992). *Stealing into Print: Fraud, Plagiarism, and Misconduct in Scientific Publishing.* Berkeley, CA: University of California Press.

Lang, T. (2004) Twenty statistical errors even you can find in biomedical research articles. *Croatian Medical Journal*, **45**(4), 361–370.

Lang, T., and Secic, M. (1997). *How to Report Statistics in Medicine: Annotated Guidelines for Authors, Editors, and Reviewers.* Philadelphia, PA: American College of Physicians.

Lapage, S. P., Sneath, P. H. A., Lessel, E. F., *et al.* (eds). (1992). *International Code of Nomenclature of Bacteria.* Washington DC: ASM Press.

Lawrence, E. L. (2011). *Henderson's Dictionary of Biology.* 15th edn. San Francisco, CA: Benjamin Cummings.

Lawrence, S. (1981). Watching the watchers. *Science News*, **119**, 331–333.

Lederer, R. (1987). *Anguished English.* New York: Dell Publishing.

Leigh, G. J. (1998). *Principles of Chemical Nomenclature: A Guide to IUPAC Recommendations.* Malden, MA: Blackwell Science.

Leki, I., Cumming, L., and Silva, T. 2008. *A Synthesis of Research on Second Language Writing in English.* London: Routledge.

Lipson, C. (2004). *Doing Honest Work in College: How to Prepare Citations, Avoid Plagiarism, and Achieve Real Academic Success*. Chicago, IL: University of Chicago Press.

Macdonald-Ross, M. (1977a). Graphics in text. In *Review of Research in Education*, No. 5, ed. L. S. Shulman. Itasca, IL: Peacock.

Macdonald-Ross, M. (1977b). How numbers are shown. *AV Communication Review*, **25**, 359–409.

Mack, K. and Skjei, E. (1979). *Overcoming Writing Blocks*. Los Angeles, CA: Tarcher. Distributed by St. Martin's Press, New York.

MacNeil, R. (1995). The glorious messiness of English. *Reader's Digest*, Oct. 1995, pp. 151–154.

Macrina, F. (2014). *Scientific Integrity*. 4th edn. Washington DC: ASM Press.

Markel, M. (1994). *Writing in the Technical Fields: A Step-by-Step Guide for Engineers, Scientists, and Technicians*. New York: IEEE Press.

Mayer, R. E. (2001). *Multimedia Learning*. New York: Cambridge University Press.

McNeill, J., Barrie, F. R., Buck, W. R., *et al.* (eds.) (2011). *International Code of Nomenclature for Algae, Fungi, and Plants (Melbourne Code). Regnum Vegetabile 154*. Koenigstein, Germany: Koeltz Scientific Books. Available online at: www.iapt-taxon.org/nomen/main.php.

Montgomery, S. L. (2003). *The Chicago Guide to Communicating Science*. Chicago, IL: University of Chicago Press.

Nelson, V. (1993). *On Writer's Block*. Boston, MA: Houghton Mifflin Co.

O'Neill, M. J. (ed.) (2013). *The Merck Index: An Encyclopedia of Chemicals, Drugs, and Biologicals*. 15th edn. New York: John Wiley & Sons.

Ogden, C. K. (1930). *Basic English: A General Introduction with Rules and Grammar*. London: Kegan Paul, Trench, Trubner.

Palmer, C. L. (2001). *Work at the Boundaries of Science Information and the Interdisciplinary Research Process*. Dordrecht, The Netherlands: Kluwer.

Pearson Education (2008). *Longman Dictionary of American English*. 4th edn. St. Laurent, Quebec, Canada: Pearson Education ESL.

Peterson, I. (1993). Going for glitz. *Science News*, **144**, 232–233.

PLoS Medicine Editors. (2008). Making sense of non-financial competing interests. *PLoS Med.* **5**(9): e199.

Raimes, A. (1988). *Grammar Troublespots: An Editing Guide for ESL Students*. New York: St. Martin's Press.

Renear, A. H. and Palmer, C. L. (2009). Strategic reading, ontologies, and the future of scientific publishing. *Science* **325**, 828–832.

Ridley, D. (2012). *The Literature Review: A Step-by-Step Guide for Students. SAGE Study Skills Series.* 2nd edn. New York: SAGE Publications.

Robbins, N. B. (2005). *Creating More Effective Graphs.* New York: Wiley-Interscience.

Rubens, P. (2002). *Science and Technical Writing: A Manual of Style.* 2nd edn. Oxford, UK: Routledge.

Safire, W. (1990). *Fumblerules: A Lighthearted Guide to Grammar and Good Usage.* New York: Doubleday.

Samuelson, P. (1994). Self-plagiarism or fair use? *Communications of the ACM,* **37**, 21–25.

Sanderlin, S. (1988). Programming instruction manuals for non-English readers. *Technical Communication,* **35**(2), 96–100.

Scanlon, P. M. (2007). Song from myself: An anatomy of self-plagiarism. *Plagiary* **2**(1), 1–11.

Schimel, J. (2012). *Writing Science: How to Write Papers That Get Cited and Proposals That Get Funded.* Oxford, UK: Oxford University Press.

Shamoo, H E. and Resnik, D. B. (2009) *Responsible Conduct of Research.* 2nd edn. Oxford, UK: Oxford University Press.

Shortland, M. and Gregory, J. (1991). *Communicating Science: A Handbook.* New York: John Wiley & Sons.

Skerman, V, B. D., McGowan, V., and Sneath, P. H. A. (1999). *Approved Lists of Bacterial Names.* Amended edn. Washington DC: ASM Press.

Simons, T. (2004). Does PowerPoint make you stupid? *Presentations,* March 24–31.

Stedman's Medical Abbreviations, Acronyms and Symbols. (2012). 5th edn. Baltimore, MD: Lippincott, Williams and Wilkins.

Stedman's Medical Dictionary. (2005). 28th edn. Baltimore, MD: Williams and Wilkins.

Studdert, V. P., Gay, C. C., Blood, D. C. (2012). *Saunders Comprehensive Veterinary Dictionary.* 4th edn. Philadelphia, PA: W. B. Saunders Co.

Swanson, E., O'Sean, A. A., and Schleyer, A. T. (1999). *Mathematics into Type.* Updated edn. Providence, RI: American Mathematical Society.

Sweller, J. (2005). Implications of cognitive load theory for multimedia learning. In *The Cambridge Handbook of Multimedia Learning,* ed. Mayer, R. E. Cambridge, UK: Cambridge University Press, Chapter 2.

Swinford, E. (2006). *Fixing PowerPoint Annoyances.* Sebastopol, CA: O'Reilly Media.

Theodosiou, T., Vizirianakis, I. S., Angelis, L., *et al.* (2011). MeSHy: Mining unanticipated PubMed information using frequencies of occurrences and concurrences of MeSH terms. *Journal of Biomedical Informatics*, **44**, 919–926.

Tufte, E. R. (2001). *The Visual Display of Quantitative Information*. 2nd edn. Cheshire, CT: Graphics Press.

Tufte, E. R. (2003). *The Cognitive Style of PowerPoint*. Cheshire, CT: Graphics Press.

University of Chicago Press Staff. (2010). *Chicago Manual of Style*. 16th edn. Chicago, IL: University of Chicago Press.

US Pharmacopeia (annual). *USP Dictionary of USAN and International Drug Names*. Rockville, MD: US Pharmacopeia.

Weiss, E. H. (1990). *100 Writing Remedies: Practical Exercises for Technical Writing*. Phoenix, AZ: Oryx Press.

Woodford, F. P. (1968). *Scientific Writing for Graduate Students: A Manual on the Teaching of Scientific Writing*. Bethesda, MD: Council of Biology Editors.

Woolsey, J. D. (1989). Combating poster fatigue: how to use visual grammar and analysis to effect better visual communications. *Trends in Neurosciences*, **12**, 325–332.

World Medical Association (WMA). (2013). World Medical Association Declaration of Helsinki: Ethical Principles for Medical Research Involving Human Subjects. *Journal of the American Medical Association*, **310** (20), 2191–2194.

Young, D. S., and Huth, E. J. (1998). *SI Units for Clinical Measurement*. Philadelphia, PA: American College of Physicians.

Index